INFORMATION RETRIEVAL THESAURUS

An annotated bibliography

Compiled by
DR. RAJENDRA KUMBHAR
M.Com.; M.Lib.I.Sc.; Ph.D.
Department of Library and Information Science,
H.P.T. Arts and R.Y.K. Science College, Nasik 422005 (Maharashtra)

Ess Ess Publications

4837/24, Ansari Road, Darya Ganj,
New Delhi-110002
✆ : 23260807, 51563444
Fax : 011-51563334
E-mail: info@essessreference.com
url:http://www.essessreference.com

First Published **2006**

ISBN: 81-7000-483-7

Rs.900/-

Published by:
Ess Ess Publications
4837/24, Ansari Road, Darya Ganj, New Delhi-110 002
Tel: 011-23260807, 41563444 Fax: 011-41563334
E-mail: info@essessreference.com
url: www.essessreference.com

Printed in India at:
Printline, New Delhi

Contents

Preface

Information explosion is one of the impacts of invention of printing technology and the emergence of democratic governments. The ever-accelerating growth of literature has put forth the need for bibliographic control.

Since 1960s information retrieval (IR) thesaurus and its auxiliary aspects have been of interest of the LIS professionals. As a result a large number of documents have been published on IR thesaurus and its various aspects. The sheer number (of documents) itself is an indicator of LIS professionals interest in IR thesaurus.

Bibliography of literature on IR thesaurus was needed to help sustain the interest of LIS professionals in IR thesaurus for it makes available the list of relevant literature. The present bibliography, I further hope, will help in literature search, in knowing various aspects of IR thesaurus, which are not yet paid attention to. The bibliography will also be useful in avoiding duplications in research on IR thesaurus.

Efforts are made to make the bibliography and entriès in it as complete as possible nevertheless, suggestions, if any, will be appreciated.

This is mainly a secondary bibliography. The entries listed in the bibliography are collected from vast number of sources. These include Library and Information Science Abstracts, Indian Library Science Abstract, actual periodicals and other compound documents such as conference and seminar volumes, books, web sites etc. I sincerely acknowledge all authors and their sources on the basis of which this book is based.

I thank Shri Sumit Sethi of Ess Ess Publications for bringing out this book at a vary short time span.

Nasik 1st January 2006

Preface

Section A
Thesaurus related bibliographies and General literature on thesaurus

Entries in this section are grouped in to two sections i.e. A1 Thesauri related bibliographies and A2 General literature on thesaurus.

Like the present bibliography earlier too efforts have been made to construct bibliographies listing literature related with IR thesaurus. Lists of thesauri have also been constructed in the past. Section A1 lists bibliographies of thesauri related literature and lists of thesauri.

The literature listed in Section A2 deals with general review of IR, definition, history, etymological reviews, clearinghouse, literature review, personal contributions towards the IR systems with thesauri, bibliometric studies, trends and research related with thesaurus, thesaurus glossaries, etc.

Section A1
Thesauri related bibliographies

1 Douglas, Kimberly and Wismer, Don.

Computer-based indexing on a small scale : bibliography.

Arlington, Virginia : Educational Resources Information Center, 1980. 19p.

One section of this bibliography lists thesauri

2 Gaster, K.

Thesaurus construction and use : selective bibliography based on material in the Aslib Library in July 1967.

Aslib Proceedings 19 (9) 1967 : 310-317.

3 Gilbert, Valerie.

A list of thesauri and subject headings held in the Aslib Library.

Aslib Proceedings 31 (6) June 1979 : 264-274.

4 Inter Organization Board for Information Systems.

Bibliography of United Nations thesauri, classifications, nomenclatures.

Geneva : Inter Organization Board for Information Systems, 1979. 252p.

5 Laureilhe, M. T.

A tentative bibliography of thesauri and subject indexes which have appeared since 1960 (31st March 1969).

Bulletin des Bibliotheques de France 14 (5) May 1969 : 203-218.

6 Laureilhe, M. T.

First supplement to the Bibliography of thesauri and list of subject-headings, published since 1960 (to December 31st 1969).

Bulletin des Bibliotheques de France 15 (1) Jan. 1970 : 21-26.

7 Laureilhe, M. T.

Fourth supplement to the Bibliography of thesauri and subject headings lists published since 1960 (to December 31st 1972).

Bulletin des Bibliotheques de France 18 (3) March 1973 : 101-107.

8 Laureilhe, M. T.

Sixth supplement to the 'bibliography of thesauri and subject headings lists' published since 1960 (to 31st December 1974).

Bulletin des Bibliotheques de France 20 (3) March 1975 : 119-127.

9 Laureilhe, M. T.

Third supplement to the Bibliography of thesauri and subject headings lists published since 1960 (to December 31st 1971).

Bulletin des Bibliotheques de France 17 (2) Feb. 1972 : 67-73.

10 MacCafferty, Maxine.

Thesauri and thesauri construction.

London : Aslib 1977. 191p.

Presents an annotated bibliography of and on thesauri.

11 van der Aa, H. J.

Thesaurus bibliography.

Amsterdam : Studiecentrum NOVI, 1977. 86p.

12 Walkley, J. and Hay, B.

An annotated list of thesauri held in the Aslib Library.

Aslib Proceedings 23 (6) June 1971 : 292-300.

Section A2
General literature on thesaurus

13 Aitchison, Jean and Clarke, Stella Dextre.

The thesaurus : a historical viewpoint, with a look to the future.

Cataloging and Classification Quarterly 37 (3-4) 2004 : 5-21.

14 Bakewell, K. G. B.

Subject indexes : production and use in the IT age.

Indexer 13 (4) Oct. 1983 : 249-251.

Reports a seminar that discussed vocabulary control and other issues related with subject indexing in the age of IT.

15 Bakewell, K. G. B. and Rowland, G.

Indexing and abstracting.

British Librarianship and Information Work 1986-1990. Volume 2. Special Libraries, Materials and Processes. Ed. by David Bromley and Angela M. Allott. London : Library Association Publishing, 1993 : 212-225.

Presents a review of developments in UK in the field of indexing and abstracting including thesauri.

16 Bearman, D.

Vocabulary control.

Archives and Museum Informatics 7 (4) Winter 1993-1994 : 6-8.

Presents a summary of activities of a workshop on vocabulary control.

17 Bergmark, D.

The effect of common words and synonyms on retrieval performance : information storage retrieval.

Ithaca, New York : Cornell University, Department of Computer Science, 1970. 44p.

18 Chowdhury, G. G.

Introduction to modern information retrieval.

London : Library Association Publishing, 1999 : 118-143.

Has a chapter on vocabulary control.

19 Cleverdon, Cyril W.

A survey of the development of information retrieval systems.

Eurim II : a European conference on the application of research in information services and libraries. Presented by Aslib. Ed. by W. E. Batten. London : Aslib, 1977 : 103-106.

20 Cleverdon, Cyril W.

Terminological control.

Essential problems in terminology for informatics and documentation. Ed. by V. I. Gorkova and I. I. Bakulina. Mosco : All-Union Institute of Scientific and Technical Information, 1979 : 32-37.

21 Coates, E. J.

The role of classification in information retrieval : action and thought in the contribution of Brian Vickery.

Journal of Documentation 44 (3) Sept. 1988 : 216-225.

Discusses about B.C. Vickery's contribution to the

development of classification and thesauri.

22 Cochrane, P. A. et al.

34th annual UIUC clinic highlights visualizing subject access.

Library Hi Tech News (142) May 1997 : 1-8.

Presents a summary of various sessions of the Clinic including thesauri and thesauri in the full text world, the role of controlled vocabulary in visualizing document associations and building and accessing vocabulary tools for networked resources.

23 Cumming, M.

Tomatoes are not the only fruit : a rough guide to taxonomies, thesauri, ontologies and the like.

Records Management Bulletin 113, April 2003 : 11-12.

24 Dahlberg, Ingetraut.

Knowledge organization and terminology : philosophical and linguistic bases.

International Classification 19(2) 1992 : 65-71.

25 Dahlberg, Ingetraut.

Major developments in classification.

Advances in librarianship. Volume 7. Ed. by M. J. Voigt and M. H. Harris. New York : Academic Press, 1977 : 41-103.

Reviews developments in the field of classification and thesauri.

26 Dahlberg, Ingetraut.

Thesaurus research : Deutsche Geselleschaft Fur Dokumentation.

EV Bulletin de I'AID 5(4) 1966 : 103-104.

27 Dahlberg, Ingetraut.

Third international study conference on classification research.

International Classification 2 (1) May 1975 : 37-44.

Report of the FID Conference (Bombay, January 1975) which has a session on thesauri construction.

28 Dale, Doris Cruger and Wilson, Betty Ruth.

A survey of the literature on subject analysis for 1984-1985.

Resources and Technical Services 30 (3) July-Sept. 1986 : 261-289.

Reviews literature on subject analysis including thesauri.

29 Diemer, A.

Classification, thesauri what comes next? The problem of the 'third generation' in documentation and information work.

Nachrichten fur Dokumentation 23 (2) Apr. 1972 : 52-57.

30 Doszkocs, T. E.

Simultaneous searching of distributed information and subject repositories on the World Wide Web.

Visualizing subject access for Twenty first Century information resources. Proceedings of the 1997 Clinic on Library Applications of Data Processing, Urbana-Champaign, Illinois, *2-4 March 1997.* Ed. by Pauline Atherton Cochrane and Eric H. Johnson (with the assistance of Sandra Roe). Urbana-Champaign, Illinois : Illinois University at Urbana-Champaign, Graduate School of Library and Information Science, 1998 : 15.

Also available at : http://www.sis.nlm.nih.gov/~doszkocs/dpc/sld001.htm

Presents a review of vocabulary control literature from 1977 to 1997.

31 Dykstra, Mary.

Subject analysis and thesauri : a background.

Art Documentation 8 (4) Winter 1989 : 173-174.

Examines role of thesauri in subject analysis.

32 Fialkowski, Konrad R.; Muraszkiewicz, Mieczyslaw R. and Tolwinska, Alicja B.

Methodology of world clearinghouse activity.

Information Processing and Management 17 (1) 1981 : 21-25.

Explains the principles and methodology of Warsaw Clearinghouse - a centre established for collecting, processing and disseminating information on thesauri and other vocabulary control tools.

33 Foskett, D. J.

Thesaurus.

Encyclopaedia of library and information science. Volume 30. Ed. By Allen Kent. New York : Marcel Dekker Inc., 1980 : 416-463.

34 Fuhr, Norbert.

Considerations in searching databases spanning 20 years.

Online Information 88. Proceedings of the 12th International Online Information Meeting, London, 6-8 December 1988. Volume 2. Oxford : Learned Information (Europe) Ltd., 1988 : 459-465.

Reviews vocabulary and other changes occurred in various databases during a span of 20 years.

35 Gallo, M. A.

Inventory of Spanish and / or Portuguese documentary languages.

International Classification 8 (1) 1981 : 28-29.

Presents a review of thesauri and other indexing languages in Spanish and or Portuguese languages.

36 Gilchrist, Alan.

Thesauri, taxonomies and ontologies : an etymological note.

Journal of Documentation 59 (1) 2003 : 7-18.

37 Grolier, E. de.

Classification one hundred years after Dewey.

Unesco Bulletin for Libraries 30 (6) Nov -Dec. 1976 : 320-329.

Examines the present state of the numerous specialized classifications and their replacement by thesauri

38 Guha, B.

Documentation and information : services, techniques and systems.

Calcutta : World Press Private Limited, 1978. 370p.

Defines thesaurus and states it's uses in a chapter on thesaurus.

39 Harman, D.

Overview of the first text retrieval conference.

Proceedings of the 14th National Online Meeting, New York, 4-6 May 1993. Ed. by Martha E. Wliams, Medford, New Jersey : Learned Information, Inc., 1993 : 181-187.

Summarizes discussions at TREC-1 conference on information retrieval techniques and tools including thesauri.

40 Harman, D.

Overview of the Second Text Retrieval Conference (TREC-2).

Information Processing and Management 31 (3) May-June 1995 : 271.

Reports ongoing research in IR techniques and tools such as thesauri as discussed in the TREC-2 conference.

41 Harris, Jessica.

Terminology change : effect on index vocabularies.

Information Processing and Management 15 (2) 1979 : 77-88.

Reports changes in the vocabulary of information science over a period of 11 years and recommends that thesauri must respond to these changes.

42 Ingwersen, Peter and Wormell, Irene.

Ranganathan in the perspective of advanced information retrieval.

Libri 42 (3) July-Sept. 1992 : 184-201.

Examines Ranganathan's approaches to knowledge organization including thesauri.

43 Jones, K. S.

Some thesauric history.

Aslib Proceedings 24 (7) July 1972 : 400-411.

44 Jones, Kevin P.

Information and the information professional.

Aslib Proceedings 43 (9) Sept. 1991 : 259-269.

Describes various aspects and properties of information – controlled vocabulary is one of them.

45 Kleinbart, Paul.

Prolegomenon to 'intelligent' thesaurus software.

Journal of Information Science 11 (2) 1985 : 45-53.

Redefines thesaurus in the context of recent developments in linguistics, AI, programming techniques and computer architecture.

46 Kunz, M.

Subject retrieval in distributed resources : a short review of recent developments.

International Cataloguing and Bibliographic Control 32 (1) Jan.-March 2003 : 17-20.

Examines recent developments in subject retrieval in the context of multilingual thesaurus and some other aspects.

47 McIlwaine, I. C.

Subject retrieval in a networked environment.

International Cataloguing and Bibliographic Control 31 (1) Jan.-March 2002 : 18-19.

Presents report of IFLA conference, which has sessions on retrieval in a multilingual environment and retrieval across multiple vocabularies.

48 McIlwaine, I. C.

Trends in knowledge organization research.

Knowledge Organization 30 (2) 2003 : 75-86.

Reviews current trends in knowledge organization including thesauri and vocabulary mapping.

49 Meikle, D.

Syndetic structure and OPACS : a literature review.

Cataloguing Australia 21 (1) March 1995 : 19-35.

Present literature review on syndetic structure in OPACs.

50 Meyriat, Jean.

Social science information languages : a comparative analysis.

International Classification 7 (2) 1980 : 61-65.

Reviews various thesauri and other terminological tools in social science.

51 Miller, P.

I say what I mean. but do I mean what I say?

Ariadne (23) March 2000. No page numbers.

Also available at : http://www.ariadne.ac.uk/issue23/metadata/

Reports activities of a Terminology Workshop, which examined the need for controlled terminologies and thesauri in providing Internet-based services.

52 Mitchell, J. S.

The road ahead for library classification systems.

Cataloguing Australia 23 (3-4) Sept.-Dec. 1997 : 41-51.

Describes various ongoing activities at the DDC including development of a new database system with an authority control file for entries in the Relative Index and linking entries from other thesauri.

53 Piggott, M.

Some post-war developments in indexing in Great Britain.

Technical services management : 1965-1990 [a festschrift volume].

New York : Haworth Press, 1996 : 259-272.

Reviews post war developments in indexing and thesauri in UK.

54 Poletylo, M.

Thesauri-origins and development.

Aktualne Problemy Informacji Dokumentacji 15 (1) 1970 : 6-9.

55 Rajan, T. N.

Indexing systems : concepts models and techniques.

Calcutta : Indian Association of Special Libraries and Information Centres (IASLIC), 1981. 270p.

A composite book on indexing which has articles on problems of indexing terminology, natural

language vis-a-vis controlled vocabulary, thesaurus in information systems, etc.

56 Redfern, Margaret.

Current research activity at the Polytechnic of North London School of Librarianship and Information Studies.

Library and Information Research News 5 (20) Dec. 1982 : 19.

Reports an ongoing project at the School of Librarianship and Information Studies, Polytechnic of North London on the search pathways in thesauri.

57 Rekha, G. and Parameswaran, M.

'Knowledge Organization', 1988-1999 : a bibliometric analysis.

SRELS Journal of Information Management 39 (4) Dec. 2002 : 355-362.

Analyzes 12 volumes of KO and identifies that vocabulary control and thesauri are some of the core topics covered by the journal.

58 Roberts, Norman.

The pre-history of the information retrieval thesaurus.

Journal of Documentation 40 (4) Dec. 1984 : 271-285.

Reviews major events in the history of thesaurus development.

59 Rowley, Jennifer and Farrow, John.

Organizing knowledge : an introduction to managing access to information. 3rd ed.

Aldershot : Gower, 2000 : 123-161.

Has a chapter on indexing and searching languages.

60 Schulte Albert, Hans G.

Classificatory thinking from Kinner to Wilkins : classification and thesaurus construction 1645-1668.

Library Quarterly 49 (1) Jan. 1979 : 42-64.

61 Scibor, E.

Thesauri and classification : an attempt at a state-of-the-art review.

Aktualne Problemy Informacji Dokumentacji 14 (6) Nov.-Dec. 1969 : 5-10.

62 Shiri, Ali Asghar and Revie, Crawford.

Thesauri on the Web : current developments and trends.

Online Information Review 24 (4) 2000 : 273-279.

PowerPoint presentation available at : http://personal.dis.strath.ac.uk/people/shiri

63 Thomas, Alan R.

Terminological problems : occurrence, causes, consequences, and solutions in guidance, counselling, and associated fields.

International Journal of Information and Library Research 1 (1)1989 : 40-52.

64 Tomov, D. T.

Some critical remarks on the stop word lists of ISI publications.

Journal of Documentation 57 (6) Nov. 2001 : 798-808.

Reports a semantic analysis of the stop word lists of publications of the ISI and lists shortcomings of the stop word list.

65 Veal, D. C.

Techniques of document management : a review of text retrieval and related technologies

Journal of Documentation 57 (2) March 2001:192-217.

Reviews document management techniques and tools including thesauri.

66 Vickery, B. C.

Thesaurus – a new word in documentation.

Journal of Documentation 16(4) 1960 : 181-189.

67 Wellisch, Hans H.

Abstracting, indexing, classification, thesaurus construction : a glossary.

Indexer 21 (2) Oct. 1998 : 101.

68 Wellisch, Hans H.

Glossary of terminology in abstracting, classification, indexing and thesaurus construction.

Australian Library Journal 51 (4) Nov. 2002 : 372-73.

69 Wellisch, Hans H.

Year's work in subject analysis : 1980.

Library Resources and Technical Services 25 (3) July-Sept. 1981 : 295-309.

Reviews literature published in 1990 on subject analysis including thesauri.

70 Wersig, G.

A new definition of 'thesaurus'.

Nachrichten fur Dokumentation 20 (2) April 1969 : 53-62.

71 Wolner, Theresa J.

Subject access literature, 1988.

Library Resources and Technical Services 33 (3) July 1989 : 240-247.

Reviews literature on subject access along with other subjects such as thesauri, subject headings, authority control.

72 Younger, Jennifer A.

Year's work in subject analysis : 1981.

Library Resources and Technical Services 26 (3) July-Sept. 1982 : 263-276.

Reviews year's publications in the field of subject analysis including vocabulary control.

Section B
Manuals/Conference Papers

Authorities such as Jean Aitchison, Dagobert Soergel, F. W. Lancaster have published comprehensive books / manuals on thesaurus construction and use. Volumes of conferences on thesaurus construction are also published. This section lists books / manuals and conference proceedings.

73 Aitchison, Jean and Gilchrist, Alan.
Thesaurus construction : practical manual.
London : Aslib, 1972. 95p.

74 Aitchison, Jean and Gilchrist, Alan.
Thesaurus construction : a practical manual. 2nd Ed.
London: Aslib, 1987.

75 Aitchison, Jean; Gilchrist Alan and Bawden, D.
Thesaurus construction and use : a practical manual. 3rd ed.
London : Aslib, 1997. 212p.

76 Aitchison, Jean; Gilchrist Alan and Bawden David.
Thesaurus construction and use : a practical manual. 4th ed.
London : Aslib IMI, 2000. 218p.

77 Alber, F. M.
On-line thesaurus design for an integrated information system.
Edmonton : Alberta University Department of Computing Science, 1972. 158p.

78 Broughton, Vanda.
Essential thesaurus construction.
London : Facet Publishing, 2005. 256p.

79 Cerny, B. A.

Development of a political service thesaurus.

Berkeley : California University, Laurence Berkeley Laboratory, 1980. 59p.

Describes methods adopted in developing a political science thesaurus.

80 Cleveland, Donald B. and Cleveland, Ana D.

Introduction to indexing and abstracting.

Littleton, Colorado : Libraries Unlimited Inc., 1983. 209p.

Discusses vocabulary control and other aspects of indexing and abstracting.

81 Croghan, Antony.

A manual on the construction of an indexing language.

London : Coburgh Publications, 1971.

82 Documentation Research and Training Centre, Banglore.

Seminar on thesaurus in information systems, jointly organized by DRTC and INSDOC. Bangalore, 1- 5 December 1975.

Bangalore : Documentation Research and Training Centre, 1975. 180p.

83 Gilchrist, Alan.

The thesaurus in retrieval.

London : Aslib, 1971. 184p.

84 Grefenstette, Gregory

Explorations in automatic thesaurus discovery.

Norwell, MA : Kluwer Academic Publishers, 1994. 320p.

Presents an automated method for creating a first-draft thesaurus from raw text.

85 Guzman, Manuel and Verstappen, Bert.

How to develop a list of index terms or thesaurus. (Human Rights Monitoring and Documentation Series ; Volume 4.) Draft.

Versoix, Switzerland : Human Rights Information and

Documentation Systems, International (HURIDOCS), 2003.

A manual for documentalists and information workers of human rights organisations. It describes the different phases involved in the process of creating index lists and thesauri and using them to index documents systematically.

Also available at : http://www.huridocs.org/tools/howtoind.htm

86 Lancaster, F. W.

Thesaurus construction and use : a condensed course.

Paris : UNESCO, 1985. 89p.

87 Orna, Elizabeth.

Build yourself a thesaurus : a step by step guide.

Norwich : Running Angel, 1983. 32p.

88 Roe, Sandra K. and Thomas, Alan R. *Eds.*

The thesaurus : review, renaissance, and revision.

New York ; London : Haworth, 2004. 209p.

A collection of twelve papers by thesaurus specialists.

Also available at: http://www.haworthpress.com/store/product.asp?sku=5134&AuthType=4

Also simultaneously co-published in Cataloging and Classification Quarterly 37 (3-4) 2004.

89 Soergel, Dagobert.

Indexing languages and thesauri : construction and maintenance.

Los Angeles : Melville Publishing Co., 1974. 632p.

90 Technical Information Center.

Energy information database, subject thesaurus.

Oak Ridge, TN : Department of Energy, Technical Information Center, 1979 : 864p.

Presents an historical account of classification and thesaurus construction activities.

91 *Thesauri for museum documentation.*

Proceedings of a Workshop held at the Science Museum, London, 24 February 1992, organized by the Museum Documentation Association, Terminology Working Group. (MDA occasional paper ; 18).

Cambridge : MDA, 1992. 106p.

92 Townley, Helen M. and Gee, Ralph D.

Thesaurus-making : grow your own word-stock.

London : Andre Deutsch, 1980. 206p.

Provides guidance in construction, updating and evaluation of thesauri.

93 Weiner, Stephen B.

A workshop on qualitative information retrieval, 18-20 November 1980.

Bethesda, MD : Center for Policy Research Inc., 1981. 66p.

Reports discussions of a workshop on IR and indexing languages.

94 United States, Department of Defense, Office of Navel Research. Project LEX.

Manual for building a technical thesaurus.

Washington, DC : Department of Defense, 1966.

Section C
Indexing languages

An index is a list of documents arranged under pre-determined subject headings. An index entry provides necessary bibliographic description about the documents listed. This includes names of author/s title of the document and other bibliographic details of the host document.

Indexing is the process of preparing an index. This process usually involves the following steps.

1. Analyzing the contents of the document to be indexed and identifying its subject.
2. Selecting standard term/s (from thesaurus, subject heading lists, classification scheme) to represent the subject identified in the first step.
3. Preparing an index entry under the selected standard subject heading with necessary bibliographical details about the document being indexed.
4. Arranging all the index entries in an alphabetical order.

In this process of indexing as can be noticed, the subject representing term/s are selected from terminological tools. Sometime the indexer has to prepare a subject heading by combining two or more terms. Thus subject-representing term/s (along with the rules of semantics and syntax) used in indexing are called indexing languages. Indexing languages are also referred to as indexing vocabularies.

Since the beginning of indexing history the LIS professionals have had interest in studying the features and aspects of indexing languages. As a result of this interest a large amount of literature has been published on indexing languages and their various aspects.

Literature dealing with indexing languages- in general is listed in this section.

95 Adam, R.

Language and information retrieval in the social sciences.

Aslib Proceedings 34, 1982 : 394-405.

96 Aitchison, Jean.

Indexing languages and indexing.

Handbook of special librarianship and information work. 6th ed. Ed. by Patti Dosset. London : Aslib, 1992 : 191-233.

97 Aitchison, Jean.

Indexing languages, classification schemes and thesauri.

Handbook of special librarianship and information work. 5th ed. Ed. by L. J. Anthony. London : Aslib, 1982 : 207-261.

98 Barite, M. G.

The notion of 'category' : its implications in subject analysis and in the construction and evaluation of indexing languages.

Knowledge Organization 27 (1-2) 2000 : 4-10.

99 Deschatalets, Gilles.

The three languages theory in information retrieval.

International Classification 13 (3) 1986 : 126-132.

100 Gebhardt, Friedrich and Stellmacher, Imant.

Opinion paper : design criteria for documentation retrieval languages.

Journal of the American Society for Information Science 29 (4) July 1978 : 191-199.

101 Hoerman, H. L. and Furniss, K. A.

Turning practice into principles : a comparison of the IFLA Principles underlying subject heading languages (SHLs) and the principles underlying the Library of Congress Subject Headings system.

Cataloging and Classification Quarterly 29 (1-2) 2000 : 31-52.

102 Hutchins, W. J.

Languages of indexing and classification.

Stevenage : Peter Peregrinus, 1979.

103 Jabrzemska, E. and Scibor, E.

Survey of indexing languages used in Polish information establishments.

International Forum on Information and Documentation 12 (2) April 1987 : 12-13.

104 Keen, E. Michael.

Aspects of computer-based indexing languages.

Computers in Libraries International 91. Proceedings of the 5th Annual Conference on Computers in Libraries, London, February 1991 : 148-151.

105 Keen, E. Michael and Digger, J. A.

A report on an information science index language test. 2 vols.

Aberystwyth : College of Librarianship, 1972.

106 Kim, C.

Retrieval languages of social sciences and natural sciences : a statistical investigation.

Journal of American Society for Information Science 33(1) 1982 : 3-7.

107 Lopes, M. I.

Principles underlying subject heading languages : an international approach.

International Cataloguing and Bibliographic Control 25 (1) Jan.-March 1996 : 10-12.

108 Maniez, J.

Database merging and the compatibility of indexing languages.

Knowledge Organization 24 (4) 1997 : 213-224.

109 Marco, J. G.

Hypertext and indexing languages : common challenges and perspectives.

Advances in knowledge organization. Knowledge organization and change. Proceedings of the 4th International ISKO Conference, Washington, DC. 15-18 July 1996. Volume 5. Frankfurt / Main : Indeks Verlag, 1996 : 87-94.

110 Moyne, J. A.

Information retrieval and natural language.

Proceedings of the 32nd Annual Meeting of the American Society for Information Science, San Francisco, 1-4 October 1969. Vol. 6. Westport, CT : Greenwood Publishing Corp., 1969 : 259-263.

111 Sharada, B. A.

Rules derivation for Kannada based indexing language using transformational grammar.

Library Science with a Slant to Documentation and Information Studies 35 (2) June 1998 : 133-138.

112 Svenonius, Elaine.

Compatibility of retrieval languages : introduction to a forum.

International Classification 10 (1) 1983 : 2-4.

113 Wall, R. A.

Indexing language structure for automated retrieval.

Information Storage and Retrieval 9 (11) Nov. 1973 : 607-617.

114 Waltz, David L.

Natural-language question-answering systems.

Proceedings of the 1975 clinic on library applications of data processing : the use of computers in literature searching and related reference activities in libraries: papers presented at the 1975 clinic on library applications of data processing, 27-30 April 1975. Urbana-Champaign. Ed. by F. Wfrid Lancaster. Urbana-Champaign : University of Illinois, Graduate School of Library Science, 1976 : 137-144.

115 Yi, H.

Indexing languages, new progress in China.

Knowledge Organization 22 (1) 1995 : 30-32.

Discusses current trends in China in indexing languages including thesauri.

Section D
Natural language

The indexing languages are categorized into two categories i.e. natural language and controlled language (vocabulary).

The subject representing terms used by authors are known as natural language terms. Natural language has its own advantages over controlled vocabulary. The literature listed in this section deals with meaning, features, advantages and uses of natural language.

116 Abramowitz, Diane.

At last, a user-oriented system : LEXIS.

Information revolution : proceedings of the 38th ASIS Annual Meeting. Volume 12. Ed. by Charles W. Husbands, Ruth L. Tighe. Washington, DC : American Society for Information Science, 1975 : 125-126.

Describes an interactive retrieval system containing full-text legal documents which aims at direct user-machine interaction without resort to thesauri.

117 Basch, R.

Searching in plain English.

Link-Up (USA) 11 (2) March-April 1994 : 14-15.

118 Baser, Kenneth H. et al.

On-line indexing experiment at Chemical Abstracts Service : algorithmic generation of articulated index entries from natural language phrases.

Journal of Chemical Information and Computer Sciences 18 (1) Feb. 1978 : 18-25.

119 Bernstein, Lionel and Williamson, Robert E.

Testing of a natural language retrieval system for a full text knowledge base.

Journal of the American Society for Information Science 35 (4) July 1984 : 235-247.

Describes 'Navigator of Natural Language Organized Data (ANNOD) - a retrieval system which combines use of probabilistic, linguistic, and empirical means to rank individual paragraphs of full text for their similarity to natural language queries proposed by users. ANNOD includes common word deletion, word root isolation, query expansion by a thesaurus.

120 Bhattacharyya, K.

The effectiveness of natural language in science indexing and retrieval.

Journal of Documentation 30 (3) Sept. 1974 : 235-254.

121 Biswas, Gautam et al.

Knowledge-assisted document retrieval : 1. The natural language interface.

Journal of the American Society for Information Science 38 (2) March 1987 : 83-96.

122 Blais, C. L.

A natural language query system to aid in navy command and control. Concepts for modifying LADDER (Language Access to Distributed Data with Error Recovery) for the retrieval of information in an operational environment.

San Diego, CA. : Naval Ocean Systems Center, 1979. 28p.

123 Bonzi, Susan and Liddy, Elizabeth D.

Testing the assumption underlying use of anaphora in natural language tests.

ASIS '88. Information Technology : planning for the next fifty years. Proceedings of the 51st Annual Meeting of the American Society for Information Science. Atlanta, Georgia, 23-27 October 1988. Volume 25. Ed. by Christine L. Borgman and Edward Y. H. Pai. Medford, New Jersey : Learned Information, Inc., for American Society for Information Science, 1988 : 23-30.

124 Chai, J. et.al

Natural Language Assistant : a dialog system for online product recommendation.

AI Magazine 23 (2) Summer 2002 : 63-75.

125 Chan, David.

Natural language interfaces.

The new information professionals. Proceedings of the Singapore-Malaysia Congress of Librarian and Information Scientists. Singapore 4-6 September 1986. Ed. by Ajita Thuraisingham. Aldershot : Gower, 1987 : 211-219.

126 Chin, D. N.

Planning intelligent responses in a natural language system.

Artificial Intelligence Review 14 (4-5) Oct. 2000 : 283-331.

127 Clark, D.

Natural language, relevancy ranking, and common sense.

IEEE Intelligent Systems 14 (4) July-August 1999 : 17-19.

128 Clemencin, Gregoire.

Querying the French Yellow Pages : natural language access to the directory.

Information Processing and Management 24 (6) 1988 : 633-649.

129 Cleverdon, Cyril.

Optimizing convenient online access to bibliographic databases.

Information Services and Use 4 (1-2) April 1984 : 37-47.

Explains the rational for using natural language instead of thesauri.

130 Cohen, Stanley M.; Dayton, David L. and Salvador, Ricardo.

Experimental algorithmic generation of articulated index entries from natural language phrases at Chemical Abstracts Service.

Journal of Chemical Information and Computer Sciences 16 (2) May 1976 : 93-99.

131 Cunningham, J.

Getting the most from Alta Vista.

Behavioral and Social Sciences Librarian 15 (1) 1996 : 53-56.

Describes the method of indexing used by Alta Vista, which uses natural language.

132 Damerau, Fred J.

Prospects for knowledge-based customization of natural language query systems.

Information Processing and Management 24 (6) 1988 : 651-654.

133 de Andrade Oliveira, Elvira.

An automatic index in natural language for UDC editions.

International Classification 2 (2) Nov. 1975 : 89-93.

134 de Heer, T.

Quasi comprehension of natural language simulated by means of information traces.

Information Processing and Management 15 (2) 1979 : 89-98.

135 Dorai, Gautham K. and Yacoob, Yaser.

Embedded grammar tags : advancing natural language interaction on the web.

IEEE Intelligent Systems 17 (1) Jan.-Feb. 2002 : 48-53.

136 Doszkocs, Tamas E.

Automatic vocabulary mapping in online searching.

International Classification 10 (2) 1983 : 78-83.

Describes the implementation of a technique for using natural language as a compatible intra- and inter-system retrieval language interface.

137 Doszkocs, Tamas E.

CITE NLM : natural language searching in an online catalog. *Information Technology and Libraries* 2 (4) Dec. 1983 : 364-380.

338 Doszkocs, Tamas E.

Natural language processing in information retrieval. *Journal of the American Society for Information Science* 37 (4) July 1986 : 191-196.

139 Doszkocs, Tamas E.

Natural-language searching as a user performance enhancement tool.

Canadian Journal of Information Science 12 (3-4) 1987 : 139-149.

140 Doszkocs, Tamas E.

Natural language user interfaces in information retrieval and data base management systems.

Online '87. Proceedings of the Conference, Anaheim, California. Part I. Weston, CT : Online Inc., 1987 : 67-72

141 Doszkocs, Tamas E. and Rapp, Barbara A.

Searching MEDLINE in English : a prototype user interface with natural language query, ranked output, and relevance feedback.

Information choices and policies. Proceedings of the 1979 ASIS Annual Meeting. Volume 16. Ed. by Roy D. Tally and Ronald R. Deultgen. White Plains, New York : Knowledge Industry Publications for American Society for Information Science, 1979 : 131-139.

142 Eichman, Thomas Lee and Coates, E. J.

Subject heading syntax and 'natural language' nominal compound syntax.

The information age in perspective. Proceedings of the 41st Annual Meeting. New York. 13-17 November 1978. Volume

15. Compiled by Everett H. Brenner. White Plains, New York : Knowledge Industry Publications for American Society for Information Science, 1978 : 126-129.

143 Evans, R.

Beyond Boolean : relevance ranking, natural language and the new search paradigm.

Proceedings of the 15th National Online Meeting, 10-12 May 1994. Ed. by Martha E. Wliams. Medford, New Jersey, Learned Information Inc., 1994 : 121-128.

144 Feldman, S. E.

Searching natural language systems : searchers know thy engine.

Searcher 2 (8) Oct. 1994 : 34-39.

145 Fidel, Raya.

Request-related criteria for the selection of search keys

1984 : Challenges to an information society. Proceedings of the 47th ASIS Annual Meeting. Compiled by Barbara Flood, Joanne Witiak and Thomas Hogan. White Plains, New York : Knowledge Industry Publications, Inc. for American Society for Information Science, 1984 : 141-143.

Explains how the request related keywords are useful in searching online information.

146 Fugmann, Robert.

The complementarity of natural and indexing languages.

International Classification 9 (3) 1982 : 140-144.

147 Fugmann, Robert.

The complementarity of natural and indexing languages.

Universal classification II : subject analysis and ordering systems. Proceedings of the 4th International Study Conference on Classification Research, FID/CR, Augsburg, 28 June-2 July 1982. Frankfurt : Indeks Verlag, 1982-83 : 86-89.

148 Fugmann, Robert.

The complementarity of natural and index language in the field of information supply : an overview of their specific capabilities and limitations.

Knowledge Organization 29 (3-4) 2002 : 217-230.

149 Gluck, M.

Generating travel paths from natural language : description of the personal navigation sub-language in two computer mediated communication systems.

Proceedings of the 55th Annual Meeting of the American Society for Information Science, Pittsburg, 26-29 Oct. 1992. Ed. by Debra Shaw, Medford, New Jersey : Learned Information Inc., For American Society for Information Science, 1992 : 26-31.

150 Hersh, W. R. and Hickam, D. H.

An evaluation of interactive Boolean and natural language searching with an online medical textbook.

Journal of the American Society for Information Science 46 (7) August 1995 : 478-489.

151 Jacsa, Pacter.

Natural language searching.

Online Information Review 28 (1) 2004 : 75-79.

Evaluates KnowledgeFinder and PubMed sorftwares that allow users to search through natural language.

152 Khelalfa, H.

Signar : generating responses in a natural language query system.

Proceedings of the 3rd International Society for Knowledge Organization (ISKO) Conference : Knowledge organization and quality management, Copenhagen, Denmark, 20-24 June 1994. Ed. by Hanne Albrechtsen and Susan Oernager. Frankfurt/Main : Indeks Verlag, 1994 : 118-126.

153 Kim, T. et al.

FromTo-CLIR : Web-based natural language interface for cross-language information retrieval.

Information Processing and Management 35 (4) July 1999 : 559-586.

154 Knapp, S. D.

Free-text searching of online databases.

Reference Librarian 5-6, 1992 : 143-153.

155 Knapp, S. D.

The contemporary thesaurus of search terms and synonyms : a guide for natural language computer searching.

Online Information Review 24 (4) 2000 : 331-322.

156 Knapp, S. D.; Cohen, L. B. and Juedes, R. R.

A natural language thesaurus for the humanities : the need for database search aid.

Library Quarterly 68(4) 1998 : 406-430.

157 Kreymer, O.

An evaluation of help mechanisms in natural language information retrieval systems.

Online Information Review 26 (1) 2002 : 30-39.

158 Kukich, Karen.

Ana's first sentences : sample output from a natural language stock report generator.

National Online Meeting 1983. Proceedings of the 4th National Online Meeting, New York, 12-14 April 1983. Ed. by Martha E. Wliams and Thomas H. Hogan. Medford, New Jersey : Learned Information, Inc., 1983 : 271-280.

159 Lancaster, F. W.; Rapport, R. L. and Penry, J. K.

Evaluating the effectiveness of an on-line natural language retrieval system.

Information Storage and Retrieval 8 (5) Oct. 1972 : 223-245.

160 Laursen, Jennie McKee.

Effectiveness of using natural language in searching volcanic stratigraphy titles.

Communicating information. Proceedings of the 43rd ASIS Annual Meeting, Anaheim, *California, 5-10 October 1980.* Volume 17. Ed. by A. R. Benenfeld and E. J. Kazlauskas. New York : Knowledge Industry Publications Inc., (for ASIS), 1980 : 191-193.

161 Le Loarer, P.

A natural language approach to an online information retrieval system.

IATUL Quarterly 1 (2) June 1987 : 107-113.

162 Lefever, M.; Freeman, B. and Schultz, L.

Managing an uncontrolled vocabulary ex-post facto.

Journal of the American Society for Information Science 23 (6) Nov.- Dec. 1972 : 339-342.

163 Leggate, P. et al.

The on-line search guide project : a prototype for a minicomputer-based aid to construction of search profiles for natural language data bases.

Oxford : University of Oxford Experimental Information Unit, 1976. 51p.

164 Lyon, M.

Language related problems in the IPC and search systems using natural language.

World Patent Information 21 (2) June 1999 : 89-95.

165 Mazlack, Lawrence J. and Feinauer, Richard A.

Establishing a basis for mapping natural-language statements onto a database query language.

Information retrieval research. Ed. by R. N. Oddy et. al. London, Butterworths, 1981 : 192-202.

166 McCray, A. T.

Natural language research program.

International Information Communication and Education 11 (2) Sept. 1992 : 256-258.

167 McKenzie, E. M.

Natural language searching : how WIN works in Westlaw.

Legal Reference Services Quarterly 18 (4) 2001 : 39-47.

168 McKeown, K.; Robin, J. and Kukich, K.

Generating concise natural language summaries.

Information Processing and Management 31 (5) Sept. 1995 : 703-733.

169 McQuire, A. R. and Eastman, C. M.

The ambiguity of negation in natural language queries to information retrieval systems.

Journal of the American Society for Information Science 49 (8) June 1998 : 686-692.

170 McWilliams, Jerry.

Automatic assignment of pre-coordinate subject headings from free-floating descriptors.

The information community : an alliance for progress. Proceedings of the 44th ASIS Annual Meeting, Washington, DC 25-30 October 1981. Volume 18. Ed. by Lois F. Lunin, Madeline Henderson and Harold Wooster. White Plains, New York : Knowledge Industry Publications Inc. for the American Society for Information Science, 1981 : 240-242.

171 Michell, Gillian.

The natural language foundations of indexing language relations.

Canadian Journal of Information Science Vol. 4. May 1979 : 99-104.

172 Ojala, M.

History lessons : ABI/INFORM.

Online 26 (1) Jan.-Feb. 2002 : 61-62.

Provides history of Abstracted Business Information (ABI/INFORM) that provided online abstracts of articles from a core list of business and management publications. The service was initiated with natural language.

173 Owei, V.

Natural language querying of databases : an information extraction approach in the conceptual query language.

International Journal of Human-Computer Studies 53 (4) Oct. 2000 : 439-492.

174 Palmquist, Ruth Ann and Singh, Pradeep.

Testing the importance of a simple thesaurus enhancement for a natural language statement of an information need.

ASIS '87 : Proceedings of the 50th ASIS Annual Meeting. Ed. by Ching-chih Chen. Medford, New Jersey : American Society for Information Science by Learned Information, 1987 : 193-195.

175 Perez-Carballo, J. and Strzalkowski, T.

Natural language information retrieval : progress report.

Information Processing and Management 36 (1) Jan. 2000 : 155-178.

176 Popovic, Mirko and Willett, Peter.

The effectiveness of stemming for natural-language access to Slovene textual data.

Journal of the American Society for Information Science 43 (5) June 1992 : 384-390.

177 Pritchard-Schoch, T.

Comparing natural language retrieval : Win and Freestyle.

Online 19 (4) July-August 1995 : 83-87.

178 Pritchard-Schoch, T.

Natural language comes of age.

Online 17 (3) May 1993 : 33-43.

179 Quint, B.

LexisNexis applies iPhrase natural language search software to key directory files.

Information Today 18 (11) Dec. 2001 : 46.

180 Radev, D. R.; Libner, K. and Fan, W.

Getting answers to natural language questions on the web.

Journal of the American Society for Information Science and Technology 53 (5) May 2002 : 359-564.

181 Redfern, Victoria.

Natural language thesaurus : a survey of student research skills and research tool preferences.

Australian Academic and Research Libraries 35 (2) June 2004 : 137-150.

Presents results of a survey that indicated the need for an online contemporary natural language thesaurus.

182 Rowe, N. C.

Inferring depictions in natural-language captions for efficient access to picture data.

Information Processing and Management 30 (3) May-June 1994 : 379-388.

183 Ruge, Gerda and Schwartz, Christoph.

Natural language access to free-text data bases : information, knowledge, evolution.

Proceedings of the 44th FID Congress, Helsinki, 28 August-1 September 1988. Ed. by Sinikka Koshiala and Ritva Launo. Amsterdam : Elsevier Science Publishers, 1989 : 153-162.

184 Sharp, J. R.

Documentation note : natural language.

Journal of Documentation 31 (3) Sept. 1975 : 191-195.

185 Shneiderman, Ben.

A note on human factors issues of natural language interaction with database systems.

Information Systems 6 (2) 1981 : 125-129.

186 Silverman, B. G.; Bachann, M. and Al-Akharas, K.

Do what I mean : online shopping with a natural language search agent.

IEEE Intelligent Systems 16 (4) July-August 2001 : 48-53.

187 Sparck Jones, Karen.

Natural language access to databases : some questions and a specific approach.

Journal of Information Science 4 (1) March 1982 : 41-48.

188 Spiegler, Israel and Elata, Smadar.

A priori analysis of national language queries.

Information Processing and Management 24 (6) 1988 : 619-631.

189 Strzalkowski, T.

Natural language information retrieval.

Information Processing and Management 31 (3) May-June 1995 : 397.

190 Tam, A. M. and Leung, C. H. C.

Structured natural-language descriptions for semantic content retrieval of visual materials.

Journal of the American Society for Information Science and Technology 52 (11) Sept. 2001 : 930-937.

Suggest a structure for natural language descriptions of the semantic content of visual materials that requires descriptors which may be taken from thesaurus and other sources.

191 Tenopir, C.

Online databases : natural language searching with WIN.

Library Journal 118 (18) Nov. 1993 : 54-56.

192 Tomaiuolo, N. G. and Packer, J.

Maximizing relevant retrieval : keyword and natural language searching.

Online 22 (6) Nov.-Dec. 1998 : 57-58 and 60.

193 Townley, H. M.

A look at natural language retrieval systems.

Information Scientist 5 (1) March 1971 : 3-15.

194 Vickery, B. C.

Classificatory principles in natural language indexing systems.

Classification in the 1970's : a discussion of development and prospects for the major schemes. Ed. by Arthur Maltby. London, Bingley, 1972 : 167-191.

195 Vleduts Stokolov, Natasha.

Concept recognition in an automatic text-processing system for the life sciences.

Journal of the American Society for Information Science 38 (4) July 1987 : 269-287.

Describes an automatic text-processing system based on natural language.

196 Young, Charlene W.; Eastman, Caroline M. and Oakman, Robert L.

An analysis of ill-formed input in natural language queries to document retrieval systems.

Information Processing and Management 27 (6) 1991 : 615-622.

Section E
Vocabulary control

Even though the natural language has many advantages it has certain lacunae also. In order to have better precision and recall there is need to control the vocabulary. The process of controlling the vocabulary used in information storage and retrieval is known as vocabulary control. The literature in this section deals meaning, need, processes and tools for vocabulary control.

197 Austin, Derek.

PRECIS.

Library Science with a Slant to Documentation 12 (4) Dec. 1975 : 89-126.

Discusses vocabulary control in PRECIS.

198 Austin, Derek.

Vocabulary control and information technology.

Aslib Proceedings 38 (1) Jan. 1986 : 1-15.

Highlights importance of vocabulary control in IT based indexing.

199 Borko, Harold and Austin, Derek.

Note commenting on 'Vocabulary control and information technology' by Derek Austin.

Aslib Proceedings 38 (6-7) June-July 1986 : 219-221.

200 Busch, J. and Jizba, L.

Organizing information content and vocabularies : Joseph Busch's journey from talking books to vocabulary markup languages.

Journal of Internet Cataloging 5 (2) 2002 : 3-19.

Narrates an interview with Joseph Busch, President of the

American Society for Information Science and Technology (ASIST) in which he discusses vocabulary control and other aspects of IR.

201 Chen, Ya-Ning; Chen, Shu-Jiun and Chung, Feng-Chien.

The feasibility study of DSpace towards a virtual cross-institutional repository.

Journal of Educational Media and Library Sciences 42 (2) Dec. 2004 : 243-256.

Describes various features including vocabulary control of Dspace – a software for creating and managing digital library.

202 Cousins, Thomas R. and Dominick, Wayne D.

The management of data bases of data bases.

The information age in perspective. Proceedings of the 41st ASIS Annual Meeting, New York, 13-17 November, 1978. Compiled by Everett H. Brenner. White Plains, New York : Knowledge Industry Publications for American Society for Information Science, 1978 : 75-78.

Discusses vocabulary control and other aspects of managing multiple databases.

203 Croydon, Stan.

Defining pattern and trends from litigation data bases.

The information community : an alliance for progress. Proceedings of the 44th ASIS Annual Meeting, Washington, DC, 25-30 October 1981. Volume 18. Ed. by Lois F. Lunin, Madeline Henderson and Harold Wooster. White Plains, New York : Knowledge Industry Publications Inc. for the American Society for Information Science, 1981 : 375-376.

Discusses the problem of vocabulary control in litigation support applications.

204 Davis, C. H.

An approach to automated vocabulary control in indexes of organic compounds, II.

Journal of Chemical Documentation 9 (4) Nov. 1969 : 252-256.

205 Dolan, Donna R.

Subject searching of the New York Times Information Bank. *Online* 2 (2) April 1978 : 26-30.

Suggests vocabulary control measures for managing the 'Information Bank' - an online database of the late edition of the New York Times and other 60 selected periodicals.

206 Dubin, D.

Dimensions and discriminability : The role of controlled vocabulary in visualizing document associations.

Visualizing subject access for Twentyfirst Century information resources. Proceedings of the 1997 Clinic on Library Applications of Data Processing, Urbana-Champaign, Illinois, 2-4 March 1997. Ed. by Pauline Atherton Cochrane and Eric H. Johnson (with the assistance of Sandra Roe). Urbana-Champaign, Illinois : Illinois University at Urbana-Champaign, Graduate School of Library and Information Science, 1998 : 39-44.

Explains the role of vocabulary control in classifying search output.

207 Fugmann, R.

Review of second edition of vocabulary control for information retrieval by F. Lancaster.

International Classification 14, 1987 : 164-166.

208 Gabriel, Erna; MacDonald, Clarice I. and Vojta, Vilma.

The vocabulary control system of the Washington Library Network.

Information revolution. Proceedings of the 38th ASIS Annual Meeting, Boston, Massachusetts, 26-30 October 1975. Volume 12. Ed. by Charles W. Husbands, Ruth L. Tighe. Washington DC : American Society for Information Science, 1975 : 14-

15.

Describes the automated vocabulary control system at the Washington Library Network.

209 Gorman, Michael.

Authority control in the context of bibliographic control in the electronic environment.

Cataloging & Classification Quarterly 38 (3-4) 2004 :11-22.

Defines authority control and vocabulary control and explains their importance.

210 Gorman, Michael.

Why teach cataloguing and classification?

Cataloging and Classification Quarterly 34 (1-2) 2002 : 1-13.

Highlights importance of teaching vocabulary control and bibliographic architecture.

211 Jackson, A. R. Haygarth.

What large users expect from secondary services producers.

Aslib Proceedings 28 (10) Oct. 1976 : 347-353.

Review the vocabulary control and other needs of large industrial users of secondary information services.

212 Klausmeier, Jane.

MICROsearch : ERIC's approach to the downloading dilemma.

National Online Meeting Proceedings 1984, New York, 10-12 April 1984. Compiled by Martha E. Wliams and Thomas H. Hogan, Medford, New Jersey : Learned Information, 1984 : 149-154.

Describes the use of MICROsearch (a program developed to search downloaded portions of the ERIC database on floppy disks) in teaching vocabulary control and other aspects of IR.

213 Klausmeier, Jane.

MICROsearch : the many uses of a downloaded database.

Microcomputers for Information Management 2 (1) March 1985 : 25-32.

Describes the use of MICROsearch (a program developed to search downloaded portions of the ERIC database on floppy disks) in teaching vocabulary control and other aspects of IR.

214 Krovetz, R. and Croft, W. B.

Lexical ambiguity and information retrieval.

ACM Transactions on Information Systems 10 (2) April 1992 :115-141.

215 Lancaster, F. W.

Vocabulary control for information retrieval.

Washington : Information Resources Press, 1972. 233p.

216 Lancaster, F. W.

Vocabulary control for information retrieval. 2nd ed.

Arlington VA : Information Resources Press, 1986.

217 MacCafferty, Maxine.

A technical information service on coal.

Aslib Proceedings 31 (10) Oct. 1979 : 445-451.

Describes vocabulary control and other efforts made by the Technical Information Service of the International Energy Agency Coal Research.

218 MacDougall, S.

Signposts on the information superhighway : indexes and access.

Journal of Internet Cataloging 2 (3-4) 2000 : 61-79.

Explains the use of information about vocabulary control and other signposts for indexing the Internet.

219 McIlwaine, I. C.

Some problems of context and terminology.

Information Studies 4 (4) Oct. 1998 : 195-201.

Discusses the problem of context and terminology, the limitations imposed by language and offers solutions thereto.

220 Milstead, J. L.

Needs for research in indexing.

Journal of the American Society for Information Science 45 (8) Sept. 1994 : 577-582.

Discusses the vocabulary and other areas of indexing, on which research is required.

221 Neelameghan, A. and Green, R.

Information indexing, searching and retrieval in multilingual and cross cultural communication : ISKO 5th International Conference, Lille, France, 25-29 August 1998 : keynote panel presentations.

Information Studies 4 (4) Oct. 1998 : 189-194.

Presents panel discussions on vocabulary control and various other issues related with indexing and searching in multilingual and cross-cultural environment.

222 Nelson, R. D. et al.

Computer editing of general subject heading data for Chemical Abstracts volume indexes.

Journal of Chemical Information and Computer Sciences 15 (2) May 1975 : 85-94.

Describes a computer program meant for the editing of subject headings of the General Subject Index of the Chemical Abstracts. This program is the first phase in the development of a vocabulary management system for general subjects.

223 Pejtersen, Annelise Mark and Austin, Jutta.

Fiction retrieval : experimental design and evaluation of a search system based on users' value criteria (Part 1).

Journal of Documentation 39 (4) Dec. 1983 : 230-246.

Discusses vocabulary control and other issues related with fiction indexing.

224 Power, G.

Information needs in social services : the community care perspective.

Assignation 14 (1) Oct. 1996 : 25-31.

Discusses vocabulary control and other aspects of information services to community care practitioners.

225 Rao, Allan Appa and Sugunamma, Gogula.

Computerised information system for libraries.

Library Science with a Slant to Documentation 24 (2) June 1987 : 122-131.

Describes vocabulary control and other components of a computerized information system.

226 Ravichandra Rao, I. K. and Iyer, Hemalatha.

Computer-based SDI : Cobol Program.

Library Science with a Slant to Documentation 13 (3-4) Sept.-Dec. 1976 : 97-112.

Describes a COBOL based SDI program which contains vocabulary control and other components.

227 Sharada, B. A.

Expressiveness in document titles.

SRELS Journal of Information Management 38 (4) Dec. 2001 : 287-294.

Discusses vocabulary control and other issues related with Kannada language database : the Kannada Nighantu (dictionary) and proposes structuring of entries in these database based on PMEST.

228 Shupak, Harris.

The evolution of a serial index.

Indexer 14 (2) Oct. 1984 : 99-102.

Describes a system developed for indexing of standards published by the American Society for Testing and Materials and the problem of vocabulary control faced during the evolution of the system.

229 Sokolov, A. V. and Firsov, G. G.

Descriptor information retrieval languages and book description.

Nauchno- Tekhnicheskaya Informatsiya; Series II (10) 1972 :18-20.

230 Stebelman, S.

Vocabulary control and the humanities : a case study of the MLA International Bibliography.

Reference Librarian (47) 1994 : 61-78.

Examines the nature of vocabulary control in humanities and explains the effect of computerization of subject authority terms through the example of MLA International Bibliography.

231 Voorbij, H. J.

Title keywords and subject descriptors : a comparison of subject search entries of books in the humanities and social sciences.

Journal of Documentation 54 (4) Sept. 1998 : 466-476.

Compares keywords and subject descriptions and concludes that the descriptors play a vital role in vocabulary control than keywords.

232 Wellisch, H. H.

Book and periodical indexing.

Journal of the American Society for Information Science 45 (8) Sept. 1994 : 620-627.

Discusses vocabulary control and other issues related with book and periodical indexing.

233 Yanez, Elva Kocalis and Kazlauskas, Edward John.

The Spanish-Speaking Mental Health Research Center Bibliographic Data Base.

RQ 19 (4) Summer 1980 : 354-359.

Describes vocabulary control and other aspects of the mental health bibliographic database of Hispanics in the United States.

Section F

Natural language vs. controlled vocabulary

The argument over the relative advantages and disadvantages of the natural and controlled vocabulary is one of the oldest one. Various experts in information storage and retrieval have expressed their opinions and experiences in the form of published literature. This section of the bibliography lists documents, which compare the two types of indexing languages i.e. natural and controlled language.

234 Ah-Ki, Estelle et al.

An experiment in software component retrieval.

Information and Software Technology 45 (10) 15 July 2003 : 633-649.

Reports results of an experiment conducted to test the relative performance of full-text and controlled vocabulary based searching of information on software components.

235 Atherton, Pauline.

Online searching of ERIC : executive summary of a five-part report with a collection of recommendations and suggestions for redesign of the ERIC record and online data base.

Syracuse, New York : ERIC Clearinghouse on Information Resources, 1979. 41p.

Reports the impact of free text and controlled vocabulary on searching the ERIC database.

236 Bechtel, Hanns.

Problems connected with free-text searching in CAS.

Proceedings of the 11th National Online Meeting, New York, 1-3 May 1990. Ed. By Martha. E. Wilams Medford, New

Jersey : Learned Information, 1990 : 37-42.

237 Benjamin, William A.

The design of a full-text company information database for multi-vendor delivery.

National Online Meeting 1983. Proceedings of the 4th National Online Meeting New York, 12-14 April 1983. Ed. by Martha E. Wliams and Thomas H. Hogan. Medford, New Jersey : Learned Information, Inc., 1983 : 33-37.

Describes the design of a full-text database containing company information, which is searchable by both a free-text and controlled vocabulary.

238 Betts, R. and Marrable, D.

Free text vs controlled vocabulary — retrieval precision and recall over large databases.

Online Information 91. Proceedings of the 15th International Online Information Meeting, London, 10-12 December 1991. Ed. by David I. Raitt. Oxford : Learned Information (Europe) Ltd., 1991 : 153-165.

239 Blair, D. C.

Full text retrieval : evaluation and implications.

International Classification 13(1) 1986 : 18-23.

240 Blair, D. C. and Maron, M. E.

An evaluation of retrieval effectiveness for a full-text document retrieval system.

Communications for the Association for Computing Machinery 28 (3) 1985 : 289-299.

241 Brundage, Christine A.

Teaching controlled vocabulary and natural language to end-users of scientific online and CD-ROM databases.

Science and Technology Libraries 10 (1) Fall 1989 : 3-13.

242 Calkins, Mary L.

Free text or controlled vocabulary? A case history step-by-step analysis...plus other aspects of search strategy.

Database 3 (2) June 1980 : 53-67.

243 Canelas, Cathryn and Westbrook, Lynn.

BI in the local high school.

College and Research Libraries News 51 (3) March 1990 : 217-220.

Describes the bibliographic instruction programme which taught the distinction between controlled vocabulary and natural language amongst many other aspects of bibliographic search.

244 Chatterjee, A.

Information retrieval languages : attributes and vocabulary - a comparative study.

Proceedings of the 15th National IASLIC Conference, Annamalainagar, Tamilnadu, India, 26-29 December 1992. Ed. Amitabha Chatterjee, Subir K. Sen and S. K. Kapoor. Calcutta : IASLIC, 1992 : 15-18.

Compares various retrieval languages and describes their characteristics.

245 Comber, Denis and Stanford, Joy.

A comparison between free text and a thesaurus controlled vocabulary in searching an online records management database.

Records Management Journal 1 (3) Autumn 1989 : 113-120.

246 Cousins, Shirley Anne.

Enhancing subject access to OPACs : controlled vocabulary vs natural language.

Journal of Documentation 48 (3) Sept. 1992 : 291-309.

247 Dubois, C. P. R.

Free text vs. controlled vocabulary : a reassessment.

Online Review 11 (4) August 1987 : 243-253.

248 Ercegovac, Z.

Minimal level cataloging : what does it mean for maps in the contexts of card catalogs, online catalogs, and digital libraries?

Journal of the American Society for Information Science 49 (8) June 1998 : 706-719.

Examines the extent of application of minimum level cataloguing rules for cataloguing maps in OCLC's databases particularly from the point of controlled vocabulary data elements and free-text data elements.

249 Feng, Suliang.

A comparative study of indexing languages in single and multidatabase searching.

Canadian Journal of Information Science 14 (2) May 1989 : 26-46.

Compares effectiveness of controlled vocabularies and other features of databases in library science.

250 Fidel, Raya.

Controlled vocabulary and free-text searching : searchers' selection of search keys.

ASIS '87. Proceedings of the 50th ASIS Annual Meeting. Ed. by Ching-chih Chen. Medford, New Jersey : American Society for Information Science (Learned Information), 1987 : 71-73.

251 Fidel, Raya.

Searchers' selection of search keys : 2. Controlled vocabulary or free-text searching.

Journal of the American Society for Information Science 42 (7) August 1991 : 501-514.

252 Fidel, Raya.

Writing abstracts for free-text searching.

Journal of Documentation 42 (1) March 1986 : 11-21.

Provides guidelines for writing abstract for free-text searching and suggests that terms in the abstract should contain index terms assigned from a controlled vocabulary.

253 Field, B. J.

Trends towards automatic indexing, I : relationship between free and controlled-language indexing and the automatic generation of controlled subject headings and classifications.

London : Institution of Electrical Engineers, 1975. 70p. (INSPEC Report R75/20).

254 Finnegan, Mark A.

Hidden assets of controlled vocabulary when free-text searching the TULSA file of Petroleum Abstracts.

Geological societies and information transfer in the electronic age. Proceedings of the 25th Meeting of the Geoscience Information Society, Dallas, Texas, 29 October - 1 November 1990. Volume 21. Ed. by Marie Dvorzak. Alexandria, Virginia : Geoscience Information Society, 1991 : 79-98.

Explains the relative advantages of free-text searching and searching based on controlled vocabulary.

255 Fremer, E. and Larsson, B.

SPIRS, WinSPIRS and OVID : a question of free-text versus thesaurus retrieval.

Bulletin of Medical Libraries Association 85(1) 1997 : 57-58.

256 Fugmann, Robert.

An examination of search strategy and an on-line bibliographic system pertaining to library and information sciences.

Special Libraries 70 (3) March 1979 : 127-134.

Asserts that the combined use of controlled and natural language terms for online searching of library and information science information will improve recall.

257 Harper, Laura G.

ECER on BRS.

Database 2 (2) June 1979 : 37-43 and 46-55.

Describes searches by bound and unbound multi-term

descriptors, controlled vocabulary, and free text in the Exceptional Child Education Resources database available on the BRS.

258 Harris, Kevin.

Part-controlled vocabulary for literature studies.

International Classification 13 (3) 1986 : 133-136.

Explains the concept of and describes the Part-controlled vocabulary i.e. a limited controlled vocabulary with freely chosen index terms which are not based on any authority procedures.

259 Harris, Kevin and Dickens, C.

Indexing a special visual image collection.

Catalogue and Index (83) Winter 1986 : 7-8.

Describes the Dickens House Classification, which has natural language extensions to the controlled vocabulary together with KWIC indexing procedures.

260 Henzler, Rolf G.

Free or controlled vocabularies : some statistical user-oriented evaluations of biomedical information systems.

International Classification 5 (1) March 1978 : 21-26.

Gives a quantitative comparison of free-text and controlled vocabulary used in indexing and retrieval.

261 Holtmann, Susanne; Nicholls, P. T. and Nicholls, Paul.

Research perspectives : women's issues searching with DIALOG OnDisc ERIC - natural language and controlled vocabulary strategies.

Laserdisk Professional 2 (3) May 1989 : 97-103.

Examines merits and demerits of free text and controlled vocabulary in formulating search strategies for searching information on women's issues.

262 Horn, M. E.

'Garbage' in, 'refuse and refuse disposal' out : making the

most of the subject authority file in the OPAC.

Library Resources and Technical Services 46 (3) July 2002 : 92 and 97-102.

Discuses the differences between the subject and keyword searches on the OPAC carried out with and without controlled vocabulary.

263 Hsieh, Ching Chun.

Full text processing of Chinese language - an experimental system for studying Chinese history literatures.

Journal of Library and Information Science (USA/Taiwan) 11 (2) Oct. 1985 : 125-142.

Describes Chinese text processor system, which uses free-text and controlled vocabulary.

264 Kaback, S. M.

ONLINE patent information : who needs indexing? We do, naturally!

World Patent Information 14 (3) August 1992 : 198-199.

Examines the relative advantages of the natural language and controlled language for searching the patents information online.

265 Khan, R. R.

MEDLARS : a critical appraisal.

Lucknow Librarian 12 (2) April-June 1980 : 53-57.

Compares MeSH vocabulary with the natural language based on titles of papers.

266 Knapp, Sara D.

Free-text searching of on-line databases.

Reference Librarian (5-6) Fall-Winter 1982 : 143-153.

Provides guidance for free-text searching of online databases.

267 Knapp, Sara D. and Gavryck, Jacqueline A.

Computer based reference service : a course taught by practitioners.

Online 2 (2) April 1978 : 65-76.

Describes a course on computer-based online reference service, which includes training on IR by using free-text and controlled vocabulary.

268 Lancaster, F. W.

The perspective : natural language versus controlled language - a new examination.

Perspectives in information management. Vol. 1. C. Oppenheim, et al Eds. London : Butterworths, 1989 : 1-23.

269 Markey, Karen; Atherton, Pauline and Newton, Claudia.

An analysis of controlled vocabulary and free text search statements in online searches.

Online Review 4 (3) Sept. 1980 : 225-236.

270 Mering, Margaret and Nowick, Elaine A.

Comparisons between Internet users' free-text queries and controlled vocabularies : a case study in water quality.

Technical Services Quarterly 21 (2) 2003 : 15-32.

271 Muddamalle, M. R.

Natural language versus controlled vocabulary in information retrieval : a case study in soil mechanics.

Journal of the American Society for Information Science 49 (10) August 1998 : 881-887.

272 Parker, J. E.

Preliminary assessment of the comparative efficiencies of an SDI system using controlled or natural language for retrieval.

Program 5 (1) Jan. 1971 : 26-34.

273 Perez, Ernest.

Text enhancement-controlled vocabulary vs. free text.

Special Libraries 73 (3) July 1982 : 183-192.

274 Regazzi, John J.

Indexing and online searching of multipurpose textual

databases : conflict or confluence.

Arlington, VA : ERIC Document Reproduction Service, 1978. 17p.

Compares the cost of using the natural language and controlled vocabulary.

275 Rowley, J. E.

A comparison between free language and controlled language indexing and searching.

Information Searching and Use 10 (3) 1990 : 147-155.

276 Rowley, J. E.

The controlled versus natural indexing languages debate revisited : a perspective on information retrieval practice and research.

Journal of Information Science 20 (2) 1994 : 108-119.

Presents an historical review of the debate concerning controlled and natural languages as used in online and CD-ROM databases.

277 Savoy, Jacques.

Bibliographic database access using free-text and controlled vocabulary : an evaluation.

Information Processing & Management 41 (4) July 2005 : 873-890.

278 Sclafani, F.

Controlled subject heading searching versus keyword searching.

Technicalities 19 (9) Oct. 1999 : 7 and 13-15.

279 Shaw, W. M.

Controlled and uncontrolled subject descriptions in the CF database : a comparison of optimal cluster-based retrieval results.

Information Processing and Management 29 (6) Nov.-Dec. 1993 : 751-763

280 Sievert, MaryEllen C. and Andrews, Mark J.

Indexing consistency in Information Science Abstracts.

Journal of the American Society for Information Science 42 (1) Jan. 1991 : 1-6.

Examines indexing consistency of descriptors drawn from small controlled vocabulary and those drawn from natural language or large controlled vocabulary.

281 Soremark, Gun.

MEDLINE versus EMBASE : comparing search quality.

Database 13 (6) Dec. 1990 : 66-67.

Compares retrieval performance of the MEDLINE and EMBASE databases by searches that used a combination of free text and controlled vocabulary.

282 Svenonius, Elaine.

Natural language vs. controlled vocabulary.

Fourth Canadian conference on information science, held at the University of Western Ontario, London (Ontario), 11-14 May 1976. Proceedings. Ottawa : Canadian Association for Information Science, 1976 : 141-150.

Compares natural and controlled vocabulary.

283 Svenonius, Elaine.

Unanswered questions in the design of controlled vocabularies.

Journal of the American Society for Information Science 37 (5) Sept. 1986 : 331-340.

Discusses various aspects of the debate free-text versus controlled vocabulary.

284 Tenopir, Carol.

Contributions of value added fields and full-text searching in full-text databases.

National Online Meeting proceedings 1985 : New York, 30 April- 2 May 1985. Compiled by Martha E. Wliams and

Thomas H. Hogan. Medford, New Jersey : Learned Information Inc., 1985 : 463-470.

Describes an experiment aimed to investigate the retrieval performance of searches based on controlled vocabulary descriptors and abstracts.

285 Tenopir, Carol.

Searching Harvard Business Review Online . . . lessons in searching a full text database.

Online 9 (2) March 1985 : 71-78.

Compares retrieval performance of full text searches carried out with abstracts, titles and controlled vocabulary terms.

286 Unruh, Betty.

Database description : Conference Papers Index.

Online 2 (3) July 1978 : 54-60.

Describes conference paper's index which is searchable by using free-text or controlled vocabulary.

287 Walker, Geraldine and Atkinson, Steven D.

Information access in the humanities : perils and pitfalls.

Library Hi Tech 9 (1) 1991 : 23-34.

Asserts the importance of multi-file searching and the need to use both natural language and controlled vocabulary terms.

Compares the retrieval effectiveness of searches based on free-text and controlled vocabulary.

Section G
Thesaurus construction

Thesaurus construction is a process that involves various activities in stages. Thesaurus is the result of the thesaurus construction activity. Thesauri are constructed by individuals and teams having common interests.

Individuals and teams involved in thesaurus construction frequently publish literature. This literature deals with the experience, experiment, difficulties faced, methods and procedures adopted by the thesaurus constructor. Once constructed the thesaurus is needed to be updated regularly. This is known as thesaurus maintenance.

The literature listed bellow deals with both these aspects i.e. thesaurus construction and maintenance.

288 Absil, J.

Conditions governing thesaurus compilation.

Cahiers de la Documentation 23 (1-2) 1969 : 40-57.

289 Aitchison, Jean.

Integration of thesauri in the social sciences.

International Classification 8 (2) 1981 : 75-85.

Describes the objectives and procedure to be adopted in the compilation cf the proposed Integrated Thesaurus of the Social Sciences.

290 Amaeshi, B.

Subject indexing in the Nigerian National Corporation Library : design of an instrument.

Library Review 50 (9) 2001 : 457-460.

Describes the method adopted for the design of a controlled vocabulary for the indexing of petroleum and gas related articles.

291 Amos, T.

The value of qualifications in the modern information world.

Business Information Review 18 (2) June 2001 : 47-55.

States that thesaurus construction and other information management skills have got impetus due to development in the information world.

292 Anderson, J. D. and Rowley, F. A.

Building an end-user thesaurus from full text.

Advances in classification research II. Proceedings of the 2nd ASIS SIG/CR : a classification research workshop. Ed. by B. H. Kwasnik and R. Fidel. Old Marlton Pike, New Jersey : Learned Information Inc., 1992 : 1-13.

293 Andre, P. Q. J.

Toward a unified agricultural thesaurus.

Quarterly Bulletin of the International Association of Agricultural Information Specialists 37 (4) 1992 : 224-226.

294 Aptagiri, D. V. and Prasad, A. R. D.

Concept grouping for thesaurus construction using NLP techniques.

Library Herald 33 (1-2) 1995 : 38-46.

295 Arms, William Y. and Arms, Caroline.

The application of clustering techniques to citation data.

England : Bath University of Technology Library, 1977. 112p.

Reports on clustering technique's application in validating thesauri.

296 Austin, Derek.

The exchange of subject information.

The interchange of bibliographic information in machine-readable form : papers given at the Western European Seminar on the Interchange of Bibliographic Information in Machine-Readable Form, sponsored by the British Library and the Library Association, held at Banbury, England, 12-16 May

1974. Ed. by R. E. Coward and M. Yelland. London : The Library Association, 1975 : 68-81.

Explains thesaurus reconciliation method.

297 Baca, Murtha.

Fear of authority? Authority control and thesaurus building for art and material culture information.

Cataloging & Classification Quarterly 38 (3-4) 2004 : 143-151.

Explains the need of authority control and method for constructing thesaurus for art and material culture information.

298 Barberena Blasquez, Elsa.

MEXICOARTE : a new means of obtaining information about the art of Mexico.

Art Libraries Journal 13 (4) 1988 : 15-19.

Reports on the development of database of Mexican art comprising references to bibliographic and visual resources and artists' biographies and the development of a thesaurus for maintaining this database.

299 Barhydt, G. C. et al.

The preparation of a thesaurus of educational terms. Final report.

Cleveland, OH : The Press of Case Western Reserve University. 1966.

300 Barlow, Caroline.

Abstracting, indexing, classification, thesaurus construction : a glossary by H. H. Wellisch. Port Aransas, TX : American Society of Indexers, Inc., 1996. 64p.

Indexer 21 (2) Oct. 1998 :101.

A book review.

301 Barlow, Caroline

Thesaurus construction and use : a practical manual by J. Aitchison, A. Gilchrist and D. Bawden. Ed. 3. London : Aslib,

1997. 212p.

Indexer 21 (3) April 1999 : 149.

A book review.

302 Barlow, Caroline.

Thesaurus construction and use : a practical manual by J. Aitchison, A. Gilchrist and D. Bawden. Ed. 3. London : Aslib, 1997. 212p.

Managing Information 8 (3) April 2001 : 61.

A book review.

303 Barrantes, Nitzia.

The Banana Thesaurus.

Quarterly Bulletin of the International Association of Agricultural Information Specialists 31 (2) 1986 : 87-91.

Describes procedure adopted in constructing the Bananas Thesaurus.

304 Barrett, H.

Authority / thesaurus at Department of Health Library.

Catalogue and Index (131) Summer 1999 : 6-9.

Briefs thesaurus / authority control activities at the Department of Health Library, UK.

305 Barth, C.

The advanced state of development of thesaurus work in the USSR and the use of Soviet experience in East Germany.

Informatika 22 (2) 1975 : 30-33.

306 Basova, I. M.

Terminological control in the field of informatics. (A case study of four years of working experience with 'Informatika' reference information system).

Proceedings of the meeting of the International Federation for Documentation Committee 'Terminology of Information and Documentation'. Moscow, 22-24 May 1976. Moscow :

All-Union Institute of Scientific and Technical Information, 1976.

Describes methods adopted for construction of informatics thesaurus.

307 Bates, Marcia.

Rethinking subject cataloguing in the online environment.

Library Resources and Technical Services 33 (4) Oct. 1989 : 400-412.

Describes the construction of 'superthesaurus' based on online searcher's descriptors.

308 Batty, David.

Microcomputers in index language design and development.

Microcomputers for Information Management 1 (4) Dec. 1984 : 303-312.

Highlights the importance of microcomputers in developing controlled vocabulary.

309 Batty, David.

Thesaurus construction and maintenance : a survival kit.

Database 12 (1) Feb. 1989 : 13-20.

Outlines basic steps in planning, construction and maintenance of a thesaurus.

310 Bauer, G.

Concept arrangement in the chemical thesaurus system. Part 1 : Concepts in non-structural chemistry.

Informatika 16 (2) 1969 : 35-41.

311 Bauer, G.

Notes on the suitable classification of terms in the chemical thesaurus system.

Informatika 16 (5) 1969 : 11-16.

312 Beffa, P.

The World Council of Churches Library : an international

library.

Bulletin of the Association of British Theological and Philosophical Libraries 8 (1) March 2001 : 5-7.

Highlights the development of thesaurus and other advancements at the WCC library.

313 Bellamy, Lois M. and Bickham, Linda.

Thesaurus development for subject cataloguing.

Special Libraries 80 (1) Winter 1989 : 9-15.

Describes methodology adopted in constructing a thesaurus of biomedical terms.

314 Belonogov, G. G.

Automatic thesaurus of descriptors.

Nauchno- Tekhnicheskaya Informatsiya; Series 2 (12) 1969 : 20-21.

315 Bennett, R.

Terminology and the computer : attention shifts to the micro.

Aslib Proceedings 46 (7-8) July-August 1994 : 188-200.

Discusses the development of an in-house terminology management tool for a networked PC environment.

316 Berardini, C.

Preparation of a thesaurus of astronomy and automation of the information processing at the Paris Meudon Observatory.

Inspel 7 (1) Jan. 1972 : 8-14.

317 Bjorklund, L.

The potential of using knowledge organising tools in collaborative system development.

Proceedings of the 3rd International Society for Knowledge Organization (ISKO) Conference : Knowledge organization and quality management. Copenhagen, Denmark, 20-24 June 1994. Ed. by Hanne Albrechtsen and Susan Oernager. Frankfurt/Main : INDEKS Verlag, 1994 : 264-271.

Explains the feasibility of using a collaborative tool for adhoc construction of a dynamic thesaurus.

318 Blagden, J. F.

Thesaurus compilation methods : a literature review.

Aslib Proceedings 20 (8) 1968 : 345-359.

319 Blamoutier, Francoise.

Training in the drafting of texts for documentation in controlled language for the purposes of automatic translation.

Third European congress on information systems and networks : overcoming the language barrier; Luxembourg 3-6 May 1977. Volume 1. Organised by the Commission of the European Communities. Munich : Verlag Dokumentation, 1977 : 495-511.

320 Blankenstein, G.

Objectives and experiences in preparing a thesaurus on 'Food and Nutrition of Man'.

Tagungsbericht der Deutschen Akademie der Landwirtschaftswissenschaften zu Berlin (105) 1970 : 97-106.

321 Boman, D. D.

Thesaurus construction for law literature.

Library Focus 9 (1- 2) 1991 : 12-22.

322 Booth, Barbara.

VIP manual : guidelines and procedures for ERIC vocabulary improvement.

Washington, DC : Educational Resources Information Center, 1978. 104p.

323 Borlund, Pia and Schneider, Jesper W.

Introduction to bibliometrics for construction and maintenance of thesauri.

Journal of Documentation 60 (5) 1 Sept. 2004 : 524-549.

324 Bovey, J. D.

Building a thesaurus for a collection of cartoon drawings.

Journal of Information Science 21 (2) 1995 : 15-22.

325 Brown, S.

CIG Annual Summer Conference, 16-18 June, Hereford : the reflective practitioner- Summary

Catalogue and Index (135) Spring 2000 : 6-7.

Highlights the need for improving skills in thesaurus construction, abstracting etc.

326 Brzicky, J.

Storage and maintenance of a thesaurus in an information system processed by computer.

Ceskoslovenska Informatika 15 (3) 1973 : 1-9.

327 Buchan, R. L.

Intertwining thesauri and dictionaries.

Information Services and Use 9 (3) 1989 : 171-175.

Describes with examples the technique of combining the functions of a dictionary and a thesaurus in a single tool.

328 Bykova, L. N. and Muzrukov, N. B.

Experience gained in establishing a bibliographical thesaurus for indexing documents relating to atomic science and technology.

Handling of nuclear information. Proceedings of the symposium organized by the International Atomic Energy Agency and held in Vienna. 16-20 February 1970. Vienna : IAEA, 1970 : 545-555.

329 Caponio, J. F. and Gillum, T. L.

Practical aspects concerning the development and use of ASTIA's thesaurus in information retrieval.

Journal of Chemical Documentation 4(1) 1964 : 5-8.

330 Carlos, Gina D'Ascenzo; Vries, John K. and Shoval, Peretz.

Constructing a thesaurus for medical knowledge.

National Online Meeting 1988. Proceedings of the 9th sNational Online Meeting, New York, 10-12 May 1988.

Compiled by Martha E. Wliams and Thomas H. Hogan. Medford, New Jersey : Learned Information Inc., 1988 : 53-58.

331 Chall, Miriam.

User needs, user aids : development of the thesaurus of sociological indexing terms.

Online information 87. Proceedings of the 11th International Online Information Meeting, London, 8-10 December 1987. Oxford : Learned Information (Europe), 1987 : 267-271.

Describes the method used for the construction of Sociological Abstract's Thesaurus.

332 Chan, L. M.

Classification present and future.

Cataloging and Classification Quarterly 21 (2) 1995 : 5-17.

Examines the role of classification in the construction of controlled vocabularies and other activities.

333 Chandran, D.

Candidate terms for thesaurus : A case study of sources of terms in the field of library and information science.

Seminar on thesaurus in information systems. Banglore : DRTC, 1975 : Paper AG.

334 Charles, Daphne.

In the beginning was the word : making English Heritage thesauri available on-line.

Cultivate Interactive 3, 29 January 2001.

Describes methods of generating and disseminating the National Monuments Record thesauri produced by English Heritage.

Also available at : http://www.cultivate-int.org/issue3/nmr/

335 Chen, H. et al.

A concept space approach to addressing the vocabulary problems in scientific information retrieval : an experiment on the worm community system.

Journal of the American Society for Information Science 48 (1) Jan. 1997 : 17-31.

Describes techniques used for building domain specific thesauri for cross-domain IR.

336 Chen, H. et al.

Automatic thesaurus generation for an electronic community system.

Journal of the American Society for Information Science 46 (3) April 1995 : 175-193.

337 Chen, Yufeng et al.

Creation of a master table for checking indication and contraindication of medicine from a knowledge base linked with a thesaurus.

Journal of Medical Systems 28 (6) Dec. 2004 : 561-573.

Reports a web-based system developed for constructing a medicine/disease thesaurus.

338 Chowdhury, G. G. and Mahapatra, M.

Applications of the theory of relational analysis in information retrieval.

Journal of Library and Information Science (India) 14 (1) June 1990 : 1-12.

Explains the possibility of applying Farradane's theory of relational analysis for various activities of IR including compilation of a relational thesaurus.

339 Chmielewska-Gorczyca.

Polyhierarchy as a means of knowledge representation.

Knowledge organization for information retrieval. Proceedings of the 6th International Study Conference on Classification Research, 16-18 June 1997, University College, London. The Hague : International Federation for Information and Documentation (FID), 1997 : 105-112.

340 Cibbarelli, Pamela; Tenopir, Carol and Ott, Retha Z.

LIBNOTES a laboratory notebook retrieval system.

The information age in perspective. Proceedings of the ASIS 41st Annual Meeting, New York, 13-17 November 1978. Volume 15. Compiled by Everett H. Brenner. White Plains, New York : Knowledge Industry Publications for American Society for Information Science, 1978 : 67-69.

Describes the thesaurus generated by Allergan Pharmaceuticals and Cibbarelli and Associates.

341 Coates, E. J.

Ranganathan's thought and its significance for the mechanisation of information storage and retrieval.

Herald of Library Science 27 (1-2) Jan.-April 1988 : 3-14.

Examines the role of classification in thesauri along with Ranganathan's influence on mechanized IR.

342 Cole, L.

Comparing contents of different INMAGIC databases.

Computers in Libraries 14 (1) Jan. 1994 : 26-29.

Contents of INMAGIC based databases are compared and the process of updating the thesauri used by these databases is described.

343 Conlon, S. P. N.; Evens, M. and Ahlswede, T.

Developing a large lexical database for information retrieval, parsing, and text generation systems.

Information Processing and Management 29 (4) July-August 1993 : 415-431.

Explains the construction of a lexical database by combining material from a number of machine-readable sources.

344 Conrad, Carleton C.

Status of indexing and classification systems and potential future trends.

Journal of Chemical Information and Computer Sciences 16 (4) Nov. 1976 : 197-201.

Discusses developments in specialized thesauri and vocabulary control.

345 Corval, Paulette and Ginocchio, Colette.

The elaboration of a bibliographical data bank for French-language documents in odontology and stomatology.

Inspel 18 (4) 1984 : 281-290.

Discusses the development of a bibliographical databank for French language documents in odontology and stomatology and the construction of faceted thesaurus for maintaining the databank.

346 Cotter, G. et al.

The National Biological Information Infrastructure : coming of age.

Online Information Review 24 (6) 2000 : 429-438.

Describes the development of controlled vocabulary at the NBII.

347 Craig, A. and Schriar, S.

Original synonyms : the genesis of the Jessica Tree.

Illinois Libraries 83 (2) Spring 2001 : 32-38.

Describes lexicographer Jessica Milstead's subject tree for the 'Find it! Programme of the Illinois State Library, which devised controlled vocabulary.

348 Craven, Timothy C.

A general versus a special algorithm in the graphic display of thesauri.

Classification research for knowledge representation and organization. Proceedings of the 5th International Study Conference on Classification Research. Toronto, Canada, 24-28 June 1991. Ed. by N. J. Williamson and H. Hudon. Amsterdam : Elsevier Science Publishers BV and FID, 1992 :

179-186.

349 Craven, Timothy C.

A NEPHIS thesaurus for computer generation of permuted cross-references.

The information age in perspective. Proceedings of the 41st Annual Meeting, New York, 13-17 November 1978. Volume 15. Compiled by Everett H. Brenner, White Plains, New York : Knowledge Industry Publications for American Society for Information Science, 1978 : 79-82.

350 Craven, Timothy C.

Automatic structure modification in the graphic display of thesauri.

*Tools for knowledge organisation and the human interface. Proceedings of the First International ISKO Conference, Darmstadt, (*Germany) *14-17 August 1990. Advances in knowledge organization, no. 1/2.* Ed. by R. Fugmann. Part I. Frankfurt/Main : Indeks. 1990 : 146-153.

Describes automatic structure simplification and automatic addition of dummy terms as an technique for modifying structure of the thesaurus.

351 Craven, Timothy C.

Concept relation structures and their graphic display.

Classification research for knowledge representation and organization. Proceedings of the 5th International Study Conference on Classification Research. Toronto, Canada, 24-28 June 1991. Ed. by N. J. Williamson and H. Hudon. Amsterdam : Elsevier Science Publishers BV and FID, 1992 : 49-60.

352 Crawford, Robert G.

Automatic thesaurus construction based on term centroids.

Canadian Journal of Information Science Vol. 4. May 1979 : 124-136.

353 Crawford, Robert G.

Dynamic dictionary updating.

Information Processing and Management. 13 (4) 1977 : 235-245.

Presents a method for updating the dictionary in a dynamic ISRS.

354 Crawford, Robert G.

The computation of discrimination values.

Information Processing and Management 11 (8-12) 1975 : 249-253.

Describes how discrimination value as a property of terms is useful in the automatic construction of thesauri.

355 Cronau, Deborah A.

Glossary of terminology in abstracting, classification, indexing and thesaurus construction by H. J. Wellisch. Medford, New Jersey : American Society of Indexers, 2001. 77p.

Australian Library Journal 51 (4) Nov. 2002 : 372-373.

A book review.

356 Crouch, C. J.

An approach to the automatic construction of global thesauri.

Information Processing and Management 26 (5) 1990 : 629-640.

Explains the feasibility of using the term discrimination value model of Salton, Yang, and Yu for the automatic construction of global thesauri.

357 Cseti, Del.

AIRS as used by the amalgamated metal workers and shipwrights' union.

Australian Special Libraries News 15 (4) Dec. 1982 : 130-135.

Describes the Alemson Information Retrieval System (AIRS)

that enables the creation and searching of an on-line thesaurus and catalogue.

358 Dahlberg, Ingetraut.

Citation codes in classification and terminology : proposal for an international standard.

International Classification 5 (2) 1978 : 91-92.

Enumerates mnemonic citation codes which indicate whether the publication is universal or special edition, language and number of editions for thesauri and classification systems, these codes are useful in establishing authority file.

359 Davidson, Robert M.

The IEA Coal data base-the development of the Coal Thesaurus and indexing strategy.

Aslib Proceedings 31 (10) Oct. 1979 : 452-459.

360 Davis, M. A.

Title keyword selection and use for optimum document retrieval : guidelines for authors.

Public and Access Services Quarterly 2 (2) 1996 : 15-23.

Explains how the searcher's natural language can be used to augment controlled vocabulary.

361 Davis, Richard A.

A curriculum in indexing and abstracting.

Indexer 10 (2) Oct. 1976 : 75-77.

Enumerates contents for courses on indexing, abstracting and thesaurus construction.

362 Dean, Rebecca J.

FAST : development of simplified headings for metadata.

Cataloging & Classification Quarterly 39 (1-2) 2004 : 331-352.

Describes a methodology to convert LCSH headings to FAST i.e. Faceted Application of Subject Terminology, headings.

363 Defriez, Philip.

Thesaurus development at the Department of Health.

Catalogue & Index (140) Summer 2001 : 1-3.

Describes methodology adopted for constructing the thesaurus at the UK Dept. of Health and explains the structure of Health Thesaurus.

364 DeHart, F. E.

Topic relevance and BSO switching effectiveness.

International Classification 9 (2) 1982 : 71-76.

Examines topic relevance (a concept which matters to thesaurus constructors) and the usefulness of BSO.

365 Delgado, Rafael Rodriguez.

Toward the integration of decimal classification and thesauri concepts.

New trends in documentation and information. Proceedings of the 39th FID Congress, University of Edinburgh, 25-28 September 1978. Ed. by Peter J. Taylor. London : Aslib, 1980 : 277-294.

Explains a method to integrate Decimal classification and thesauri concepts to construct a megathesaurus.

366 Devadason, F. J.

Postulate-Based Permuted Subject Indexing Language as a metalanguage for computer-aided generation of information retrieval thesaurus.

International Forum on Information and Documentation 8 (1) Jan. 1983 : 22-29.

Discusses the usefulness of POPSI in thesaurus construction.

367 Devadason, F. J. and Balasubramanian, V.

Automated system for generating thesaurus from subject representations.

Annals of Library Science and Documentation 25 (1-4) March-Dec. 1978 : 79-85.

Reports a coding scheme developed for augmenting the subject strings to make them suitable for generating a thesaurus.

368 Devadason, F. J. and Balasubramanian, V.

Computer generation of thesaurus from structured subject-propositions.

Information Processing and Management 17 (1) 1981 : 1-11.

Describes the use of subject headings structured according to postulates and principles for facet analysis, as the input for generating thesauri.

369 Dextre Clarke, Stella G.

Integrating thesauri in agricultural science.

Compatibility and integration of order system. Research Seminar. Proceedings of the TIP/ISKO Meeting, Warwaw, 13-15 September 1996. Warwaw : Wydawnictwo SBP, 1996 : 111-122.

370 Dextre, S. G. and Clark, T. M.

A system for machine-aided thesaurus construction.

Aslib Proceedings 33 (3) March 1981 : 102-112.

371 Diaz, Irene et al.

Generating domain representations using a relationship model.

Information Systems 30 (1) March 2005 : 1-19.

Explains the use of automatic domain analysis in the creation of controlled vocabulary.

372 Diaz, Irene. et al.

Semi-automatic construction of thesaurus applying domain analysis techniques.

International Forum on Information and Documentation 23 (2) April-June 1998 : 11-19.

373 Dillon, Martin and Caplan, P.

A technique for evaluating automatic term clustering.

Journal of the American Society for Information Science 31

(2) March 1980 : 89-96.

Describes with examples automatic and manual thesaurus generation and compares their effectiveness.

374 Dimitrova, G.

Thesaurus semiotics and thesaurus lexicography.

International Classification 19(2) 1992 : 86.

375 Diodato, Virgil.

Modern algebra and information science.

Journal of the American Society for Information Science 34 (4) July 1983 : 257-261.

Explains the use of modern algebra in establishing syndetic structures in thesaurus.

376 Doran, K.

Metadata for corporate intranet.

Online 23 (1) Jan.-Feb. 1999 : 42-44 and 46-50.

Describes efforts towards creation of controlled vocabulary for managing databases on the Weyerhaeuser Library's Intranet.

377 Dovbenko, M. A. and Umanski, A. N.

A comparative analysis of information retrieval thesauri and normalised scientific and technical terminologies with the aim of their coordinated development.

International Forum on Information and Documentation 5 (4) Oct. 1980 : 9-11.

Suggests procedure for the correlation of thesauri construction and maintenance with terminological work.

378 Duncan, Elizabeth B. and McAleese, Ray.

Intelligent access to databases using a thesaurus in graphical form.

Online information 87. Proceedings of the 11th International Online Information Meeting, London, 8-10 December 1987.

Oxford : Learned Information (Europe), 1987 : 377-387.

Reports a pilot experiments in the construction of a graphical thesaurus as a potential interface to an information system and its effect on students understanding.

379 Edelblute, T.

A Pro-Cite authority file on a network.

Technical Services Quarterly 12 (3) 1995 : 29-40.

Describes the creation of a subject authority file for agriculture, using the Pro-Cite bibliographic management software.

380 Eichhorn, M. M. and Reinecke, R. D.

Development and implementation of a thesaurus for the visual sciences.

Journal of Chemical Documentation 9 (2) May 1969 : 114-118.

381 Fabian, Claudia.

The CERL thesaurus file.

Cataloging & Classification Quarterly 39 (1-2) 2004 : 413-420.

Explains the development of the thesaurus of The Consortium of European Research Libraries, which lists place names, printers, publishers, and persons related to early printing.

382 Field, B. J.

Semi-automatic development of thesauri using free-language vocabulary analyses. Part 1.

London : INSPEC, Institution of Electrical Engineers, 1975. 37p.

383 Fishel, Carolyn C.

CINAHL list of subject headings : a nursing thesaurus revised.

Bulletin of the Medical Library Association 73 (2) April 1985 : 153-159.

Explains the logic and procedures adopted in revising the

thesaurus of Cumulative Index to Nursing and Allied Health Literature.

384 Fong, Colin.

Thesaurus construction and use : a practical manual by J. Aitchison, A. Gilchrist and D. Bawden. Ed. 3. London : Aslib, 1997. 212p.

Australian Library Journal 48 (3) Aug. 1999 : 292.

A book review.

385 Foo, S. et al.

Automatic thesaurus for enhanced Chinese text retrieval.

Library Computing 19 (3-4) 2000 : 270-280.

Suggests procedure for generating an automatic Chinese thesaurus to provide related terms to a user's queries to enhance retrieval effectiveness.

386 Foo, S. et al.

Automatic thesaurus for enhanced Chinese text retrieval.

Library Review 49 (5-6) 2000 : 230-239.

Suggests procedure for generating an automatic Chinese thesaurus to provide related terms to a user's queries to enhance retrieval effectiveness.

387 Fourie, Ina.

Thesaurus construction and use: a practical manual by J. Aitchison, A. Gilchrist and D. Bawden. Ed. 3. London : Aslib, 1997. 212p.

Electronic Library 16 (4) August 1998 : 266.

A book review.

388 Freeman, Frank H.

Building a thesaurus for a diffuse subject area.

Special Libraries 67 (4) April 1976 : 220-222.

Describes procedures and problems in constructing a thesaurus for soft-sciences, interdisciplinary field such as leadership.

389 Frieband, Susan J. and Burnum, Judy.

The US Trade Representative (USTR) trade thesaurus : development, innovation and use.

Information Services and Use 8 (5- 6) 1988 : 239-248.

390 Frost, C. O.

Title words as entry vocabulary to LCSH terms and derived terms from title in bibliographic records with implications for subject access in online catalogs.

Cataloguing and Classification Quarterly 10 (1-2) 1989 : 165-179.

391 Fujiwara, Y. et al.

A dynamic thesaurus for intelligent access to research databases.

Information, knowledge, evolution. Proceedings of the 44th FID Congress, Helsinki, 28 August-1 September 1988. Ed. by Sinikka Koshiala and Ritva Launo. Amsterdam : Elsevier Science Publishers, 1989 : 173-181.

Describes thesaurus construction methods, which used formats to input terms based on expertise.

392 Gershon, M. R.

Building a management services thesaurus.

O and M Bulletin 24 (1) Feb. 1969 : 19-26.

393 Ghose, Amitabha and Dhawle, Anand S.

Problems of thesaurus construction.

Journal of the American Society for Information Science 28 (4) July 1977 : 211-217.

394 Ghose, Amitabha and Dhawle, Anand S.

Theoretical foundations of thesaurus construction.

Seminar on thesaurus in information systems. Banglore : DRTC, 1975 : Paper AB.

395 Giles-Peters, A.

Experiments in the mechanical construction of cross-database thesauri

Online Information 93. Proceedings of the 17th International Online Information Meeting. London, 7-9 December 1993. Ed. by David I. Raitt and Ben Jeapes. Oxford : Learned Information (Europe) Ltd, 1993 : 137-147.

396 Gillman, P.

Transferring text.

C and L Applications 6 (9) May 1993 : 9-11.

Describes the construction of a health care thesaurus involving the movement of text between different application programs.

397 Gillum, T. L.

Compiling a technical thesaurus.

Journal of Chemical Documentation 4, 1964 : 29-32.

398 Gillum, T. L. et al.

Philosophy of and guidelines for revision of the thesaurus of ASTIA descriptors.

Arlington, VA : Armed Services Technical Information Agency, 1961.

399 Goethals, F.

The use and compilation of a thesaurus.

Cahiers de la Documentation 23 (1-2) 1969 : 20-39.

400 Goodwin, R. and Minion, R.

Progress towards a Canadian polar information system.

Proceedings of the 15th Polar Libraries Colloquy, Bipolar information initiatives : the needs of polar research. Cambridge, 3-8 July 1994. Ed. by D. W. H. Walton, W. Mls and C. M. Phlips. Bluntisham, UK : Bluntisham Books for Polar Libraries Colloquy Steering Committee, 1995 : 138-141.

Reports on the development of geographic thesauri at CPIS.

401 Gopinath, M. A.

Curricula in teaching classification and indexing in advanced courses in library and information science : a case study.

Library Science with a Slant to Documentation and Information Studies 36 (1) March 1999 : 3-9.

Presents curriculum for the design of classification schemes and vocabulary control devices.

402 Gopinath, M. A.

Information retrieval thesaurus : its structure, function and construction.

Librarian 2, 1985 : 1-7.

403 Gordon, A. S.

Browsing image collections with representations of commonsense activities.

Journal of the American Society for Information Science and Technology 52 (11) Sept. 2001 : 925-929.

Describes a methodology for creating networks of subject terms by manually representing a large number of common sense activities that are broadly related to image subject terms.

404 Gor'kova, V. I.; Azgaldov, E. G. and Chernyi, A. I.

Essential problems in terminology for informatics and documentation : some methodological recommendations on dictionary development.

Moscow : All Union Institute of Scientific and Technical Information, 1980. 111p.

405 Gorman, G. E.

Information retrieval in New Testament studies.

Bulletin of the Association of British Theological and Philosophical Libraries (7) Nov 1976 : 10-16.

Reports a project undertaken to construct a thesaurus for the compilation of an index to New Testament literature.

406 Gornostaev, Yu M. and Rappich, H.

Basic methodological points concerning the production of compatible thesauri.

Informatika 19 (6) 1972 : 23-29.

407 Green, Rebecca.

The development of a relational thesaurus.

Advances in knowledge organization. Volume 5. Knowledge organization and change. Proceedings of the 4th ISKO International Conference, Washington, DC. 15-18 July 1996. Frankfurt : Indeks Verlag, 1996 : 72-79.

408 Greengrass, Alan R.

The Information Bank Thesaurus.

The information age in perspective. Proceedings of the 41st Annual Meeting, New York, 13-17 November 1978. Volume 15. Compiled by Everett H. Brenner. White Plains, New York : Knowledge Industry Publications for American Society for Information Science, 1978 : 137-140.

Discusses the processes involved in development of the New York Times Information Bank Thesaurus.

409 Greer, F. L.

User vocabulary in thesaurus development.

Perceptual and Motor Skills 21, 1965 : 827-837.

410 Grefenstette, Gregory.

Explorations in automatic thesaurus discovery.

Journal of Documentation 51 (4) Dec. 1995 : 447-448.

Presents an automated method for creating a first-draft thesaurus from raw text.

411 Greig, Eugenie.

LCSH update.

Cataloguing Australia 14 (2-3) June-Sept. 1988 : 19-22.

412 Groll, H.

Thesaurus problems : considerations relating to the compilation of a legal thesaurus in German.

International Journal of Law Libraries 2 (1) March 1974 : 13-19.

413 Grosch, A. N.

Thesaurus construction : a small collection of nonscientific reports.

Special Libraries 60 (2) Feb. 1969 : 87-92.

414 Gu, H. et al.

A methodology for partitioning a vocabulary hierarchy into trees.

Artificial Intelligence in Medicine 15 (1) Jan. 1999 : 77-98.

Demonstrates a methodology for partitioning a hierarchical controlled medical vocabulary into trees.

415 Guntzer, U. et al.

Automatic thesaurus construction by machine learning from retrieval sessions.

Information Processing and Management 25 (3) 1989 : 265-273.

Describes an IR system called TEGEN which uses searcher's actual search behaviour to generate thesaurus entries automatically.

416 Gupta, D. K. and Tripathi, G. N.

Exploration and production of thesaurus : its helpfulness in indexing in a library and information systems.

Seminar on thesaurus in information system. Banglore : DRTC, 1975 : Paper CF.

417 Guy, Louis Gavet.

A mathematical formulation of keyword compression for thesauri.

Information Processing and Management 13 (3) 1977 : 189-200.

Illustrates a method for concentrating the set of keywords of a thesaurus.

418 Haaland, Ooyvind.

Offshore platform documentation : a systematic approach to solving linguistic problems in the Norwegian oil industry.

International Forum on Information and Documentation 14 (2) April 1989 : 18-21.

Reports efforts made for the preparation and distribution of a word list containing terms approved by Norwegian oil industry.

419 Hammond, William.

Construction of the N.A.S.A. thesaurus : computer processing support.

Maclean, VA : Aries Corporation, 1968. 14p.

420 Hanqing, H. et al.

Computer aided compilation of permuted index of Chinese Thesaurus.

Journal of the China Society for Scientific and Technical Information 17 (4) August 1998 : 281-286.

421 Hariri, Mehrangiz.

Dynamics of a thesaurus : a quantitative approach.

Ann Arbor, Michigan : University Microforms International, 1980. 102p.

Examines the dynamic features of thesaurus and suggests a quantitative method to measure the changes.

422 Haynes, David.

Thesaurus construction using a micro.

Library Micromation News (13) July 1986 : 8-12.

Explains usefulness of microcomputer in thesaurus construction.

423 Heinze, C.

The tasks, main function and construction of the thesaurus of

the East German Council of Ministers.
Informatika 19 (5) 1972 : 14-18.

424 Hemmasi, H.

ARIS music thesaurus : another view of LCSH.

Library Resources and Technical Services 36 (4) Oct. 1992 : 487-503.

Describes attempts to construct a micro-thesaurus i.e. ARIS music thesaurus from a macrothesaurus i.e. LCSH.

425 Hemmasi, H.

The Music Thesaurus Project at Rutgers University.

New Jersey Libraries 28 (2) Spring 1995 : 21-23.

426 Hermann, P. et al.

Construction and application of the non-ferrous metals thesaurus.

Informatika 19 (1) 1972 : 29-36.

427 Hickey, Carol et al.

Vocabulary mapping for terminology services.

Journal of Digital Information : 4 (4) 2003. No page numbers.

Also available at: http://www.jodi.ecs.soton.ac.uk/Articles/v04/i04/Vizine-Goetz/

Describes a project aimed to add value to controlled vocabularies by making inter-vocabulary associations.

428 Hines, T. C. and Harris, J. L.

Columbia University School of Library Service system for thesaurus development and maintenance.

Information Storage and Retrieval 7 (1) June 1971 : 39-50.

429 Hino, S.

INIS thesaurus and correction routines for descriptor file.

Dokumentesyon Kenkyu 21 (5) May 1971 : 145-151.

430 Hoffmann, G.

Investigations into the construction of thesauri for patent literature.

Informatika 19 (1) 1972 : 37-39.

431 Hoffmann, G.

Investigations on constructing thesauri for patent literature.

Informatika 18 (3) 1971 : 27-31.

432 Holm, B. E. and Rasmussen, L. E.

Development of a technical thesaurus.

American Documentation 12 (3) 1961 : 184-190.

433 Hudon, Michele.

Preparing terminological definitions for indexing and retrieval thesauri : a model.

Advances in knowledge organization. Volume 5. Knowledge organization and change. Proceedings of the 4th International ISKO Conference, Wahington, DC, 15-18 July 1996. Frankfurt / Main : Indeks Verlag, 1996 : 363-369.

434 Huntley, K.; Veverka, M. J. and Golden, M.

The FDA's medical dictionary for Drug Regulatory Affairs alpha test.

Drug Information Journal 29 (4) Oct.-Dec. 1995 : 1133-1143.

Described thesaurus construction activity of the Food and Drug Administration (USA).

435 Ivanova, N. S.

On the automatic compilation of a thesaurus.

Nauchno- Tekhnicheskaya Informatsiya; Series 2 (6) 1969 : 17-20.

436 Jacobs, C.

If a picture is worth a thousand words, then.

Indexer 21 (3) April 1999 : 119-121.

Provides guidance in the design and implementation of a thesaurus for image indexing.

437 James, Stuart.

Thesaurus construction and use : a practical manual by J. Aitchison, A. Gilchrist and D. Bawden. Ed. 3. London : Aslib, 1997. 212p.

Library Review 48 (1-2) 1999 : 104-105.

A book review.

438 Janas, Jurgen M.

Automatic recognition of the part-of-speech for English texts.

Information Processing and Management 13 (4) 1977 : 205-213.

Describes a system of automatic recognition of the part-of-speech for English texts, which can be adopted for automatic indexing and automatic thesaurus construction.

439 Janos, J.

A typical means of expressing grammatical relations in retrieval languages.

Ceskoslovenska Informatika 16 (12) 1974 : 667-672.

440 Jantz, R. C.

An approach to managing vocabulary for databases on the Web.

Cataloging and Classification Quarterly 28 (3) 1999 : 55-66.

Proposes a combination of interactive and manual processes for effective management of vocabulary for searching web-based databases.

441 Jimba, Samuel Wodi.

A thesaurus for indexing Nigerian newspapers-a research report.

Library Scientist. 12, 1985 : 60-68.

Describes the method adopted in constructing a thesaurus for newspaper indexing.

442 Joudrey, D. N.

A new look at US graduate courses in bibliographic control.

Cataloging and Classification Quarterly 34 (1-2) 2002 : 59-101.

Identifies thesaurus construction as one of the primary areas in the US graduate courses in bibliographic control.

443 Joythi, T.

Construction of information retrieval thesaurus on nervous diseases terms using Prolog.

SRELS Journal of Information Management 40 (1) 2003 : 13-22.

444 Kapterev, A. I.

Professional environment as an information analysis object.

Knowledge Organization 20 (4) 1993 : 201.

Stages in compilation and study of different professional thesauri are examined as an item in the information analysis of professional environment.

445 Kazlauskas, Edward John and Holt, Thomas D.

The application of a minicomputer to thesaurus construction.

Journal of the American Society for Information Science 31 (5) Sept. 1980 : 363-368.

446 Kerckhove, P.

Compilation of the C.R.I.C. thesaurus.

Cahiers de la Documentation 23 (1-2) 1969 : 5-14.

Describes method used for constructing thesaurus for cement and concrete.

447 Kerckhove, P.

Criteria for the selection and writing out of keywords for an encyclopaedic thesaurus.

Cahiers de la Documentation 24 (2) 1970 : 49-77.

448 Kertesz, R.

Methods for compiling and up-dating a controlled vocabulary.

Probleme de Informare si Documentare 8 (2) Feb. 1974 : 132-147.

449 Kim, C.

Theoretical foundations of thesaurus-construction and some methodological consideration for thesaurus-updating.

Journal of the American Society for Information Science 24 (2) March-April 1973 : 148-156.

Abstract available at: http://slis6000.slis.uwo.ca/601/test/documents/doc0627/html

450 Kim, Chai and Kim, S. D.

Consensus vs frequency : an empirical investigation of the theories for identifying descriptors in designing retrieval thesauri.

Information Processing and Management 13 (4) 1977 : 253-258.

451 King, H.

Developing a thesaurus at GCHQ.

Catalogue and Index (138) Winter 2000 : 8.

Describes the development of UK Government Communications Headquarter's Thesaurus.

452 Klatt, M. J.

An aid for total quality searching : developing a hedge book.

Bulletin of the Medical Library Association 82 (4) Oct. 1994 : 438-441.

Explains the development of a hedge book i.e. a lists of terms, related to particular subject that supplements or replaces controlled vocabulary.

453 Klaus, H.

Understandings of thesauri in the online dialogue : implications for construction and display.

Cataloguing Australia 25 (1-4) March-Dec. 1999 : 120-139.

454 Knypl, E. T.

Building a polythematic thesaurus (exemplified by the thesaurus of the Chemical Establishment in Oswiecim).

Aktualne Problemy Informacji Dokumentacji 16 (3) 1971 : 4-10.

455 Kramer, R.; Nikolai, R. and Habeck, C.

Thesaurus federations : loosely integrated thesauri for document retrieval in network based on Internet technologies.

Journal of Digital Libraries 1(2) Sept. 1997 : 122-131.

Presents an approach for integration of distributed and heterogeneous thesaurus databases and the integration of multilingual and monolingual thesauri.

Also available at : http://www.bubl.ak.uk/journals/lis/fj/ijodl/v01n0297.htm#3thesaurus

456 Kriek, R.

The compilation of a personal documentation system.

Library cooperation : trends, possibilities and conditions. Proceedings of the 8th meeting of IATUL, Enschede, 28 May – 1 June 1979. Ed. by Nancy Fjallbrant. Goteborg, Sweden : IATUL, Chalmers University of Technology, 1979 : 187-189.

Describes contents for a course on personal documentation system which includes indexing, thesaurus construction and other relevant aspects.

457 Kulik, A. N.

Acquisition for an integrated network of information retrieval systems and the thesaurus.

Nauchno- Tekhnicheskaya Informatsiya; Series 2 (12) 1972 : 23-29.

458 Landau, Herbert B. and Byer, Wendy L.

Production of a hierarchical chemical thesaurus.

Journal of Chemical Information and Computer Sciences 16 (3) August 1976 : 141-146.

Reports on the construction of hierarchical chemical thesaurus using a computer system known as Hierarchical Indented Thesaurus System (HITS).

459 Lang, F. H.

The automated compilation of thesauri and concepts for dictionaries and specialist terminologies.

Nachrichten fur Dokumentation 24 (6) Dec. 1973 : 231-238.

460 Lazarescu, G.

Considerations on the elaboration and use of a thesaurus for selective dissemination of information.

Studii si Cercetari de Documentare 14 (2) June 1972 : 127-133.

461 Lazarescu, G.

Contribution to a Romanian thesaurus for education.

Studii si Cercetari de Documentare 15 (2) June 1973 : 131-146.

462 Lazinger, Susan S.

Producing an LCSH authority list for special libraries with dBASE.

Electronic Library 8 (1) Feb. 1990 : 8-14.

463 Leontyeva, T. M. and Margaritov, V. B.

Towards a system of thesauri for a pure and applied chemical information retrieval system : word-stock analysis and recommendations.

Nauchno- Tekhnicheskaya Informatsiya; Series II (2) 1971 : 21-28.

464 Lewis, George R.

Introducing and administering online information retrieval service.

Agricultural Libraries Information Notes 3 (7/8) July /August 1977 : 1-6.

Discusses cost of thesaurus construction amongst other costs involved in creating and maintaining an IR system.

465 Li, Kar Wing and Yang, Christopher C.

Automatic construction of English / Chinese Parallel Corpora. *Journal of the American Society for Information Science and Technology* 54 (8) June 2003 : 730-742.

Describes method used for constructing an English – Chinese parallel corpus automatically from web for cross-lingual IR.

466 Litoukhin, J.

Toward an integrated thesaurus of the social sciences.

International Classification 7 (2) 1980 : 56-59.

Describes various attempts made so far and under progress for construction of integrated thesaurus of social sciences.

467 Little, K.

Constructing a thesaurus of environmental protection terms.

Cataloguing Australia 19 (3-4) Sept.-Dec. 1993 : 222-232.

468 Lobova, L. V.

Main principles of building a linguistic software for large automated information retrieval systems for science and technology.

New trends in documentation and information. Proceedings of the 39th FID Congress, University of Edinburgh, 25-28 September 1978. Ed. by Peter J. Taylor. London : Aslib, 1980 : 234-241.

Describes activities aimed at developing a software and thesaurus for Soviet S & T information retrieval.

469 Loginov, B. R. et al.

Creation and use of authority files in the State Central Scientific Medical Library.

International Cataloguing and Bibliographic Control 25 (4) Oct. –Dec. 1996 : 80-81.

470 Lohr, H. et al.

Aligning a working thesaurus with super-ordinate thesauri.

Informatika 19 (6) 1972 : 30-34.

471 Lucarelli, Anna.

Semantic authority control and the new Soggettario.

Cataloging & Classification Quarterly 39 (1-2) 2004 : 353-364.

Proposes a pre-coordinated controlled vocabulary as a renewal of the subject headings for the Italian Library Catalogues (Soggettario).

472 Lucke, W. and Kruger, D.

Construction of thesauri in the field of heavy engineering : experiences and results.

Informatika 18 (3) 1971 : 22-26.

473 Luk, Johnny and Yang, Christopher C.

Automatic generation of English / Chinese thesaurus based on a parallel corpus in laws.

Journal of the American Society for Information Science and Technology 54 (7) May 2003 : 671-682.

474 Lukenbill, W. B.

Historical resources in the local church : a field report on a largely gay and lesbian congregation.

American Archivist 61 (2) Fall 1998 : 384-399.

Explains the need and method adopted to construct controlled vocabulary to catalogue church archives.

475 Lupnitz, M.

Construction of a thesaurus for a computerized information retrieval system (IRS).

Tagungsbericht der Deutschen Akademie der Landwirtschaftswissenschaften zu Berlin (105) 1970 : 69-79.

476 Ma, W. Y. and Manjunath, B. S.

A texture thesaurus for browsing large aerial photographs.

Journal of the American Society for Information Science 49 (7) 15 May 1998 : 633-648.

Describes methods adopted in constructing a texture thesaurus and its application in browsing aerial photographs.

477 Mackesy, Eileen M.

The MLA Thesaurus of Linguistic, Literary, and Folkloric Terms : a work in progress.

The information community : an alliance for progress. Proceedings of the 44th ASIS Annual Meeting, Washington, DC 25-30 October 1981. Volume 18. Ed. by Lois F. Lunin, Madeline Henderson and Harold Wooster. New York : Knowledge Industry Publications Inc., 1981 : 324-327.

478 Maixner, V.

Towards compensation laws in constructing thesauri.

Information Storage and Retrieval 6 (5) Dec. 1970 : 383-385.

479 Malherbe, P. M.

Government Gazette Index - an index of the Government Gazette of the Republic of South Africa.

South African Journal of Library and Information Science 53 (2) June 1985 : 95-101.

Reports the development of thesaurus and indexing the Government Gazette of the Republic of South Africa.

480 Mali, Hafedh and Rada, Roy.

Merging thesauri : principles and evaluation.

IEEE Transactions on Pattern Analysis and Machine Intelligence 10(2) 1988 : 204-220.

481 Mandersloot, W. G. B.; Douglas, E. M. B. and Spicer, N.

Thesaurus control - the selection, grouping, and cross-referencing of terms for inclusion in a coordinate index word list.

Journal of the American Society for Information Science 21 (1) Jan.-Feb. 1970 : 49-57.

482 Marder, Joan V.

The development of the British Education Thesaurus : a personal account.

Education Libraries Journal 32 (1) Spring 1989 : 2-8.

483 Markey, Karen.

Online searching of ERIC : suggestions for improvement from the special project.

Syracuse, New York : ERIC Clearinghouse on Information Resources, 1979. 23p.

Suggests improvements in the ERIC vocabulary.

484 Marle, G. A. and Skaliks, M.

Some statistics about the searching behaviour of users of the OPAC of the Twenty University library.

IATUL Proceedings (New Series) 3, 1994 : 75-96.

Describes the creation and integration of descriptors and their conversion into a thesaurus.

485 Martin, M. Marlene.

Subject indexing in the new Ethnographic Bibliography of North America.

Behavioral and Social Sciences Librarian 11 (1) 1991 : 13-26.

Reviews problems encountered in creating the Subject Thesaurus for the supplement to the Fourth edition of the Ethnographic Bibliography of North America.

486 Martin, W. A.

Toward an integral multi-file on-line bibliographic database.

Journal of Information Science 2 (5) Nov. 1980 : 241-253.

Reports an attempt to generate common retrieval vocabulary for multi-file online databases.

487 Martinez, K.

The Research Libraries Group : new initiatives to improve access to art and architecture information.

Inspel 32 (1) 1998 : 8-22.

Examines various activities of the RLG including its support for maintaining thesauri for the Arts.

488 Martinez, S. J. et al.

Computer processing of thesaurus data.

Proceedings of the 32nd Annual Meeting of the American Society for Information Science, San Francisco, 1-4 October 1969. Volume 6. Westport, CT : Greenwood Publishing, 1969 : 269-275.

489 McKnight, Mark.

Improving access to music : a report of the MLA Music Thesaurus Project Working Group.

Notes 45 (4) June 1988 : 714-721.

Identifies need for music thesaurus and suggests method for its compilation.

490 McNitt, William H.

Development of the PRESNET subject descriptor thesaurus.

American Archivist 52 (3) Summer 1989 : 358-364.

Describes steps involved in creating, maintaining and using PRESNET – the Presidential Libraries Information Network thesaurus.

491 Miller, P.

The thesaurus of geographic names.

Burisa (134) Sept. 1998 : 13-14.

States the need for thesaurus of geographic names and efforts made for constructing the same.

492 Miller, U.

Thesaurus construction : problems and their roots.

Information Processing and Management 33 (4) July 1997 : 481-493.

Analyses some general problems of thesaurus construction and suggests methodological and methodical ways of solving problems in thesaurus construction.

493 Miller, U.

Thesaurus construction and new information environment.

Encyclopaedia of library and information science. Volume 68. Ed. by Allen Kent. New York : Marcel Dekker Inc., 2001 : 319-345.

494 Miller, U.; Iie, M. and Vibe, A. M.

Sport thesauri construction in different languages : linguistic problems and their solutions.

Papers : 10th Scientific Congress, Paris, 10-12 June 1997. Paris : International Association for Sports Information, 1997 : 137-160.

495 Milstead, Jessica L.

Methodologies for subject analysis in bibliographic databases.

Information Processing and Management 28 (3) 1992 : 407-431.

Highlights importance of upgrading thesauri for effective machine-aided indexing.

496 Milstead, Jessica L. and Berger, M. C.

The Engineering Information thesaurus development project.

Information Services and Use 13 (1) 1993 : 71-80.

Describes method adopted by Engineering Information, Inc. in constructing a thesaurus for organizing its databases.

497 Mojzisek, J.

Methodology of thesaurus construction, Part 1.

Ceskoslovenska Informatika 15 (7-8) 1973 : 53-71.

498 Moorcroft, H.

Reflections on constructing an Aboriginal and Torres Strait Islander Thesaurus.

Cataloguing Australia 20 (4) Dec. 1994 : 108-111.

499 Moskovich, V. A.

The statistical distribution method of thesaurus construction : present situation and future prospects. Part 1.

Nauchno- Tekhnicheskaya Informatsiya Series; II (3) 1972 : 12-21.

500 Moureau, M. and Delaunay, J.

Principles and development of a thesaurus applied to the example of the oil industry.

ANRT Information et Documentation (2) June 1972 : 57-78.

501 Musen, M. A. et al.

Development of a controlled medical terminology : knowledge acquisition and knowledge representation.

Methods of Information in Medicine 34 (1-2) March 1995 : 85-95.

Explains the knowledge acquisition and representation system's usefulness in developing controlled medical terminology.

502 Mustafa-Elhadi, Widad.

The contribution of terminology to the theoretical conception of classificatory languages and document indexing.

*Tools for knowledge organisation and the human interface. Proceedings of the 1st International ISKO Conference, Darmstadt, (*Germany) *14-17 August 1990. Advances in knowledge organization, no. 1/2.* Ed. by R. Fugmann. Part I. Frankfurt/Main : Indeks. 1990 : 98-106.

Explains the role of linguistics in the analysis of semantic relationships used by documentalists in conceiving thesauri.

503 Negulyaev, G. A.

Construction of the thesaurus of elementary statements.

Nauchno- Tekhnicheskaya Informatsiya ; Series II (5) 1973 : 8-15.

504 Negulyaev, G. A.; Pokras, Y. L. and Kolesnikova, L. I.

Automated vocabulary selection for retrieval thesauri.

Nauchno- Tekhnicheskaya Informatsiya; Series 2 (2) 1973 : 16-24.

505 Neville, H. H.

Feasibility study of a scheme for reconciling thesauri covering a common subject.

Journal of Documentation 26 (4) Dec. 1970 : 313-336.

506 Neville, H. H.

Thesaurus reconciliation.

Aslib Proceedings 24 (11) Nov. 1972 : 620-626.

507 Nielsen, M. L.

A framework for work task based thesaurus design.

Journal of Documentation 57 (6) Nov. 2001 : 774-797.

Explains a method of thesaurus design that used group interviews, recollection of information needs and word association tests to collect data and content analysis and discourse analysis to analyze data.

508 Nielsen, Marianne Lykke.

Thesaurus construction : key issues and selected readings.

Cataloging and Classification Quarterly 37 (3-4) 2004 : 57-74.

509 Nutter, J. T.; Fox, E. A. and Evens, M. W.

Building a lexicon from machine-readable dictionaries for improved information retrieval.

Literary and Linguistic Computing 5(2) 1990 : 129-137.

510 Nwali, L. O.

Principles of agricultural thesaurus construction and utilization in Nigeria.

Quarterly Bulletin of the International Association of Agricultural Information Specialists 37 (4) 1992 : 201-204.

511 Nyahoda, Phillip.

Towards a Southern African thesaurus.

Zimbabwe Librarian 22 (1-2) 1990 : 28-29.

Describes ongoing efforts for the construction of a Southern African thesaurus.

512 Nyahoda, Phillip

Towards an indigenous Southern African thesaurus.

African Research and Documentation 56, 1991 : 43-45.

Describes principles of thesaurus construction i.e. (i) establishing terminology with a bias towards Southern Africa (ii) the choice of a suitable format for thesaurus construction.

513 Oliver, D. E. et al.

Representation of change in controlled medical terminologies.

Artificial Intelligence in Medicine 15 (1) Jan. 1999 : 53-76.

Presents a model for developing controlled vocabulary in medical science.

514 O'Neil, M. and Payne, C.

Read Codes Version 3 : a user led terminology.

Methods of Information in Medicine 34 (1-2) March 1995 : 187-192.

Explains how the user led terminology helps to maintain dynamic terminology.

515 O'Neill, Edward T.

Computer generation of a subject authority file.

Information interaction : proceedings of the 44th ASIS Annual Meeting, Columbus, Ohio, 17-21 October 1982. Volume 19. Ed. by A. E. Petrarca, C. I. Taylor and R. S. Kohn. White

Plains, New York : Knowledge Industry Publications, Inc., (for ASIS), 1982 : 220-223.

516 Orlinkov, L. L. and Malyatskii, V. S.

A descriptor information retrieval system for welding.

Nauchno- Tekhnicheskaya Informatsiya; Series 1 (5) 1969 : 15-16.

517 Ornager, Susanne and Johne, Mogens.

Changes in thesaurus construction caused by the use of Boolean searching.

Seventh International Online Information Meeting. London, 6-8 December 1983. Oxford : Learned Information, 1983 : 167-173.

518 Oruma, B.

Developing the Nigerian agricultural thesaurus.

Quarterly. Bulletin of the International Association of Agricultural Information Specialists 27 (4) 1982 : 111-115.

519 Ovens, Cora S. H.

Methodology for constructing a thesaurus in the linguistics and literature fields.

South African Journal of Library and Information Science 57 (1) March 1989 : 45-50.

520 Padmanabhan, V. S. and Amba, K. N.

Some factors to be considered in the compilation of a thesaurus for leather and allied industries.

Seminar on thesaurus in information system. Banglore: DRTC, 1975 : Paper CE.

521 Palatova, R. P.

Developing a descriptor retrieval system for the abstract journal Pipeline Transport.

Nauchno- Tekhnicheskaya Informatsiya; Series 1 (5) 1969 : 13-15.

522 Papier, L. S. and Cortelyou, E. H.

Use of a technical word association test in the preparation of a thesaurus.

Journal of Documentation 18(4) 1962 : 183-187.

523 Park, Y. C. and Choi, K. S.

Automatic thesaurus construction using Bayesian networks.

Information Processing and Management 32 (5) Sept. 1996 : 543-553.

524 Patenall, Diane.

Records management : three years' experience at the Records Management Office of New South Wales.

Archives and Manuscripts 7 (5) Nov. 1979 : 252-255.

Explains changes made due to new policies at New South Wales Record Management Office, which includes creation of a functional thesauri.

525 Peniston, Silvina.

Online thesauri and classification schemes.

Its News (16) May 1988 : 44-49.

Describes construction and use of online thesauri and classification schemes.

526 Petersen, Toni.

Developing a new thesaurus for art and architecture.

Library Trends 38 (4) Spring 1990 : 644-658.

Narrates the processes and policies adopted in the construction of the AAT.

527 Pickens, Keith.

Adapting ERIC to New Zealand.

New Zealand Libraries 46 (6) Sept. 1990 : 22-24.

Suggests an adaptation of ERIC thesaurus to produce a New Zealand Thesaurus of Education.

528 Poletylo, M.

Principles of thesaurus construction for mechanised information retrieval systems.

ANRT Information et Documentation (2) June-July 1970 : 43-46.

529 Pollard, Richard.

Hypertext presentation of thesauri used in on-line searching.

Electronic Publishing Review 3 (3) August 1990 : 155-172.

Examines merits and demerits of hypertext for the on-line presentation of thesauri.

530 Prasad, K. N.; Mahajan, S. K. and Thyagarajan, K.

Work and time analysis for rendering terms in a thesaurus derived from faceted classification schedule : a case study with lathe production.

Seminar on thesaurus in information systems. Banglore : DRTC, 1975 : Paper BD.

531 Preisler, W.

The importance, construction and testing of a thesaurus.

Informatika 17 (6) 1970 : 4-18.

532 Preisler, W.

Types of thesaurus and problems concerning their compilation.

Informatika 20 (4) 1973 : 9-16.

533 Rada, Roy.

Maintaining thesauri and metathesauri.

International Classification 17 (3- 4) 1990 : 158-164.

Describes computer systems helpful in maintaining thesauri and metathesauri.

534 Rada, Roy. et al.

Creating and evaluating entry terms.

Journal of Documentation 44 (1) March 1988 : 19-41.

535 Rada, Roy. et al.

Development and application of a metric on semantic nets. I *EEE Transactions on Systems, Man and Cybernetics* 19(1) 1989 : 17-30.

536 Rahmann, M. and Samulowitz, H.

Planning and compilation of a specialized thesaurus.

Nachrichten fur Dokumentation 19 (6) Dec. 1968 : 222-226.

537 Raizada, A. S. et al.

Principles of thesaurus construction and Indian Science Abstracts indexing system.

Seminar on thesaurus in information systems. Banglore : DRTC, 1975 : Paper AE.

538 Ramsey, M. C.

A collection of visual thesauri for browsing large collections of geographic images.

Journal of the American Society for Information Science 50 (9) July 1999 : 826-834.

Suggests a method for automatic generation of visual thesauri of large collections of geo-spatial media using fuzzy, unsupervised machine-learning techniques.

539 Ravichandra Rao, I. K.

Semi automatic construction of thesaurus.

Seminar on thesaurus in information system. Banglore : DRTC, 1975 : Paper BB.

540 Rector, A. L.

Faithfulness or comparability.

Methods of Information in Medicine 35 (3) Sept. 1996 : 218-219.

A critical appraisal of M. S. Tuttle and S. J. Nelson's article entitled 'a poor precedent' and J. J. Cimino's article entitled 'formal descriptions and adaptive mechanisms for changes in controlled medical vocabularies'.

541 Rees-Potter, Lorna K.

Dynamic thesaural systems : a bibliometric study of terminological and conceptual change in sociology and economics with application to the design of dynamic thesaural systems.

Information Processing and Management 25 (6) 1989 : 677-691.

Explains the use of citation, co-citation and citation context analysis in updating thesauri.

542 Rees-Potter, Lorna K.

Dynamic thesauri : the cognitive function.

*Tools for knowledge organisation and the human interface. Proceedings of the 1st International ISKO Conference, Darmstadt, (*Germany) *14-17 August 1990. Advances in knowledge organization, no. 1/2.* Ed. by R. Fugmann. Part II. Frankfurt/Main : Indeks. 1990 : 145-150.

Reports an ongoing project of constructing and maintaining a thesaurus semi-automatically.

543 Rolling, L. N.

Compilation of thesauri for use in computer systems.

Information storage and retrieval Vol. 6, 1970 : 341-350.

544 Rolling, L. N.

Graphic display devices in thesaurus construction and use.

Aslib Proceedings 23 (11) Nov. 1971 : 591-594.

545 Rolling, L. N.

Regulating the interrelation of terms in a computer-aided system.

Nachrichten fur Dokumentation 24 (2) April 1973 : 60-64.

546 Rolling, L. N.

The role of graphic display of concept relationships in indexing retrieval vocabularies.

Classification research. Proceedings of the 2nd International Study Conference. Ed. by Atherton Pauline. Copenhagen : Munksgaard, 1965 : 295-320.

547 Rolls, M. J.

Non-conventional literature in agriculture-the user's view.

Quarterly Bulletin of the International Association of Agricultural Information Specialists 27 (1) 1982 : 25-29.

Describes Agricultural Extension and Rural Development Centre's (AERDC) collections of non-conventional literature and the development of thesaurus for storage and retrieval of information about the non-conventional literature in agriculture.

548 Rosenbaum, H. D.

The co-ordination of work on thesauri in the GDR : a contribution to the improvement of information activities.

Informatika 19 (1) 1972 : 16-21.

549 Rosenbaum, H. D.

The development of a compatible search language for national and international information systems of CMEA countries.

Informatika 21 (4) 1974 : 28-30.

550 Rossall, H.

Setting up a general practice library.

Librarians World 9 (5) 2000 : 83-85.

Describes the development of thesaurus and other modernization works carried out at a general practice library at the Fisher Medical Centre (FMC) in Skipton, North Yorkshire, UK.

551 Rostron, R. M.

Construction of thesaurus.

Aslib Proceedings 20 (3) 1968 : 181-187.

552 Roux, P. J. A. and Rykheer, J. H.

Developing a South African master thesaurus for community information.

South African Journal of Library and Information Science 58 (2) June 1990 : 174-179.

553 Roy, P. B. and Banerjee, S. B.

Basic considerations for designing a thesaurus for an information system for social science subject with special reference to Jute trade.

Seminar on thesaurus in information systems. Banglore : DRTC, 1975 : Paper AH.

554 Rugg, G.

The future of smart systems in information science.

Perspectives in Information Management 3 (2) 1993 : 150-165.

Presents a thematic review of the experts systems including automatic indexing and automatic thesaurus construction.

555 Saarti, J.

Fiction indexing and the development of fiction thesauri.

Journal of Librarianship and Information Science 31 (2) June 1999 : 85-92.

556 Salmond, Rachel.

Thesaurus construction and use : a practical manual by J. Aitchison, A. Gilchrist and D. Bawden. Ed. 4. London : Aslib IMI, 2000. 218p.

Australian Library Journal 51 (3) August 2002 : 261.

A book review.

557 Salton, G.

Experiments in automatic thesaurus construction for information retrieval.

New York : Cornell University, 1971. 27p.

558 Salton, G.

Experiments in automatic thesaurus construction for information retrieval : information storage and retrieval.

Ithaca, New York : Cornell University, Department of Computer Science, 1970. 28p.

559 Sand, W. and Sawicki, L

Work performed in connection with the construction of a national system of thesauri.

Aktualne Problemy Informacji Dokumentacji 17 (5) 1972 : 3-6.

560 Satija, M. P.

Thesaurus construction and use : a practical manual by A. Aitchison, A. Gilchrist and D. Bawden. Ed. 3. London : Aslib, 1997. 212p.

Asian Libraries 8 (1) 1999 : 357.

A book review.

561 Schaarschmidt, K.; Osada, N. and Kopcke, W.

The clinic-specific thesaurus : a means of 'lean documentation' in pediatric surgery.

Methods of Information in Medicine 36 (3) August 1997 : 207-213.

Describes how the frequency of diagnoses in paediatric surgery was used to develop diagnostic codes i.e. a clinic specific thesaurus.

562 Schon, J.

The Thesaurus of Engineering and Scientific Terms (TEST) : history of development and construction.

Nachrichten fur Dokumentation 21 (3) June 1970 : 110-113.

563 Schoonbaert, D.

Automatic mapping of free-text to thesaurus : good policy?

Bulletin of Medical Libraries Association 85 (4) 1997 : 439-440.

564 Schwanhausser, G.

An automatically produced thesaurus.

Seminar on thesaurus in information system. Banglore : DRTC, 1975 : Paper BA.

565 Schwartz, Candy and Noreault, Terry.

Human-assisted thesaurus generation : a first step.

The information age in perspective. Proceedings of the 41st Annual Meeting, New York, 13-17 November 1978. Volume 15. Compiled by Everett H. Brenner, White Plains, New York : Knowledge Industry Publications for American Society for Information Science, 1978 : 291-294.

Narrates an experiment attempted to provide semantic, thesaurus-type information derived from and specific to a given collection.

566 Scibor, E.

Principles of building a national system of thesauri in the GDR.

Aktualne Problemy Informacji Dokumentacji 18 (1) 1973 : 16-20.

567 Sedelow, S. Y. and Sedelow, W. A.

Thesauri and concept-lattice semantic nets.

Proceedings of the 3rd International Society for Knowledge Organization (ISKO) Conference : Knowledge organization and quality management. Copenhagen, Denmark, 20-24 June 1994. Ed. by Hanne Albrechtsen and Susan Oernager, Frankfurt/Main : INDEKS Verlag, 1994 : 350-357.

Explains the usefulness of Formal Concept - Lattice in thesaurus construction.

568 Sedelow, W. A. and Sedelow, S. Y.

Multicultural / multilingual electronically mediated communication.

Social Science Computer Review 12 (2) Summer 1994 : 242-249.

Modeling of semantic space is discussed with specific reference to a National Science Foundation funded project on knowledge representations in thesauri.

569 Shearer, James R.

A practical exercise in building a thesaurus.

Cataloging and Classification Quarterly 37 (3-4) 2004 : 35-56.

570 Sheffield, Philip.

Encouraging people to find out faster : the British Education Index and the British Education Thesaurus as resources.

Learning Resources Journal 5 (3) Oct. 1989 : 58-61.

Describes purposes and development of BEI and the BET.

571 Shephard, M. and Watters, C.

Computer generation of thesaurus.

Seminar on thesaurus in information system. Banglore : DRTC, 1975 : Paper BC.

572 Shneiderman, Ya A.

Constructing a materials dictionary.

Nauchno- Tekhnicheskaya Informatsiya; Series II (9) 1969 : 17-23.

573 Sneiderman, C. A. and Bicknell, E. J.

Computer-assisted dynamic integration of multiple medical thesaurus.

Computers in Biology and Medicine 22(1-2) Jan.–March 1992 : 134-145.

574 Soergel, D.

Automatic and semi-automatic methods as an aid in the construction of indexing languages and thesauri.

International Classification 1 (1) May 1974 : 34-39.

575 Sokolov, A. V.

Concerning the efficient make-up of an information retrieval thesaurus.

Nauchno- Tekhnicheskaya Informatsiya; Series II (1) 1970 : 35-41.

576 Spackman, A.; Gilbert, D. and Glastonbury, B.

Scoping the language of the personal social services.

Assignation 13 (3) April 1996 : 13-18.

Describes method of thesaurus construction which uses terms in clinical practice and Social Terms Scoping Project (a project which tests terms used within personal social services).

577 Sparck, Jones K.

Automatic thesaurus construction and relation of a thesaurus to indexing terms.

Aslib Proceedings 22(5) 1970 : 226-228.

578 Spiteri, L. F.

The essential elements of faceted thesauri.

Cataloging and Classification Quarterly 28 (4) 1999 : 31-52.

Examines principles of facet analysis adopted in thesaurus construction and also extent of their adoption.

579 Sprunger, Kent.

XREF : a subject thesaurus generator created with WordPerfect 5.0.

OCLC Micro 5 (2) April 1989 : 9-10.

Gives details of XREF - a WordPerfect macro that generates a cross-referencing subject thesaurus from a simple input files.

580 Stanley, Janet L.

African art and AAT.

Art Documentation 4 (3) Fall 1985 : 103-105.

Reports a method through which African art terms were supplied to ATT.

581 Starska, D.

Methods of building a thesaurus : the problem of a

representative set of documents.

Aktualne Problemy Informacji Dokumentacji 17 (5) 1972 : 7-14.

582 Strater, H. H.

Problem of thesaurus construction for education.

Council for Europe. EUDISED Technical Studies 3. Strasbourg : Documentation Centre for Education in Europe, 1969 : 23-51.

583 Study Group for Law Libraries and Documentation Services, West Germany.

Study Group for Law Libraries and Documentation Services : resolution to produce a uniform legal thesaurus and a uniform classification for all legal libraries in the German Federal Republic.

Bibliotheksdienst (5) May 1973 : 229-231.

584 Stumm, D.

When is a forest fire a bushfire? Towards an Australian Pictorial Thesaurus.

Cataloguing Australia 25 (1-4) March-Dec. 1999 : 140-146.

585 Svenonius, Elaine.

Definitional approaches in the design of classification and thesauri and their implications for retrieval and for automatic classification.

Knowledge organization for information retrieval. Proceedings of the 6th International Study Conference on Classification Research, 16-18 June 1997, University College, London. The Hague : International Federation for Information and Documentation (FID), 1997 : 14-17.

586 Svenonius, Elaine.

Design of controlled vocabularies.

Encyclopaedia of library and information science. Volume 45 (Supplement 10). Ed. by Allen Kent. New York : Marcel Dekker Inc., 1990 : 82-109.

587 Svenonius, Elaine.

Design of controlled vocabularies in the context of emerging technologies

Library Science with a Slant to Documentation 25 (4) Dec. 1988 : 215-227.

Examines issues involved in the design and development of thesauri and other vocabulary control devices their role in the information technology environment.

588 Svenonius, Elaine and Schmierer, Helen F.

Current issues in the subject control of information.

Library Quarterly 47 (3) July 1977 : 326-346.

Discusses problems posed by synonyms and alternative form of a name in an authority file and suggest remedies such as indexing vocabulary convertibility.

589 Tarker, Barbara.

Interactive evolution in an information center.

ASIS '87: Proceedings of the 50th ASIS Annual Meeting. Ed. by Ching-chih Chen. Medford, New Jersey : American Society for Information Science by Learned Information, 1987 : 220-224.

Traces the development of MATRIS - the Manpower and Training Research Information System of the US Department of Defense (DoD) and describes its various projects including the creation of controlled vocabulary.

590 Technical Information Center, Department of Energy.

Subject thesaurus permutated listing.

Oak Ridge, TN : Department of Energy, Technical Information Center, 1981. 240p.

Explains use of permuted listing to prepare and search thesaurus entries.

591 Thomas, Alan R.

Teach yourself thesaurus : exercises, readings, resources.

Cataloging and Classification Quarterly 37 (3-4) 2004 : 23-34.

Reviews readings, exercises and resources useful in thesaurus construction.

592 Thomas, P. A

Some problems in compiling a thesaurus of transportation and planning terms.

Aslib Proceedings 23 (11) Nov. 1971 : 595-606.

593 Thomas, Sarah E.

Improved access to agricultural literature through a comprehensive, detailed agricultural thesaurus.

Quarterly Bulletin of the International Association of Agricultural Information Specialists 36 (1-2) 1991 : 80-82.

Describes cooperative efforts aimed at constructing a single, unified thesaurus for agricultural databases.

594 Tikhonova, L.

Automation of information processes in the sphere of culture.

Resource Sharing and Information Networks 9 (1) 1993 : 125-129.

Reports ongoing efforts to integrate isolated thesauri.

595 Tomita, Tetsuo and Hattori, Kazutoshi.

Compilation of thesaurus and total index of 'Nihon-Kagaku-Gijutsu-Shi Taikei' and analysis of its documents.

International Classification 2 (1) May 1975 : 11-21.

Describes the method adopted for the construction of a thesaurus for the source book 'Nihon Kagaku-Gijutsu-Shi Taikei' (History of Science and Technology in Japan from 1850-1960).

596 Tomlinson, Daphne and Cordiner, Daphne.

Design and implementation of an online private information retrieval system for a technology-based consultancy.

Online Review 10 (6) Dec. 1986 : 339-351.

Reports on the construction of thesaurus for newly emerging technical subjects.

597 Torre, D. S.

KSR : Keywording for subject retrieval.

Art Documentation 14 (2) Summer 1995 : 29-35.

Reports the KSR project aimed at developing hierarchic symbols and controlled vocabulary for cataloguing slides and photographs.

598 Trickey, Keith V.

Thesaurus construction and use : a practical manual by J. Aitchison, A. Gilchrist and D. Bawden. Ed. 3. London : Aslib, 1997. 212p.

Journal of Librarianship and Information Science 31 (1) Mar 1999 : 49-50.

A book review.

599 Tseng, Yuen-Hsien.

Automatic thesaurus generation for Chinese documents.

Journal of the American Society for Information Science and Technology 53 (13) 2002 : 1130-1138.

600 Tseng, Yuen-Hsien.

Networked information services for retrospective data.

Journal of Information, Communication and Library Science 9 (2) Dec. 2002 : 27-39.

Describes planning, development and current status of the Socio-Cultural Research Center's network information services, which has also developed a thesaurus.

601 Tyulenev, A. E.

Method of creating a geological information retrieval descriptor language for 'Exogenic mineral deposits'.

Nauchno- Tekhnicheskaya Informatsiya; Series 2 (8) 1972 : 15-19.

602 Van Driel, M.

Archives and automation in the Netherlands : a survey.

ADPA 4 (3) 1984 : 41-47.

Efforts for the development of a thesaurus for managing archives database and other activities related with archive's automation project are reported.

603 Vandendorpe, James; Evens, Martha and Wang, Yih Chen.

Relational thesauri in information retrieval.

Journal of the American Society for Information Science 36 (1) Jan. 1985 : 15-27.

Reports an experiment in the development of relational thesaurus and its use.

604 Virgona, Thomas.

Design and implementation of contemporary thesauri.

Canadian Journal of Information and Library Science 27 (4) Dec. 2003 : 58.

Reviews print and web literature on thesaurus construction.

605 Walker, A.

Building an Australian thesaurus : indexing Australian historical photographs.

Cataloguing Australia 19 (3-4) Sept.-Dec. 1993 : 268-279.

Describes the compilation of a thesaurus for indexing historical photographs.

606 Wall, E.

Final report on first revision of the thesaurus of ASTIA descriptors.

Arlington, VA : Armed Services Technical Information Agency, 1962.

607 Wall, E.

Symbiotic development of thesauri and information systems : a case history.

Journal of the American Society for Information Science 26 (2) March - April 1975 : 71-79.

608 Wall, E.

Vocabulary building and control techniques.

American Documentation 20 (2) April 1969 : 161-164.

609 Warner, Amy J.

A linguistic approach to the automatic hierarchical organization of phrases.

ASIS'90. Information in the year 2000 : from research to applications. Proceedings of the 53rd Annual Meeting of the American Society for Information Science, Toronto, Canada, 4-8 November 1990. Volume 27. Ed. by Diane Henderson. Medford, New Jersey : Learned Information, Inc., 1990 : 220-227.

Describes the automatic hierarchical organization of phrases as a step in automatic thesaurus construction.

610 Watters, C. and Shepherd, Michael.

Computer-generation of thesaurus.

Library Science with a Slant to Documentation 12 (2) June 1975 : 40-54.

611 Weber, H. and Richter, G.

Supervision and updating of the thesaurus for oil and natural gas.

Informatika 20 (1) 1973 : 29-35.

612 Werder, H.

Computer-assisted elaboration and maintenance of a thesaurus.

Informatika 19 (3) 1972 : 25-32.

613 Wheeler, Gill.

Maintaining a controlled vocabulary for a large online database service.

Computers in Libraries International 91. Proceedings of the

5th Annual Conference on Computers in Libraries, London, February 1991 : 115-119.

Discusses issues involved in the maintenance of a thesaurus of INSPEC – an online database.

614 Whitehead, Cathleen.

Mapping LCSH into thesauri : the AAT Model.

Beyond the book : extending MARC for subject access. Boston : Hall, 1990 : 81-98.

615 Wiggins, R.

Beyond the spider : the accidental thesaurus.

Searcher 10 (9) Oct. 2002 : 68-77.

Explains the need and procedure for automatic generation of thesaural capability into search engine.

Full text available at : http://www.infotoday.com/searcher/oct02/wiggins.htm

616 Will, Leonard.

Thesaurus construction and use : a practical manual by J. Aitchison, A. Gilchrist and D. Bawden. Ed. 3. London : Aslib, 1997. 212p.

Managing Information 5 (3) March 1998 : 42.

A book review.

617 Will, Leonard.

Thesaurus consultancy.

Cataloging and Classification Quarterly 37 (3-4) 2004 : 75-85.

Reviews the role and functions of a consultant in thesaurus construction.

Alos available at : http://www.willpowerinfo.co.uk/thesconsult.rtf

618 Wolff Terroine, M.; Rimbert, D. and Rouault, B.

Improved statistical methods for automatic construction of a medical thesaurus.

Methods of Information in Medicine 11 (2) April 1972 : 104-113.

619 Wolff Terroine, M.; Simon, N. and Rimbert, D.

Use of a computer for compiling and holding a medical thesaurus.

Methods of Information in Medicine 8 (1) Jan. 1969 : 34-40.

620 Zahawi, Faria.

Industrial information in the Arab countries.

Information systems design for socio-economic development : retrospect and prospect. Proceedings. FID Symposium, Brussels, 30 September - 2 October 1975, held on the 80th anniversary of the International Federation for Documentation. The Hague : International Federation for Documentation, 1976 : 64-68.

Discusses activities related with translation of thesauri into Arabic.

621 Zhu, Shilin and Yuye, Shen.

Establishing a united retrieval system of forestry documents in China.

Information systems for forestry-related subjects : access, search techniques and user needs. Proceedings of the Meeting of the IUFRO Subject Group S6.03 Information Systems and Terminology, Swiss Federal Institute of Forestry Research, Birmensdorf, and the Swiss Federal Institute of Technology, Zurich, 21-24 June 1888. Ed. by Alois Kempf and Rosemarie Louis. Birmensdorf (Switzerland) : IUFRO Subject Group S6.03, 1988 : 87-93.

Reports efforts made in the Institute of Scientech Information, Chinese Academy of Forestry to establish a united retrieval system including the compilation of the subject thesaurus of forestry and other developments.

Section H
Thesaural relationships

An IR thesaurus differs from a language thesaurus on account of thesaural relationships. The three types of thesaural relationships i.e. (1) Equivalence (2) Hierarchical and (3) Associative relationship enable to show / identify which term is broader / narrower to which other term and which two or more terms are associated with each other.

Thesaural relationships give the IR thesaurus its special feature. As such number of professionals have written about the nature of these relationships. Literature is also written about methods of establishing thesaural relationships. This section lists literature on thesaural relationships.

622 Atanasiu, P. and Gercu, N.

Relationships between the key-words of thesauri.

Studii si Cercetari de Documentare 13 (3) Sept. 1971 : 213-224.

623 Bean, C. A.

The semantics of hierarchy.

Information Studies 4 (4) Oct. 1998 : 217-219.

States that controlled medical vocabularies are domain knowledge bases and that much of the knowledge in a controlled vocabulary is contained within its syndetic structure.

624 Bean, C. A.

The semantics of hierarchy : axplicit parent- child relationships in MeSH tree structures.

Advances in knowledge organization. Volume 6. Structure and relations in knowledge organization. Proceedings of the 5th International ISKO Conference, Lille, 25-29 August 1998.

Wurzburg, Germany : Ergon Verlang, 1998 : 133-138.

625 Bean, Carol.

Analysis non-hierarchical associative relationships among Medical Subject Headings (MeSH) : anatomical and related terminology.

Advances in knowledge Organization. Volume 5 .Knowledge organization and change. Proceedings of the 4th International ISKO Conference 15-18 July 1996, Washington, DC. Frankfurt/Main : Indeks Verlag, 1996 : 80-86.

626 Craven, Timothy C.

Thesaural relations in a concept-network management system for customizing of permuted index displays.

Information Processing and Management 20 (5-6) 1984 : 603-610.

Explains the role of thesaural relations in managing concept-network.

627 Dextre Clarke, S. G.

Thesaural relationships.

Relationships in the organization of knowledge. Ed. by C. A. Bean. and R. Green. Dordrecht : Kluwer, 2000 : 37-52.

628 Doszkocs, Tamas E

AID, an Associative Interactive Dictionary for online searching.

Online Review 2 (2) June 1978 : 163-173.

Explains a method for automatic generation and display of related terms, synonyms, broader and narrower terms and other semantic associations for given search concepts.

629 Doszkocs, Tamas E.

An associative interactive dictionary for online bibliographic searching.

Information technology 78. Ed. by J. Moneta. North-Holland : Publishing Company, 1978 : 489-492.

Describes the automatic generation and display of related terms, broader and narrower terms, and other semantic associations for given search concepts to be used for an online bibliographic retrieval.

630 Doszkocs, Tamas E.

Implementing an associative search interface in a large online bibliographic database environment.

New trends in documentation and information. Proceedings of the 39th FID Congress, University of Edinburgh, 25-28 September 1978. Ed. by Peter J. Taylor. London : Aslib, 1980 : 295-297.

Explains the process developed by NLM for automatic generation and display of related terms, broader and narrower terms and other semantic associations.

631 Gopinath, M. A.

Equivalence relations in information retrieval thesaurus.

Library Science with a Slant to Documentation 22 (1) March 1985 : 57-63.

Examines equivalence relationships in a textile technology thesaurus and an energy thesaurus.

632 Foskett, A. C.

Cutter to Austin.

Cataloguing Australia 2 (3-4) July-Dec. 1976 : 12-18.

Discusses semantic relationship between terms in thesauri as analyzed by the CRG.

633 Hudon, Michele.

A preliminary investigation of the usefulness of semantic relations and of standardized definitions for the purpose of specifying meaning in a thesaurus.

Advances in knowledge organization Vol. 6 Structures and relations in knowledge organization. Proceedings of the 5th ISKO International Conference, Lille, France, 25-29 August

1998. Wurzburg, Germany : Ergon Verlag, 1998 : 139-145.

634 Maniez, J.

Relationship in thesauri : some critical remarks.

International Classification 15 (3) 1988 : 133-138.

635 Molholt, Pat.

Standardization of inter-concept links and their usage.

Advances in knowledge organization. Volume 5. Knowledge organization and change. Proceedings of the 4th International ISKO Conference, Washington, D.C. 15-18 July 1996. Frankfurt/Main : Indeks Verlag, 1996 : 65-71.

636 Molholt, Pat.

Standardizing and codifying related term links for improved information retrieval.

Tools for knowledge organisation and the human interface. Proceedings of the 1st International ISKO Conference, Darmstadt, (Germany) *14-17 August 1990. Advances in knowledge organization, no. 1/2.* Ed. by R. Fugmann. Part I. Frankfurt/Main : Indeks. 1990 : 267-275.

Discusses findings of a literature survey in the context of proposed research on the related term structure for the Art and Architecture Thesaurus.

637 Neelameghan, A.

Non – hierarchical associative relationships : their types and computer generation of RT links.

Seminar on thesaurus in information systems. Banglore : DRTC, 1975 : Paper AA.

638 Neelameghan, A. and Ravichandra Rao, I. K.

Non-hierarchical associative relationships : their types and computer-generation of RT links.

Library Science with a Slant to Documentation 13 (1) March 1976 : 24-42.

639 Rajan, T. N.

Related terms in thesaurus.

Seminar on thesaurus in information systems. Banglore : DRTC, 1975 : Paper AC.

640 Seetharama, S.

Term-concept relationship in an information retrieval thesaurus.

Library Science with a Slant to Documentation 13 (2) June 1976 : 67-73.

Examines representation of compound concepts in thesauri.

641 Seetharama, S.

Term - concept relationships in an information retrieval thesaurus.

Seminar on thesaurus in information systems. Banglore : DRTC, 1975 : Paper AJ.

642 Sridhar, M. S.

A mathematical approach to relations in thesauri.

Journal of Library and Information Science (India) 5 (1) June 1980 : 76-87.

Provides mathematical approach for establishing thesaural relationships.

643 Willetts, Margaret.

An investigation of the nature of the relation between terms in thesauri.

Journal of Documentation 31 (3) Sept. 1975 : 158-184.

Examines associative relationships in 10 thesauri.

Section I

Thesaurus construction standards (for Monolingual thesaurus)

By adopting appropriate standards and guidelines one can perform a particular task in uniform, consistent and logical way. Standards also help to perform the task efficiently. Standards and guidelines are results of critical, logical thinking of experts. As such the products / activities based on standards are always of a better quality. Considering such a usefulness of standards and guidelines various national and international agencies have produced standards and guidelines for thesaurus construction and maintenance. This section lists standards and guidelines meant for the construction of monolingual thesauri. This section also lists literature discussing various aspects of standards and guidelines meant for the construction of monolingual thesauri.

644 Aitchison, Jean.

Subject control : thesaurus construction standards.

Standards for the international exchange of bibliographic information. Ed. by I. C. McIlwaine, London : Library Association Publishing, 1991 : 128-136.

Reviews existing thesaurus construction standards and presents a futuristic view about the same.

645 American National Standards Institute.

American national standard guidelines for thesaurus structure, construction, and use.

New York : American National Standards Institute, 1974. 20p.

646 American National Standards Institute.

American National Standard guidelines for thesaurus structure, construction and use. (ANSI Z39.19-1980).

New York, American National Standards Institute, 1980.

647 American National Standards Institute.

ANSI / NISO Z39-19 : 1993. Guidelines for construction, format and management of monolingual thesauri.

Bethesda MD : National Information Standards Organization Press, 1994.

Also available at : http://www.niso.org/standards/resources/Z39-19.pdf

648 British Standards Institution.

British standards 5723 : 1979 - Guidelines for the establishment and development of monolingual thesauri.

London : British Standards Institution, 1979.

649 British Standards Institution.

BS 5723 : Guidelines for the establishment and development of monolingual thesauri. 2nd ed.

London : British Standards Institution, 1987.

650 Dahlberg, I.

DIN 32 705 : the German standard on classification systems-a critical appraisal.

International Classification 19 (4) 1992 : 201-204.

Criticizes the exclusion of a convergence of classification systems and thesauri in the form of faceted classification and faceted thesauri from the German standard on the development of classification systems.

651 Fayen, Emily.

A new standard for controlled vocabularies.

Indexer 24 (2) Oct. 2004 : 62-65.

Reviews ANSI / NISO Z39.50 standard for thesaurus construction and its proposed revision.

652 Hoffmann, G.

On the standardization of subject thesauri in patent literature.

Zentralinstitut fur Information und Dokumentation Zeitschrift 15 (5) Oct. 1968 : 215-220.

653 International Organization for Standardization.

ISO 2788 : Guidelines for the establishment and development of monolingual thesauri.

Geneva : International Organization for Standardization, 1974.

654 International Organization for Standardization.

ISO 2788 : Guidelines for the establishment and development of monolingual thesauri. 2nd ed.

Geneva : International Organization for Standardization, 1986.

655 International Organization for Standardization.

ISO 5963 : Documentation - methods for examining documents, determining their subjects and selecting indexing terms.

Geneva : International Organization for Standardization , 1985.

656 Jones, Kevin P.

Problems associated with the use of compound words in thesauri, with special reference to BS 5723 : 1979.

Journal of Documentation 37 (2) June 1981 : 53-68.

657 Krooks, D. A. and Lancaster, F. W.

The evolution of guidelines for thesaurus construction.

Libri 43 (4) Oct.-Dec. 1993 : 326-342.

Presents a review of literature dealing with guidelines for thesaurus construction.

658 Leski, K.

Standards in thesauri development.

Aktualne Problemy Informacji Dokumentacji 19 (5) 1974 : 3-8.

659 Lorch, W. T.

International guidelines for thesauri : a description of the Third Unesco draft.

Nachrichen fur Dokumentation 21 (2) April 1970 : 72-75.

660 Maines, M.

Guidelines for thesaurus construction.

Informatics 1: Proceedings of a conference held by the Aslib Coordinate Indexing Group on 11-13 April 1973 at Durham University. London: Aslib, 1973 : 118-125.

661 Office of Education. Panel on Educational Terminology.

Rules for thesaurus preparation.

Washington, DC : US Government Printing Office, 1969.

662 RBMS Bibliographic Standards Committee.

Thesaurus construction and maintenance guidelines. (RBMS manual ; 13).

Chicago : American Library Association, Association of College and Research Libraries, Rare Books and Manuscripts Section, 1998.

Guidance on the choice of options and local decisions in applying NISO Z39.19 to the development of existing thesauri and the construction of additional controlled vocabularies for rare books and manuscripts.

Also available at : http://www.rbms.nd.edu/rbms_manual/thesaurus_construction.shtml

663 Roe, Sandra K. and Thomas, Alan R.

An interview with Dr. Amy J. Warner (June 2003).

Cataloging and Classification Quarterly 37 (3-4) 2004 : 193-198.

Shares experience about the revision of Z39.19 Guidelines for the Construction, Format, and Management of Monolingual Thesauri.

664 Somers, H. L.

Observations on standards and guidelines concerning thesaurus construction.

International Classification 8(2) 1981 : 69-74.

Compares the existing standards and guidelines for thesaurus construction and management.

665 Spiteri, L. F.

The use of facet analysis in information retrieval thesauri : an examination of selected guidelines for thesaurus construction.

Cataloging and Classification Quarterly 25 (1) 1997 : 21-37.

666 Sub-panel on Classification and Indexing of Committee on Scientific and Technical Information (COSATI).

Guidelines for the development of information retrieval thesauri.

Washington, DC : Committee on Scientific and Technical Information, COSATI, 1967.

667 UNESCO.

Guidelines for the establishment and development of monolingual scientific and technical thesauri for information retrieval. CS/MC/20.

Paris : UNESCO, 1970.

668 UNESCO.

Guidelines for the establishment and development of monolingual thesauri for information retrieval. CS/WS/500.

Paris : UNESCO, 1971.

669 UNESCO.

Guidelines for the establishment and development of monolingual thesauri for information retrieval. 2nd rev. ed. PGI-81/WS/15.

Paris : UNESCO, 1981. 64p.

670 Zamfirescu, M.

Guidelines for the establishment and development of monolingual thesauri for documentary research (1).

Probleme de Informare si Documentare 7 (5) May 1973 : 436-445.

671 Zamfirescu, M.

Guidelines for the establishment and development of monolingual thesauri for documentary retrieval (continued).

Probleme de Informare si Documentare 7 (7) July 1973 : 652-661.

Section J

Literature related with thesaurus construction softwares

Thesaurus construction and maintenance is a complex task. It involves a large amount of repetitive activities. Computers are very good for repetitive work. Many efforts are made to make use of this and other features of computer and other information technologies for library and information activities. Development of software for thesaurus construction and maintenance is one such effort. Today many softwares are developed for thesaurus construction and maintenance. Literature is published on various aspects of thesaurus construction and maintenance softwares. This section lists literature dealing with thesaurus construction softwares.

As many softwares for thesaurus construction and maintenance are available in the market one has to be very judicious in selecting appropriate software. To help in the selection of appropriate software for thesaurus construction and maintenance experts have written literature containing criteria for evaluation of thesaurus construction and maintenance software. So this section also lists literature that deals with the evaluation of softwares for thesaurus construction and maintenance.

672 Brandt, D. S.
Ovid searching software.
Library Software Review 15 (3) Fall 1996 : 141-148.
Describes Ovid searching software, which among other features allows mapping of controlled vocabularies.

673 Cnowdhury, G. G.; Neelameghan, A. and Chowdhury, S.
Vocabulary control online in MicroIsis databases : a Pascal interface.
ASTINFO Newsletter 9(3) 1994 : 11-18.

674 Chowdhury, G. G.; Neelameghan, A. and Chowdhury, S.

Vocabulary control online in MicroISIS databases : a Pascal interface.

Microcomputers for Information Management 11 (4) Dec. 1994 : 295-305.

Describes VOCON.PAS - a Pascal based program used in MicroISIS software for developing controlled vocabulary.

675 Chowdhury, G. G.; Neelameghan, A. and Chowdhury, S.

VOCON : Vocabulary control online in MicroIsis databases.

Knowledge Organization 22(1) 1995 : 18-22.

676 Cibbarelli, P.

Cibbarelli's surveys : user ratings of Information Navigator software.

Computers in Libraries 13 (2) Feb. 1993 : 38-39.

Presents integrated online software designed for housekeeping operations and thesauri.

677 Flood, G.

Yell builds thesaurus management tool.

Information World Review (188) Feb. 2003 : 1.

Describes 'ThesBulider' a thesaurus management software developed by Applied Psychology Research.

678 Ganzmann, Jochen.

Criteria for the evaluation of thesaurus software.

International Classification 17 (3-4) 1990 : 148-157.

Copies available at: http://www.willpower.demon.co.uk/ganzmann.htm

679 Gillum, T. L.; George, R. H. and Leitmeyer, J. E.

An autoencoder for clinical and regulatory data processing.

Drug Information Journal 29 (1) Jan.-March 1995 : 107-113.

Describes an autoencoder i.e. a computerized terminology processing system developed by Merck Research Laboratories,

Pennsylvania.

680 Graef, Jean.

Thesaurus software.

Montague Institute Review October 2001. No page numbers.

Also available at: http://www.montague.com/abstracts/thessoft.html

Discusses software for creating and maintaining a thesaurus. It is only abstract. Full text on the web is restricted to members of the Montague Institute.

681 Jyothi, T.

Construction of information retrieval thesaurus on nervous system diseases terms using Prolog.

SRELS Journal of Information Management 40 (1) March 2003 : 13-22.

682 Karisiddappa, C. R. and Prasad, A. R. D.

Declarative programming and thesaurus construction

IASLIC Bulletin 38 (4) Dec. 1993 : 161 -165.

Explains the application of declarative programming in thesaurus construction.

683 Massimiliano, G. and Negrini, G.

A tool to guide the logical process of conceptual structuring

Proceedings of the 3rd International Society for Knowledge Organization (ISKO) Conference : Knowledge organization and quality management. Copenhagen, Denmark, 20-24 June 1994. Ed. by Hanne Albrechtsen and Susan Oernager, Frankfurt/Main : INDEKS Verlag, 1994 : 342-349.

Describes CLASTHES – a software architecture designed to generate a thesaurus with a poly-hierarchical facet based structure.

684 Milstead, Jessica L.

Specifications for thesaurus software.

Information Processing and Management 27 (2-3) 1991 : 165-175.

685 Milstead, Jessica L.

Thesaurus management software.

Encyclopaedia of Library and Information Science. Volume 51. Ed. by Allen Kent. New York : Marcel Dekker Inc., 1993 : 389-407.

686 Milstead, Jessica L.

Thesaurus software packages.

ASIS'90. Information in the year 2000 : from research to applications. Proceedings of the 53rd Annual Meeting of the American Society for Information Science, Toronto, Canada, 4-8 November 1990. Volume 27 ed. by Diane Henderson, Medford, New Jersey : Learned Information, Inc., 1990 : 3-15.

Describes and compares thesaurus construction softwares.

687 Milstead, Jessica L.

Thesaurus software packages for personal computers.

Database 13 (6) Dec. 1990 : 61-65.

Reviews thesaurus construction softwares.

688 Noordhof, Margaret.

Indexing with AUTHEX.

Computers in Libraries 11 (1) Jan. 1991 : 25-26.

Describes AUTHEX, a microcomputer program developed to produce printed periodical indexes, portions, of this program can be used for thesaurus construction.

689 Riesland, Melissa A.

Tools of the trade : vocabulary management software.

Cataloging and Classification Quarterly 37 (3-4) 2004 : 155-176.

Suggests criteria for evaluation of thesaurus management softwares.

690 Ritzler, Claus.

Comparative study of PC-supported thesaurus software.

International Classification 17 (3-4) 1990 : 138-147.

Compares INDEX, PROTERM and TMS – softwares meant for thesaurus construction.

691 Rowley, Jennifer.

Thesaurus modules in text management software.

Text retrieval : information first. Proceedings of the Institute of Information Scientists 1990 Text Retrieval Conference, London, 1990. *Ed. by Peter Gillman. London : Taylor Graham, 1991 : 16-33.*

692 Soergel, Dagobert.

Software support for thesaurus construction and display.

Proceedings of the 5th ASIS SIG/CR Classification Research Workshop. Advances in Classification Research. Volume 5. Held at the 57th ASIS Annual Meeting, Oct. 16-20, 1994, Alexandria, VA. - Silver Spring, MD : American Society for Information Science, Special Interest Group / Classification Research, 1994 : 157-184.

693 Valauskas, E. J.

Indexing magazines with bibliographic software on the Macintosh.

Database 17 (3) June 1994 : 101-104.

Describes software used for constructing a thesaurus for magazine indexing on Macintosh.

694 Wilson, Ruth.

The BookshelF thesaurus : treasure or trauma.

Library Review 40 (6) 1991 : 42-49.

Describes the thesaurus module of BookshelF – a library software.

695 Wright Jan C.

Thesaurus software and keyword constellation construction. *A to Z : The Newsletter of STC's [Society for Technical Communication's]* 5 (1) January 2002 : 3-5.

Also available at : http://www.stcsig.org/idx/index.html

Section K

Websites listing thesaurus construction softwares

Number of websites provide list of thesaurus construction and maintenance softwares. This section provides names and URLs of such websites.

696 Ganzmann, Jochen.
Checklist for Thesaurus Software.
http://www.willpower.demon.co.uk/criteria.htm

697 Milstead, J. L.
Thesaurus management software.
http://www.asindexing.org.thessoft.shtml

698 Thesaurus-building tools and software.
http://www.darmstadt.gmd.de/~lutes/thestools.html

Section L

Lists of thesaurus construction softwares

A great variety of thesaurus construction and maintenance software is available. This section provides names and web address of thesaurus construction and maintenance softwares. The bibliographical entries in this section are arranged under following three sub-categories.

L1 Softwares having modules for thesaurus construction and maintenance

L2 Standalone softwares for thesaurus construction and maintenance

L3 Multi-user softwares designed for cooperative use

Section L1

Softwares having modules for thesaurus construction

699 Adlib / Databasix

700 Bibliotech / Comstow; Inmagic

701 CAIRS / CAIRS

702 Livelink Collections Server Webtop Thesaurus Manager / Open Text Corporation

703 MTM / OECD

704 Oracle Text / Oracle

705 STAR / Cuadra Associates

Section L2

Standalone softwares for thesaurus construction

706 a.k.a. / Synercon Management Consulting

707 Amicus Thesaurus / LBA Consulting Partners Limited

708 BEAT / Josep Sau

709 Cognatrix / LGO Systems

710 IC INDEX / AGI-Information Management Consultants

711 Lexico / Project Management Enterprises

712 MIDOSThesaurus / Progris

713 Multilingual Thesaurus (MLT) / OPI - Information Processing Centre

714 MultiTes / M

715 OSTI Thesaurus software package / Energy Science and Technology Software Center

716 SchemaServer / Schema Logic

717 Semaphore Taxonomy Manager / APR Smartlogik

718 STRIDE / Questans

719 SuperThes / Federal Environment Agency, Austria.

720 Synema / Syndetics Research

721 TAT (Thesaurus Administration Tool) / European Parliament

722 TCS-8 / Liu-Palmer

723 TemaTres / R020 Bibliotecología y Ciencias de la Información

724 TERM MANAGER / Cardbox Software

725 TermMaster / Dagobert Soergel

726 Term Tree 2000 / A.C.S. - Active Classification Solutions

727 Term tree / Tony Gill

728 Thesaurus Builder / Trias Politica

729 Thesaurus Master Data Harmony

730 TheW and THSRS / Timothy Craven

731 THSAR / MaxThink

732 tmCAKE / dTinf, The ReuseCompany

733 Trias Politica Thesaurus Builder / Trias Politica

Section L3
Multi-user softwares designed for cooperative use

734 LinKFactory / Language & Computing nv

735 MetaTagger Studio / Interwoven

736 Synaptica / Synapse Corporation

737 WebChoir / WebChoir Inc.

738 Wordmap / Wordmap Ltd.

Section M
Structure and description of thesaurus

An IR thesaurus always adopts a very special entry and display structure. There exist a great variety as far as the structure of IR thesaurus is concerned. The literature listed in this section deals with structure and description of thesaurus. More specifically the literature in this section deals with entry structure, display format and methods adopted in organizing the thesaural entries. The literature in this section also deals with strengths and weaknesses of a particular thesaurus, features of a particular thesaurus, reviews and opinions about a particular thesaurus, as well as comparisons of two or more thesauri.

739 Abe, Shin'ichi and Horie, Koshi.

Introducing the Thesaurus Society homepage : walking through medical terminology.

Igaku Toshokan (Journal of the Japan Medical Library Association) 50 (2) 2003 : 183-185.

740 Anjaneyulu, V.

NASA thesaurus in information retrieval.

Seminar on thesaurus in information system. Banglore : DRTC, 1975 : Paper CC.

740a Anzola, M. Constanza.

Thesaurus on seed science and technology.

Quarterly Bulletin of the International Association of Agricultural Information Specialists 31 (2) 1986 : 79-86.

Describes the structure and use of the Thesaurus on Seed Science and Technology.

741 APA boosts psychology with vocabulary.

Information World Review (204) July -August 2004 : 7.

Examines vocabulary of American Psychological Association that enables effective searching of the database.

742 Australian Historic Records Register Thesaurus.

Archives and Manuscripts 25 (2) Nov. 1997 : 388-389.

743 Backus, Joyce E. B.; Davidson, Sara and Rada, Roy.

Searching for patterns in the MeSH vocabulary.

Bulletin of the Medical Library Association 75 (3) July 1987 : 221-227.

744 Bakewell, K. G. B.

Reference books for indexers.

Indexer 15 (3) April 1987 : 131-140.

Describes thesauri and other tools useful for indexers.

745 Bakewell, K. G. B.

The Unesco : IBE Education Thesaurus (second edition) : a description and assessment.

Education Libraries Bulletin 19 (2) Summer 1976 : 9-19.

Critically evaluates the International Bureau of Education's thesaurus and compares it with other thesauri on education.

746 Ballew, Randy; Duncan, Thomas and Blasingame, Mike.

Relational data structures for implementing thesauri.

Berkeley : University of California, Museum Informatics Project. Information Systems and Technology, 1999. 23p.

Also available at: http://www.mip.berkeley.edu/mip/related/thesaurus/thesaurus.pdf

Explains the implementation of Z39.19 compliant thesauri in SQL database and also includes entity -relational model for a thesaurus structure.

747 Barthe, K.

GIFAS rationalized French : a controlled language for

aerospace documentation in French.

Technical Communication 46 (2) May 1999 : 220-229.

748 Bedford, Stephen.

The thesaurus is dead.

Records Management Bulletin (115) August 2003 : 3-6.

Considers the problems and solutions related with the 'keyword AAA thesaurus' meant for Records Management.

749 Berman, Barbara L.

Form headings in subject cataloguing.

Library Resources and Technical Services 33 (2) April 1989 : 134-139.

750 Berman, Sanford.

Prejudices and antipathies : a tract on the LC subject heads concerning people.

Journal of Academic Librarianship 19 (4) Sept. 1993 : 246.

751 Berman, Sanford.

Prejudices and antipathies : a tract on the LC subject heads concerning people.

Library Review 43 (3) 1993 : 54-55.

752 Berman, Sanford.

Prejudices and antipathies : a tract on the LC subject headings concerning people.

Technicalities 13 (4) April 1993 : 14-15.

753 Berman, Sanford.

Prejudices and antipathies : a tract on the LC Subject Heads Concerning People.

WLW Journal 16 (3) Fall 1993 : 24-25.

754 Berman, Stanford.

'Teen' subject headings : a selection from the Hennepin County Library authority file.

Technical Services Quarterly 2 (1-2) Fall-Winter 1984 : 191-212.

755 Berman, Sanford.

Tools for tinkering.

Technical Services Quarterly 2 (1-2) Fall-Winter 1984 : 213-221.

Describes vocabulary control tools, which help to improve access to subject catalogue.

756 Berman, Sanford.

Unreal! Hennepin County library Subject Headings for Fictional Characters and Places.

Public Library Quarterly 13 (3) 1993 : 91.

757 Bertrand Gastaldy, Suzanne; Davidson, Colin H. and Gastaldy, S. Bertrand.

Improved design of graphic displays in thesauri through technology and ergonomics.

Journal of Documentation 42 (4) Dec. 1986 : 225-251.

Evaluates thesaurus display formats.

758 Bielicka, Lycyna Anna; Paciejewski, Janusz and Scibor, Eugeniusz.

Classification and indexing languages in Poland (1974-1986). Part 1.

International Classification 14 (2) 1987 : 23-28.

Describes problems of indexing languages including thesauri.

759 Bielicka, Lycyna Anna; Paciejewski, Janusz and Scibor, Eugeniusz.

Classification and indexing languages in Poland (1974-1986). Part 2.

International Classification 14 (2) 1987 : 85-89.

Describes problems of indexing languages including thesauri.

760 Biswas, S. C. and Smith, F.

Term and cross-reference structure in computerized deep structure indexing system.

International Classification 15 (3) 1988 : 139-144.

Describes the term structure and cross reference structure of the Deep Structure Indexing System.

761 Blagden, J. F.

Structured thesauri.

Aslib Proceedings 23 (3) March 1971 : 139-143.

762 Blake, L. and Stallings, E. T.

Arranging roots : classification and subject headings for genealogical collections.

Library Resources and Technical Services 41 (4) Oct. 1997 : 335-346.

763 Blamoutier, F.

Vocabulary problems in the thesaurus for the economics of energy.

Banque des Mots (5) 1973 : 83-96.

764 Boere, M.

Treasures of the women's movement.

Feminist Collections 22 (1) Fall 2000 : 19-21.

Describes the thesaurus and explains its application in online search.

765 Boll, J. J. et al.

Library of Congress Subject Headings.

Cataloging and Classification Quarterly 1 (2-3) 1982 : 123-133.

766 Bolshakov, Igor A.

Thesaurus in word processors : what should it be?

International Forum on Information and Documentation 16 (2) April 1991 : 3-11.

Suggests a new thesauri structure to be used in word processing.

767 Booth, Barbara.

A 'new' ERIC Thesaurus, fine-tuned for searching.

Online 3 (3) July 1979 : 20-29.

768 Bottle, R. T.

Thesaurus, controlled indexing and the incidence of synonyms and related terms.

Informatics 1: Proceedings of a conference held by the Aslib Coordinate Indexing Group on 11-13 April 1973 at Durham University. London : Aslib, 1974 : 145-153.

769 Brand, Alice A. and Kinzie, Lenora A.

A comparison of online access to psychoanalytic literature.

Database 7 (1) Feb. 1984 : 54-55 and 58-63.

Describes databases in the field of psychoanalysis and compares them considering various criteria including controlled vocabulary.

770 Bronson, Roberta J.

Creative ways to locate MeSH subheading information.

Medical Reference Services Quarterly 13 (1) Spring 1994 : 73-80.

771 Bronson, Roberta J.

MeSH chemical headings and pharmacologic action.

Medical Reference Services Quarterly 16 (3) Fall 1997 : 45-53.

772 Bronson, Roberta J.

NLM's MeSH vocabulary file.

Medical Reference Services Quarterly 11 (2) Summer 1992 : 47-57.

Scope, searching strategies and special features of the on-line MeSH Vocabulary File are discussed.

773 Bronson, Roberta J.

Two chemical dictionary files : CHEMLINE and CHEMID.

Medical Reference Services Quarterly 11 (1) Spring 1992 : 1-16.

Describes and compares the two chemical dictionaries of the MEDLARS.

774 Brown, Charles.

Computerizing the regulations : finding all the regulations that apply, automatically.

Government Executive. July 1980 : 20-21.

Describes the Code of Federal Regulations and its thesaurus.

775 Brown, James W.; Sitts, Maxine K. and Yarborough, Judith.

ERIC : what it can do for you / how to use it.

Information Reports and Bibliographies 4 (5) 1975 : 3-12.

Describes ERIC's features including the thesaurus of ERIC Descriptors.

776 Browne, Glenda.

Scope notes for LISA subject headings.

Online Review 16 (1) Feb. 1992 : 3-16.

Examines scope notes given for subject headings in the LISA online user manual edition 1 and 2.

777 Brunner, Theodore F.

The Thesaurus Linguae Graecae : classics and the computer.

Library Hi Tech 9 (1) 1991 : 61-67.

778 Busch, J. A.

Building and accessing vocabulary resources for networked resource discovery and navigation.

Visualizing subject access for Twentyfirst Century information resources. Proceedings of the 1997 Clinic on Library Applications of Data Processing, 2-4 Mar 1997. Urbana-Champaign, Illinois. Ed. by Pauline Atherton Cochrane and Eric H. Johnson (with the assistance of Sandra Roe). Urbana-Champaign, Illinois : Illinois University at Urbana-Champaign,

Graduate School of Library and Information Science, 1998 : 148-156.

Describes and compares AAT, Union List of Artist Names and Thesaurus of Geographic Names and their usefulness in Internet searches.

779 Busch, Joseph.

A method for evaluating the multiple relations between subject descriptors-related terms in the Thesaurus of Engineering and Scientific Terms : a pilot study.

The information age in perspective. Proceedings of the 41st Annual Meeting, New York, 13-17 November 1978. Volume 15. Compiled by Everett H. Brenner. White Plains, New York : Knowledge Industry Publications for American Society for Information Science, 1978 : 59-62.

780 Byrne, C. C. and McCracken, S. A.

An adaptive thesaurus employing semantic distance, relational inheritance and nominal compound interpretation for linguistic support of information retrieval.

Journal of Information Science 25 (2) 1999 : 113-131.

Describes structure of the National Information Infrastructure Testbed for Diagnostic and Prognostic Maintenance of Equipment and Processes' thesaurus.

781 Campbell, D. J.

EJC thesaurus of engineering terms.

Journal of Documentation 21, 1965 : 136-139.

782 Carter, Andrew J.

Literature analysis system of the Office of Road Safety.

Australian Special Libraries News 12 (1) March 1979 : 59-62.

Describes thesauri and other components of Literature analysis system of the Office of Road Safety.

783 Casey, A.

Standard terminology for nursing : results of the nursing, midwifery and health visiting terms project.

Health Informatics 1 (2) May 1995 : 41-43.

Describes nursing thesaurus.

784 Chan, David F.

Computer-aided visualization of database structural relationships.

Communicating information. Proceedings of the 43rd ASIS Annual meeting, Anaheim, California, 5-10 October 1980. Volume 17. Ed. by A. R. Benenfeld and E. J. Kazlauskas. New York : Knowledge Industry Publications, Inc., 1980 : 358-360.

Illustrates usefulness of interactive computer graphic displays for thesaural displays.

785 Chan, Lois Mai.

Alphabetical arrangement and subject collocation in Library of Congress subject headings.

Library Resources and Technical Services 21 (2) Spring 1977 : 156-169.

786 Chan, Lois Mai.

Library of Congress subject headings : principles and application.

Australian Library Review 13 (2) May 1996 : 226-227.

787 Chan, Lois Mai.

Library of Congress Subject Headings : principles and application.

Cataloging and Classification Quarterly 23 (1) 1996 : 127-130.

788 Chan, Lois Mai.

The Library of Congress Classification System in an online environment.

Cataloging and Classification Quarterly 11 (1) 1990 : 7-25.

Describes LCC's controlled vocabulary and other features.

789 Chan, Lois Mai.

The period subdivision in subject headings.

Library Resources and Technical Services 16 (4) Fall 1972 : 453-459.

790 Chan, Lois Mai.

The principle of uniform headings in Library of Congress Subject Headings.

Library Resources and Technical Services 22 (2) Spring 1978 : 126-136.

791 Chan, Lois Mai and Hodges, T.

Entering the millennium : a new century for LCSH.

Cataloging and Classification Quarterly 29 (1-2) 2000 : 225-234.

792 Chan, Lois Mai and O'Neill, Edward T.

FAST (Faceted Application of Subject Terminology) : a simplified vocabulary based on the Library of Congress Subject Headings.

IFLA Journal 29 (4) 2003 : 336-342.

793 Chan, Lois Mai and Vizine-Goetz, D.

Errors and obsolete elements in assigned Library of Congress Subject Headings : implications for subject cataloging and subject authority control.

Library Resources and Technical Services 41 (4) Oct. 1997 : 295-322.

794 Chartron, Ghislaine.

Lexicon management tools for large textual data bases : the Lexinet system.

Journal of Information Science 15 (6) 1989 : 339-344.

Suggests a methodology for comparing existing terminology

with the terminology detected by the Lexinet system.

795 Cimino, J. J.

Formal descriptions and adaptive mechanisms for changes in controlled medical vocabularies.

Methods of Information in Medicine 35 (3) Sept. 1996 : 202-210.

Presents taxonomy for describing the semantic changes that occur in a standard controlled medical vocabulary.

796 Cimino, J. J.

Vocabulary and health care information technology : state of the art.

Journal of the American Society for Information Science 46 (10) Dec. 1995 : 777-782.

Critically reviews controlled medical vocabularies.

797 Cipolla, W. R.

Music subject headings : a comparison.

Library Resources and Technical Services 18 (4) Fall 1974 : 387-397.

798 Clack, Doris Hargrett.

The adequacy of Library of Congress Subject Headings for black literature resources.

Library Resources and Technical Services 22 (2) Spring 1978 : 137-144.

799 Cochrane, P. A.

Improving LCSH for use in online catalogs revisited : what progress has been made? What issues still remain?

Cataloging and Classification Quarterly 29 (1- 2) 2000 : 73-89.

Describes structure of relationships between headings in the LCSH and links between the LCSH headings, LC class numbers or other vocabularies.

800 Coen, J. A.

An investigation of indirect subdivision by place in Library of Congress subject headings.

Library Resources and Technical Services 13 (1) Winter 1969 : 62-78.

801 Colbach, R.

Thesaurus structure and generic posting.

Handling of nuclear information. Proceedings of the symposium organized by the International Atomic Energy Agency and held in Vienna, 16-20 February 1970. Vienna : IAEA, 1970 : 585-595.

802 Comparison of UDC with descriptor systems.

FID Bulletin 17(10) 1967 : 106.

803 Conway, M. O.

Characteristics of subject headings in the Library of Congress BOOKSM Database.

Library Resources and Technical Services 37 (1) Jan. 1993 : 47-58.

804 Coppin, Ann S.

The Lunar Science Institute.

Sci-Tech News 29 (4) Oct. 1975 : 97, 112 and 114.

Describes activities of the Lunar Science Institute, Houston, Texas and its Thesaurus of Lunar Science Terms.

805 Cujba, A.

National polythematic thesaurus.

Probleme de Informare si Documentare 7 (3) March 1973 : 190-209.

806 Currier, S. and Wake, S.

Negotiating subject access : resource discovery on the Web.

Library and Information Briefings (97) May 2001 : 1-14.

Reports results of High-Level Thesaurus project on cross

searching.

807 Dadlez, Eva M.

Catalyst resources for women on BRS.

Database 6 (4) Dec. 1983 : 32-43.

Describes controlled vocabulary and other aspects of Catalyst - a non-profit organisation working to foster the full participation of women in business and professional life.

808 Dahlberg, Ingetraut.

Conceptual compatibility of ordering systems.

International Classification 10 (1) 1983 : 5-8.

Asserts the need of compatibility between ordering systems such as classification and thesauri.

809 Dalhberg, Ingetraut.

New trends in classification.

New trends in documentation and information. Proceedings of the 39th FID Congress, University of Edinburgh, 25-28 September 1978. Ed. by Peter J. Taylor. London : Aslib, 1980 : 214-222.

Reports research on contents and structure of elements of classification systems and thesauri in US.

810 Danky, James P.

Newspapers and their readers : the United States Newspaper Program's List of Intended Audience Terms.

Cataloging and Classification Quarterly 6 (4) Summer 1986 : 85-106.

811 Davies, J. Eric.

Mechanical engineering information organization, part I : subject term authorities.

IATUL Proceedings 7 (2) Dec. 1974 : 60-74.

Reviews mechanical engineering terms in TEST, NASA Thesaurus, Subject Headings for Engineering and the Thesaurofacet.

812 Dealy, Jacqueline.

Canadian literacy thesaurus / thesaurus canadien d'alphabetisation.

Canadian Journal of Information and Library Science 19 (1) April 1994 : 44-45.

813 Detant, M.

The thesaurus and indexing in the mechanised documentation system of Euratom.

Cahiers de la Documentation 23 (1-2) 1969 : 58-82.

814 Drabenstott, K. M.

Period subdivisions in the Library of Congress Subject Headings system - some thoughts and recommendations for the future.

Cataloging and Classification Quarterly 15 (4) 1992 : 19-45.

815 Drabenstott, K. M.; Dede, B. A. R. and Leavitt, M.

The changes of meaning in subdivided subject headings.

Cataloging and Classification Quarterly 28 (3) 1999 : 19-43.

816 Drabenstott, K. M.; Simcox, S. and Fenton E. G.

Do patrons understand Library of Congress Subject Headings?

Technicalities 19 (1) Jan. 1999 : 1 and 6-9.

817 Drabenstott, K. M.; Simcox, S. and Fenton, E. G.

End-user understanding of subject headings in library catalogs.

Library Resources and Technical Services 43 (3) July 1999 : 140-160.

818 Drabenstott, K. M.; Simcox, S. and Williams, M.

Do librarians understand the subject headings in library catalogs?

Reference and User Services Quarterly 38 (4) Summer 1999 : 369-387.

819 Drabenstott, K. M. and Weller, M. S.

The exact-display approach for online catalog subject searching.

Information Processing and Management 32 (6) Nov. 1996 : 719-745.

820 Dykstra, Mary.

LC subject headings disguised as a thesaurus.

Library Journal 113 (4) 1 Mar 1988 : 42-46.

821 Eastman, Caroline M.

Overlaps in postings to thesaurus terms : a preliminary study.

ASIS '88. Information Technology : planning for the next fifty years. Proceedings of the 51st Annual Meeting of the American Society for Information Science, Atlanta, Georgia, 23-27 October 1988. Volume 25. Ed. by Christine L. Borgman and Edward Y. H. Pai. Medford, New Jersey : Learned Information, Inc., 1988 : 181-184.

Examines the patterns of term overlap in MeSH and its implications.

822 Efthimiadis, E. N. and Afifi, M.

Population groups : indexing, coverage, and retrieval effectiveness of ethnically related health care issues in health sciences databases.

Bulletin of the Medical Library Association 84 (3) July 1996 : 386-396.

Thesauri of MEDLINE, PsycINFO and EMBASE are examined to know the representation given to population groups.

823 Eisner, Michael.

New thesaurus qualities of ARBOR.

Tools for knowledge organisation and the human interface. Proceedings of the 1st International ISKO Conference, Darmstadt, (Germany) *14-17 August 1990. Advances in knowledge organization, no. 1/2.* Ed. by R. Fugmann. Part I.

Frankfurt/Main : Indeks. 1990 : 155-160.

Describes thesaurus qualities of ARBOR database designed to index different objects of classical archaeology and art history.

824 Engineers Joint Council.

Study of engineering terminology and relationships among engineering terms : final report.

New York, Engineer's Joint Council, 1963.

825 Epstein, Barbara A.

The terminology of psychiatry : DSM-III, Medical Subject Headings and the Thesaurus of Psychological Index Terms.

Medical Reference Services Quarterly 3 (1) Spring 1984 : 49-66.

Reviews the terminology in the Third edition of the Diagnostic and Statistical Manual (DSM-III) of the APA in relation to the thesaurus terms available in MeSH and the Thesaurus of Psychological Index Terms.

826 Exon, M.

Keyword file titling and the GADM Thesaurus : implications for librarians.

Cataloguing Australia 16 (3-4) Sept.-Dec. 1990 : 58-60.

Describes keyword file titling and the General Administrative Thesaurus of Australia.

827 Fabian, Claudia.

Hand Press Book Database und CERL Thesaurus.

Zeitschrift fur Bibliothekswesen und Bibliographie 51 (4) July–Sept. 2004 : 229-235.

Describes HPB's database and thesaurus of the Consortium of European Research Libraries.

828 Fichte, B. and Bauer, G.

The subject thesaurus for silicon organic chemistry, suitable for integration with a chemical thesaurus system.

Zentralinstitut fur Information und Dokumentation Zeitschrift 15 (6) Dec. 1968 : 259-264.

829 Fikar, Charles R.

Making sense of central nervous system infections at the reference desk.

Medical Reference Services Quarterly 23 (3) Fall 2004 : 33-38.

Discusses and presents terminology related with some aspects of infections of the central nervous system.

830 Fikar, Charles R.

Making sense of liver enzymes, liver function tests, and hepatobiliary disorders at the reference desk.

Medical Reference Services Quarterly 22 (3) Fall 2003 : 15-22.

Discusses terminology related with various aspects of the laboratory diagnosis of certain diseases of liver.

831 Fink, E. E.

The Getty Information Institute : a retrospective.

D-Lib Magazine 5 (3) March 1999. No page numbers.

Reviews the achievements of the Getty Information Institute with special reference to vocabulary tools created by the institute i.e. ATT, Getty Thesaurus of Geographic Names, Union List of Artist Names etc.

Also available at: http://www.dlib.org/dlib/march99/fink/03fink.html

832 Fizames, C.

How to improve the medical quality of the coding reports based on WHO-ART and COSTART use.

Drug Information Journal 31 (1) Jan.-March 1997 : 85-92.

Reports on the weaknesses of the WHO-ART and COSTART terms used for auto-encoding of subjects in medical databases.

833 Flor, P. et al.

A controlled vocabulary for nursing and allied health in Norway.

Health Information and Libraries Journal 18 (1) March 2001 : 10-19.

834 Foster, Jane et al.

When is a thesaurus not a thesaurus : the GCHQ story continues.

Catalogue & Index (140) Summer 2001 : 12.

Describes Corporate Keyword Hierarchy – a taxonomy with a classification scheme and thesaural features developed at the Govt. Communications Headquarters, UK and also explains how the taxonomy building was made essential by the lacunae in the thesaurus.

835 Fountain, J. F.

Headings for children's materials : an LSCH / Sears Companion.

School Library Media Quarterly 22 (2) Winter 1994 : 118.

836 Fox, Nick et al.

The ERIC Thesaurus : an analysis.

Education Libraries Bulletin 21 (3) Autumn 1978 : 14-30.

837 Frost, Carolyn O. and Dede, Bonnie A.

Subject heading compatibility between LCSH and catalog files of a large research library : a suggested model for analysis.

Information Technology and Libraries 7 (3) Sept. 1988 : 288-299.

838 Fugmann, Robert.

POLIDCASYR : the polymer documentation system of IDC.

Journal of Chemical Information and Computer Sciences 19 (2) May 1979 : 64-68.

Describes controlled vocabulary developed for explaining nonstructural concepts.

839 Fuhr, Norbert.

Models for retrieval with probabilistic indexing.

Information Processing and Management 25 (1) 1989 : 55-72.

Describes role of controlled vocabulary in retrieval models based on probabilistic indexing.

840 Gabbard, Paula Beversdorf.

LCSH and PRECIS in music : a comparison.

Library Quarterly 55 (2) April 1985 : 192-206.

841 Gault, L. V.; Shultz, M. and Davies, K. J.

Variations in Medical Subject Headings (MeSH) mapping : from the natural language of patron terms to the controlled vocabulary of mapped lists.

Journal of the Medical Library Association (JMLA) 90 (2) April 2002 : 173-180.

Compares the mapping of natural language terms used by the users to the MeSH interfaces on the MEDLINE database.

Also available at : http://www.pubmedcentral.nih.gov// articlerender.fcgi?artid=100762

842 Gilchrist, Alan.

Interim report on HANDVOC project.

European coordination of information concerning disabled persons. Ed. by A. Pedotti and R. Andrich. Milan : Commission of the European Communities, 1984 : 155-169.

843 Glastonbury, B.

Database of social research methodology.

New Technology in the Human Services 10 (4) 1997 : 21-22.

Describes the CD-ROM database of social research methodology, which provides bibliography, abstract, terms search and thesaurus for social science research methodology.

844 Goossens, P. and Pairon, E.

Library of Congress Subject Headings in Dutch and French.

Linking of automated library functions : library systems seminar, The Hague, 20-22 April 1983. The Hague : Pica-Bureau, 1983 : 68-77.

845 Gordon, Dena.

Controlled vocabularies in business databases : a fresh book.

National Online Meeting. Proceedings 1982. Compiled by Martha E. Wliams and Thomas H. Hogan. Medford, New Jersey : Learned Information, Inc., 1982 : 133-143.

Evaluates recall and precision performances of thesauri used by three bibliographic business databases.

846 Gould. J.

The vocabulary of sociology.

The phenomenon of sociology : a reader in the sociology of sociology. Ed. by. E. A. Tiryakin. New York : Appleton-Century-Crofts, 1971 : 313-324.

847 Gravesteijn, J.

Presentation of an arrow-diagram thesaurus of the earth sciences.

ANRT Information et Documentation (8) Oct. 1968 : 21-28.

848 Grecu, N.

Concept-analysis in the natural sciences towards compatibility between specialist vocabularies and thesauri.

Studii si Cercetari de Documentare 11 (4) 1969 : 307-313.

849 Greenberg, J.

Subject control of ephemera : MARC format options.

Popular Culture in Libraries 4 (1) 1996 : 71-91.

Lists and describes controlled vocabulary tools for ephemeral material.

850 Grosch, A. N.

Computer-based subject authority files at the University of

Minnesota libraries.

Journal of Library Automation 5 (4) Dec. 1972 : 230-243.

851 Gueniot, Y. and Laureilhe, M. T.

On some thesauri.

Bulletin des Bibliotheques de France 14 (5) May 1969 : 181-202.

852 Gueniot, Y. and Laureilhe, M. T.

Some thesauri

Bulletin des Bibliotheques de France 15 (1) Jan. 1970 : 5-19.

853 Gunn, Katherine L. and Burk, C. F.

A decentralized, cooperative, indexing project : Canadian Index to Geoscience Data.

Third open conference on information science in Canada, Quebec, 8-10 May, 1975. Proceedings. Ed. by E. Marshall, M. Pare. Ottawa : Canadian Association for Information Science, 1975 : 243-252.

Describes the cooperative indexing programme and the thesaurus used for the same.

854 Hall, Elaine N.

W (h)ither LCSH?.

Cataloguing Australia 10 (2) June 1984 : 3-11.

855 Hane, P. J.

EBSCO releases EBSCOhost Web 6.0

Information Today 19 (8) Sept. 2002 : 3.

Describes EBSCO Publishing's EBSCOhost Web6.0 an enhanced version of its flagship EBSCOhost interface, which has features such as thesauri for CINAHL, MEDLINE and PsycINFO.

856 Hass Weinberg, Bella.

Multiple sets of human indexing for civil engineering documents : comparison of structure and occurrence rates in full text.

Science and Technology Libraries 2 (3) Spring 1982 : 13-33.

Methodological problems of comparing terms from different sources are discussed.

857 Hass Weinberg, Bella and Cunningham, Julie A.

The design of online thesauri

National Online Meeting 1988. Proceedings of the Ninth National Online Meeting, New York, 10-12 May 1988. Compiled by Martha E. Wliams and Thomas H. Hogan. Medford, New Jersey : Learned Information Inc., 1988 : 411-419.

Compares the formats of on-line thesauri with their printed counterparts.

858 Hauzner, I.

Different conceptions of retrieval languages and thesauri.

Ceskoslovenska Informatika 13 (2) 1971 : 9-17.

859 Hemmasi, H.

The music thesaurus : function and foundations.

Notes 50 (3) March 1994 : 875-882.

860 Hildenbrand, S.

Information for equality : the documentation center of the Women's Institute in Madrid.

Wilson Library Bulletin 68 (7) March 1994 : 45-47.

Describes thesaurus for Spanish women and other features of the documentation center of the Women's Institute, Madrid .

861 Hill, Linda L.

Geographic indexing for bibliographic databases.

Resource Sharing and Information Networks 4 (2) 1989 : 1-12.

Explains the advantages of computer graphic display over word-based indexing and provides variations of geographic indexing terminology.

862 Holley, Robert P.

Constraints of the 3 x 5 card.

Cataloging and Classification Quarterly 4 (1) Fall 1983 : 29-35.

Explains obstacles in the use of LC Subject Headings such as obsolete terminology and the need of comprehensive cross-referencing for using controlled vocabulary.

863 Horowitz, Roberta S. et al.

Concurrence in content descriptions : author versus Medical Subject Headings (MeSH).

Information interaction. Proceedings of the 45th ASIS Annual Meeting, Columbus, Ohio, 17-21 October 1982. Volume 19. Ed. by A. E. Petrarca, C. I. Taylor and R. S. Kohn. White Plains, New York : Knowledge Industry Publications, Inc., (for ASIS), 1982 : 139-140.

864 Houldsworth, A. and Eisenschitz, T. S.

Computerised litigation support in solicitors' offices.

Law Librarian 24 (2) June 1993 : 82-87.

Describes a computerized litigation support system and the controlled vocabulary used by the system.

865 Houser, J.

The visual vocabulary of the graphical environment.

Searcher 4 (1) Jan. 1996 : 18-23.

866 Houtart, E.

The CREDOC dictionary.

Cahiers de la Documentation 23 (1-2) 1969 : 15-19.

Describes a law thesaurus.

867 Hyams, P.

MAID has substance : it's just a shame about the hype.

Monitor (181) March 1996 : 2-3.

Heights features of MAID – 'the online business information service' and states that considerable value is added to it by its controlled vocabulary.

868 ILO Thesaurus : Labour, employment and training terminology.

Library Review 48 (1-2) 1999 : 104-105.

869 Islam, M.

Subject headings authority list (SHAL) : a computerization project at CDA Library.

Third open conference on information science in Canada, Quebec, 8-10 May, 1975. Proceedings. Ed. by E. Marshall, M. Pare. Ottawa : Canadian Association for Information Science/L'Association Canadienne des Sciences de l'Information, 1975 : 31-37.

870 Ivankin, V. I.

An experimental descriptive dictionary for the automobile industry with partial formulation of the links between descriptors.

Nauchno- Tekhnicheskaya Informatsiya; Series 2 (4) 1969 : 11-14.

871 Iwe, J. I.

Linguistics and information processing : provision of syntactic and semantic consistency in the language of Library of Congress Subject Headings (LCSH) pertaining to literature and librarianship : a comparative analysis.

Cataloging and Classification Quarterly 32 (2) 2001 : 107-126.

872 Jablonski, S.

The pre-constructed vocabulary : a procrustean bed.

Bulletin of the Medical Library Association 61 (1) Jan. 1973 : 21-23.

873 Jacso, P.

Savvy searchers do ask for direction.

Online and CD-ROM Review 23 (2) April 1999 : 99-102.

Examines strengths and weaknesses of online thesauri of DIALOG and DataStar.

874 Jacso, P.

WebSPIRS 4.0 : JavaScript Search Software.

Library Software Review 17 (4) Dec. 1998 : 244-269.

Discusses selection of search terms, thesaurus display and other features of WebSPIRS 4.0 information retrieval software made available to subscribers to SilverPlatter online databases.

875 Jones, K. P.

Basic structures for thesaural systems.

Aslib Proceedings 23 (11) Nov. 1971 : 577-590.

876 Jones, Susan.

A thesaurus data model for an intelligent retrieval system.

Journal of information science *19, 1993 : 167-178.*

Presents an entity-relationship data model for a thesaurus structure.

877 Kahn, Tamar Joy and Orr, Cecily.

BIOETHICSLINE : an overview for searchers.

Medical Reference Services Quarterly 3 (3) Fall 1984 : 1-21.

Describes the BIOETHICSLINE File (BIOETHICS)- a bibliographic database on bioethics and the Bioethics thesaurus.

878 Kassel, A.

Here they come! : database producers on the Web.

Searcher 5 (7) July-August 1997 : 26-31.

Describes Internet products and services including thesauri delivered on the web.

879 Kennedy, J. and Kossmann, C. E.

Nomenclatures in medicine.

Bulletin of the Medical Library Association 61, 1973 : 238-252.

880 Kent, R. E.

Implications and rules in thesauri.

Proceedings of the 3rd International Society for Knowledge Organization (ISKO) Conference : Knowledge organization and quality management. Copenhagen, Denmark, 20-24 June 1994. Ed. by Hanne Albrechtsen and Susan Oernager, Frankfurt/Main : INDEKS Verlag, 1994 : 154-160.

Explains the application of Formal Concept Analysis to the study of rule generation in whole language semantic space as in thesauri.

881 Khosh Khui, A.

Effects of subject specificity : part 1 - specificity of LC Subject Headings and depth of subject analysis in monographic records.

Technical Services Quarterly 4 (2) Winter 1986 : 59-67.

882 Khosh Khui, A.

Efforts of subject specificity : part 2 - relationship of LC subject headings specificity and class notation length.

Technical Services Quarterly 4 (3) Spring 1987 : 33-39.

883 Kim, Chai.

Retrieval language of social sciences and natural sciences : a statistical investigation.

Journal of the American Society for Information Science 33 (1) Jan. 1982 : 3-7.

Analyzes the retrieval language of social sciences and natural sciences to test whether the facts on relative frequency matches with theoretical distribution of Zipf's law.

884 Kirkman, J.; Snow, C. and Watson, I.

Controlled English in international documentation.

New trends in documentation and information : proceedings of the 39th FID Congress, University of Edinburgh, 25-28

September 1978. Ed. by Peter J. Taylor. London : Aslib, 1980 : 70-76.

Describes the 'Controlled English' project of University of Wales Institute of Science and Technology.

885 Kirtland, Monika.

Macro - and microthesauri : changes occurring in MeSH-derived thesauri and a solution to some related search handicaps.

Journal of the American Society for Information Science 32 (4) July 1981 : 249-252.

Describes Cancer Information Thesaurus – a thesaurus derived from MeSH.

886 Kirtland, Monika; Atherton, Pauline and Harper, Shirley.

Integrating borrowed records into a database : impact on thesaurus development and retrieval.

Database 3 (4) Dec. 1980 : 26-33.

Compares the thesaurus of LABORLIT database with the inverted dictionary of terms found in a sample of Management Contents records.

887 Kulik, A. N.

Thesaurus of Scientific and Technical Terms : an outline and an analysis of vocabulary distribution.

Nauchno- Tekhnicheskaya Informatsiya Series 1 (9) 1974 : 26-34.

888 Lavell, Cherry.

Thesauri for museum documentation : the proceedings of a workshop held at the Science Museum, London 24 February 1992.

Indexer 19 (1) April 1994 : 71-72.

889 Learned, B. P.; Sigala, S. and Petersen, T.

Giving up the ABCs : an interview with Toni Petersen.

Art Documentation 18 (2) 1999 : 30-33.

Presents an interview with Toni Petersen who was actively involved in the creation of the Art and Architecture Thesaurus.

890 Leontyeva, T. M. and Margaritov, V. B.

Statistical analysis and quantitative characteristics of the elements of a thesaurus system.

Nauchno- Tekhnicheskaya Informatsiya; Series II (10) 1970 : 19-25.

891 Leska, M. and Leski, K.

Thesaurus on information science.

Aktualne Problemy Informacji Dokumentacji 17 (3) 1972 : 9-13.

892 Levery, F.

The problems of documentary vocabulary and the organization of dictionaries and thesauri.

Storage and retrieval of information : a user-supplier-dialogue. Proceedings. 18-30 June 1968. Neuly-sur-Seine : North Atlantic Treaty Organization, Advisory Group for Aerospace Research and Development, 1968 : 21-39.

893 Levery, F.

The problems raised by documentary language and the structuring of dictionaries and thesauri.

TA Informations 13 (1) 1972 : 1-8.

894 London, Gertrude.

A classed thesaurus as an intermediary between textual, indexing and searching languages.

Revue Internationale de la Documentation 32(4) 1965 : 145-149.

895 Lopez-Huertas, M. J.

Thesaurus structure design : a conceptual approach for improved interaction.

Journal of Documentation 53 (2) March 1997 : 139-177.

Explains usefulness of discourse analysis in designing thesaurus structure.

896 Main, D. W.

Scottish Business Periodicals Index.

Scottish Libraries (49) Jan.-Feb. 1995 : 16.

Describes the creation of a subject index to periodicals dealing with Scottish business and the thesaurus compiled for the same.

897 Mandelstam, Michael.

Thesaurus on equipment for disabled people.

Journal of Documentation 44 (2) June 1988 : 144-158.

Describes the Disabled Living Foundation's thesaurus.

898 Markham, J. W. and Avery, B. F.

LCSH and the ASFIS Thesaurus : an update.

Electronic information and publications : looking to the electronic future, let's not forget the archival past. Proceedings of the 24th Annual Conference of the International Association of Aquatic and Marine Science Libraries and Information Centers (IAMSLIC) and the 17th Polar Libraries Colloquy (PLC), Reykjavik, Iceland, 20-25 September 1998. Ed. by James W. Markham, Andrea L. Duda and Martha Andrews. Fort Pierce, Florida : IAMSLIC, 1999 : 347-353.

Compares LCSH and the ASFIS Thesaurus.

899 Martin, Sabine and Bergerhoff, Gunter.

Chemical Abstracts Online : a study of the quality of controlled terms.

Journal of Chemical Information and Computer Sciences 31 (1) Feb. 1991 : 147-152.

Explains the quality features of the controlled terms used by the online CAS.

900 McCray, A. T. and Nelson, S. J.

The representation of meaning in the UMLS.

Methods of Information in Medicine 34 (1-2) March 1995 : 193-201.

Describes the Unified Medical Language System.

901 Meredith, Sydney.

News from SA : the thesaurus and revised user aids.

Online 86. Proceedings of the Conference, Chicago, Illinois, 4-6 November 1986. Weston, CT : Online Inc., 1986 : 163-167.

902 Meyer, E.; Jansen, R. and Sens, E.

The IDC thesaurus system.

Nachrichten fur Dokumentation 23 (5) Oct. 1972 : 203-211.

903 Micco, Helen Mary.

A comparison of subject access systems in medicine LCSH, MeSH, PRECIS.

ASIS '85. Proceedings of the 48th ASIS Annual Meeting 1985. Las Vegas, Nevada, 20-24 October 1985. Volume 22. Ed. by Carol A. Parkhurst. White Plains, New York : Knowledge Industry Publications Inc. for the American Society for Information Science, 1985 : 41-53.

904 Micco, Helen Mary.

An exploratory study of three subject access systems in medicine : LCSH, MeSH, PRECIS.

Ann Arbor, Michigan : University Microforms International, 1980. 163p.

905 Michard, A. and Pham Dac, D.

Description of collections and encyclopaedias on the Web using XML.

Archives and Museum Informatics 12 (1) 1998 : 39-79.

Discusses limitations of present vocabulary control tools used in cataloguing art works and proposes a cooperative production of multilingual and multicultural systems using XML.

906 Middleton, Michael.

The way that information professionals describe their own discipline : a comparison of thesaurus descriptors.

New Library World 105 (11-12) 2004 : 429-435.

Compares the treatment given to information professionals and their activities in thesauri.

907 Miller, Peter W.

Structural characteristics of thesauri.

London : City University, Centre for Information Science, 1982 : 55p.

Describes structural characteristics of 6 thesauri.

908 Miller, U.

The Sport Database : some comments.

Online and CD-ROM Review 20 (2) April 1996 : 67-74.

Compares and comments on the print and CD-ROM version of the Sport Thesaurus.

909 Milstead, J. L.

ASIS Thesaurus of information science in librarianship.

Library Quarterly 65 (2) April 1995 : 243-244.

910 Milstead, J. L.

Invisible thesauri : the year 2000.

Online CD- ROM Review 19(2) 1995 : 93-94.

911 Milstead, J. L. and Ward, Suzanne.

Ei Thesaurus.

Database 16 (6) Dec. 1993 : 80-81.

912 Miyajima, T.

A study of specialized terminology : the problem of technical terms.

International Classification 9, 1982 : 152-154.

913 Mochel, G. and Wisner, R.

Thesaurus in economics.

Informatika 18 (4) 1971 : 26-30.

914 Molnar, I.

Designing a new type of thesaurus structure.

Tudomanyos es Muszaki Tajekoztatas 19 (3) March 1972 : 149-169.

915 Molnar, I.

Thesaurus on computer techniques in Hungarian, II : Comparative statistical analysis of the thesaurus.

Tudomanyos es Muszaki Tajekoztatas 21 (2) Feb. 1974 : 81-93.

916 Moys, E. A. et al.

Moys classification and thesaurus for legal materials.

Managing Information 8 (8) Oct. 2001 : 61.

917 NASA thesaurus 1994 edition, NASA SP-7096.

Information Processing and Management 32 (1) Jan. 1996 : 117-118.

918 Neamtu, O.

Towards new types of thesauri.

Studii si Cercetari de Documentare 11 (1) March 1969 : 35-40.

919 Negrini, Giliola.

Organizing the literary work of art - a common aim for Finland and Italy.

Signum 36 (4) 2003 : 91-95.

Compares 'Kaunokki' the Finnish Thesaurus for Fiction with and the Thesaurus of Italian Literature.

920 Nestel, B.; Gijsbers, G. and Ballantyne, P.

A mini thesaurus as an aid to the management of agricultural research.

Quarterly Bulletin of the International Association of Agricultural Information Specialists 37 (4) 1992 : 215-223.

Describes a mini thesaurus of agriculture based on the AGROVOC Thesaurus.

921 Newton, Mary.

SPIRES tailored to a special library : a mainframe answer for a small online catalog.

Database 12 (1) Feb. 1989 : 48-53.

Describes controlled vocabulary and other aspects of the Motor Vehicle Manufacturers Association's (Detroit, Michigan) library's Document Retrieval Subsystem.

922 Nicholson, D.

Subject-based interoperability : issues from the High Level Thesaurus (HILT) Project.

International Cataloguing and Bibliographic Control 32 (1) Jan.-March 2003 : 14-16.

Describes the first phase of the project.

923 Nicholson, D.; Dunsire, G. and Neill, S.

HILT : moving towards interoperability in subject terminologies.

Journal of Internet Cataloging 5 (4) 2002 : 97-111.

Explains interoperability feature of High-Level Thesaurus.

924 Nixon, J. M.

Review of CAB International's CD-ROM database AgECONCD.

Journal of Agricultural and Food Information 3 (1) 1995 : 93-97.

Describes controlled vocabulary and other aspects of AgECONCD - a CD-ROM database produced by CAB International, UK.

925 Ohman, E.

The criticism of UDC by H. Arntz in the light of investigations into concordances between UDC and thesauri.

Nachrichten fur Dokumentation 23 (2) April 1972 : 65-68.

926 Oldenkamp, D. M.

The new WilsonWeb.

Searcher 11 (3) March 2003 : 17-25.

Describes thesaurus and other features of H. W. Wilson Company's WilsonWeb's new interface.

927 Ostrove, G. E.

Music subject cataloging and form / genre implementation at the Library of Congress.

Cataloging and Classification Quarterly 32 (2) 2001 : 91-106.

Discusses treatment given to form and genre of music in the LCSH.

928 Pack, T.

Free reference resources on the Web.

Link-Up (USA) 15 (5) Sept.-Oct. 1998 : 22.

Describes free reference resources on the web including thesauri.

929 Pack, Thomas.

Cyber-touring the world's best buildings.

Information Today 21 (7) July-August 2004 : 21-22.

Provides information about the notable architectural websites and the website of ATT.

930 Pajona, P.

INSEAD : business and management thesaurus.

Managing Information 1 (5) May 94 : 47.

931 Palatova, R. P.

Structure of a thesaurus for pipeline transport (using Referativnyi Zhurnal 'Pipeline Transport').

Nauchno- Tekhnicheskaya Informatsiya Series ; II (1) 1973 : 18-21.

932 Palmer, Jospeph W.

Subject authority control and syndetic structure - myth and realities. An inquiry into certain subject heading practices and some questions about their implications.

Cataloging and Classification Quarterly 7 (2) Winter 1986 : 71-95.

933 Parekh, Harsha.

The Unesco-IBE education thesaurus : an evaluation.

Seminar on thesaurus in information system. Banglore : DRTC, 1975 : Paper CG.

934 Pearce, H. J.

Thesaurus of disability index terms.

Indexer 20 (4) Oct. 1997 : 227.

935 Pelissier, D.

Focus on Unesco databases and information services.

Information Development 9 (4) Dec. 1993 : 247-250.

Describes databases and thesauri at the Unesco Clearing House.

936 Petersen, Toni.

Art and Architecture Thesaurus.

American Archivist 57 (3) Summer 1994 : 562-564.

937 Petersen, Toni.

Art and Architecture Thesaurus.

Journal of the American Society for Information Science 46 (2) March 1995 : 152-160.

938 Petersen, Toni.

Subject control in visual collections.

Art Documentation 7 (4) Winter 1988 : 131-135.

Describes ATT and its use in deriving subject representing terms for database of visual collections.

939 Petersen, Toni.

The AAT : a model for the restructuring of LCSH.

Journal of Academic Librarianship 9 (4) Sept. 1983 : 207-210.

940 Petersen, Toni.

The AAT in the MARC format.

Art Documentation 8 (4) Winter 1989 : 181-182.

941 Pilz, J.

Thesaurus for the joint system of the machine tool industry and its incorporation into the thesaurus of the Ministerium fur Verarbeitungsmaschinen- und Fahrzeugbau.

Informatika 18 (1) 1971 : 26-28.

942 Pokras, Yu L.

A descriptor information retrieval language for specialisation and cooperation in the machine-building industry.

Nauchno- Tekhnicheskaya Informatsiya; Series II (5) 1969 : 12-15.

943 Poletylo, M.

The structure of the thesaurus of the International Nuclear Information System (INIS).

Aktualne Problemy Informacji Dokumentacji 16 (6) 1971 : 23-29.

944 Posnett, N. W.

Thesaurus of Land Resource Terms and its relationship with a feature card system.

Quarterly Bulletin of the International Association of Agricultural Information Specialists 27 (3) 1982 : 74-86.

Describes the thesaurus of land resource terms and its use with feature card system.

945 Poznanin, L. P. and Vlasova, V. F.

On the necessity for creating a thesaurus for biology and its structure.

Nauchno- Tekhnicheskaya Informatsiya; Series II (9) 1972 : 23-24.

946 Preisler, W.

On the structure of a thesaurus.

Informatika 19 (1) 1972 : 22-28.

947 Price, Richard.

PRECIS reassessed.

Catalogue and Index (87) Winter 1987 : 4-6.

Presents a comparative account of subject terms (based on PRECIS) in BNB, in a general thesaurus and more specialized thesauri.

948 Proud, Barbara.

Subject access and the special library.

Cataloguing Australia 7 (4) Oct.-Dec. 1981 : 18-20.

Discusses the inadequacies of several well-known classification schemes and thesauri from special libraries point of view.

949 Quijano-Solis, A.; Moreno-Jimenex, P. M. and Figueroa-Servin, R.

Automated authority files of Spanish-language subject headings.

Cataloging and Classification Quarterly 29 (1-2) 2000 : 209-223.

950 Ralston, N. M.

Controlled vocabularies for MEDLARS databases.

Medical Reference Services Quarterly 14 (2) Summer 1995 : 25-34.

951 Rao, Chandershekhar.

Thesaurus of cell biology.

Library Herald 22 (4) Jan. 1984 : 217-220.

Elaborates the coverage and structure of the cell biology thesaurus.

952 Roberts, N.

Concepts, structures and retrieval in the social sciences up to c.1970.

Social Science Information Studies 5 (2) April 1985 : 55-67.

Compares 20 thesauri so as to analyze work / concept relationship and concept structuring in social sciences.

953 Rolland-Thomas, Paul.

Thesaural codes : an appraisal of their use in the Library of Congress Subject Headings.

Cataloging and Classification Quarterly 16 (2) 1993 : 71-91.

Examines compatibility of thesaural codes used in LCSH.

954 Rorvig, M. E.; Turner, C. H. and Moncada, J.

The NASA image collection visual thesaurus.

Journal of the American Society for Information Science 50 (9) July 1999 : 794-798.

955 Rothwell, D. J.

SNOMED-based knowledge representation.

Methods of Information in Medicine; 34 (1 -2) March 1995 : 209-213.

Describes SNOMED - a universal standardized vocabulary and data structure suitable for maintaining computer based patient record.

956 Rowley, J. E. et al.

The use of INFO, a database management system, in teaching library and information studies at Manchester Polytechnic.

Education for Information 6 (1) March 1988 : 71-82.

Describes vocabulary control and other features of 'INFO' - a database management package used in teaching by the Department of Library and Information Studies at Manchester Polytechnic.

957 Sardar, Ziauddin.

The Information Unit of the Hajj Research Centre.

Aslib Proceedings 30 (5) May 1978 : 158-164.

Describes the Information Unit of the Hajj Research Centre at the King Abdul Aziz University, Jeddah, Saudi Arabia and its thesaurus, which is developed for indexing their technical material.

958 Schiff, E.

The Thesaurus of Engineering Terms and its revised edition the Thesaurus of Engineering and Scientific Terms.

Tudomanyos es Muszaki Tajekoztatas 16 (11-12) Nov.-Dec. 1969 : 863-875.

959 Schuyler, P. L.

The UMLS Metathesaurus : representing different views of biomedical concepts.

Bulletin of the Medical Library Association 81 (2) April 1993 : 217-222.

960 Scibor, Eugeniusz and Jabrzemska, Eleonora.

Thesaurus of Common Topics (TCT) : origin, functions, structure.

Information Processing and Management 21 (1) 1985 : 5-10.

Describes the Thesaurus of Common Topics that covers interdisciplinary areas.

961 Senf, W.

IDC-Thesaurus and its reorganization.

Bonn Bad Godesborg, West Germany : Bundesministerium fur Forschung und Technologie, 1979. 69p.

Reviews the West German Internationale Dokumentationsgesellschaft fur Chemie IDC-Thesaurus and its reorganization.

962 Shaw, Margaret.

Developments in overseas data bases and their relevance to Australia.

ARLIS/ANZ News (16) Dec. 1983 - Feb. 1984 : 5-9.

Reviews important indexing projects under way in the USA and elsewhere and describes ATT.

963 Shaw, W. M.

Retrieval expectations, cluster-based effectiveness, and performance standards in the CF database.

Information Processing and Management 30 (5) Sept.-Oct. 1994 : 711-723.

Describes methods used to investigate retrieval performance of controlled and uncontrolled vocabulary of cystic fibrosis (CF) database, a sub-set of MEDLINE.

964 Sheppard, Judy and Schleffler, Diane.

Subject headings for information and referral.

California Librarian 37(3) 1976 : 14-17.

965 Silver, D. P.

An introduction to the population / family planning thesaurus.

Overview 3 (1-2) Spring 1975 : 8-11.

966 Smith, Inese A.

Development of indexing systems at the National Youth Bureau.

Catalogue and Index (73) Summer 1984 : 1-4.

Describes use of custom-designed thesaurus on youth, developed for a new indexing system.

967 Sobel, Samuel and Singh, Surjit.

United Nations Bibliographic Information System (UNBIS).

Unesco Journal of Information Science, Librarianship and Archives Administration 2 (4) Oct.-Dec. 1980 : 220-226.

Describes UNIBIS and its objectives one of which is to use vocabulary aligned with other major international lists and thesauri.

968 Sorrentine, Sherrill; Fierberg, Joan and Goodchild, Eleanor,

Y.

CATLINE as an acquisitions tool for health and patient education materials.

Bulletin of the Medical Library Association 66 (4) Oct. 1978 : 458-460.

Describes CATLINE along with the MeSH thesaurus used for managing information in the CATALINE database.

969 Speight, F. Y.

What is 'the Thesaurus of Engineering Terms' developed by the Engineers Joint Council (EJC).

Bulletin de l' AID 5(4) 1966 : 29-43.

970 Spurgen, Charles.

Index language devices in various thesaurus : a comparative study.

Annals of Library Science and Documentation 1984 : 77-92.

971 Squires, S. J.

Access to biomedical information : the unified medical language system.

Library Trends 42 (1) Summer 1993 : 127-151.

Describes the UMLS used for accessing the biomedical information.

972 Stiff, M.

MDA archaeological objects thesaurus.

Indexer 21 (1) April 1998 : 52-53.

973 Stodulski, A.

RCN library nursing thesaurus : a thesaurus of terms used in nursing, midwifery, health visiting and related areas.

Health Libraries Review 12 (3) Sept. 1995 : 229-230.

974 Strong, Gary W. and Drott, M. Carl.

A thesaurus for end-user indexing and retrieval.

Information Processing and Management 22 (6) 1986 : 487-

492.

Explains the construction of a faceted hierarchical thesaurus meant for end user indexing and retrieval.

975 Studwell, William E.

A tale of two decades, or, the decline of the fortunes of LC subject headings.

Western Association of Map Libraries Information Bulletin 25 (2) March 1994 : 73-74.

976 Studwell, William E.

Cutterism, codism, and consumerism : the past, present, and future of LC subject access.

Technical Services Quarterly 9 (1) 1991 : 19-25.

977 Studwell, William E.

Game shows, elevators, full plates, and other allegories : a look at the present state and future possibilities of LC subject headings.

Serials Librarian 23 (3-4) 1993 : 241-243.

978 Studwell, William E.

Game shows, elevators, full plates, and other allegories : look at the present state and future possibilities of LC Subject Headings.

Western Association of Map Libraries Information Bulletin 24 (2) March 1993 : 103-106.

979 Studwell, William E.

How stable is the cataloging process? Part 2 : some possible solutions.

Behavioral and Social Sciences Librarian 15 (2) 1997 : 71-74.

980 Studwell, William E.

Ignore it and it will go away :...but it's still there!

Technicalities 17 (4) April 1997 : 1 and 13.

981 Studwell, William E.

LC's head in the sand, or, why the Subject Cataloging Manual is not enough.

Technical Services Quarterly 10 (3) 1993 : 45-50.

982 Studwell, William E.

Library of Congress subject headings relating to the social sciences : some suggestions for improvement.

Behavioral and Social Sciences Librarian 12 (1) 1993 : 9-20.

983 Studwell, William E.

Map libraries and a subject heading code.

Western Association of Map Libraries Information Bulletin 18 (2) March 1987 : 157-158.

984 Studwell, William E.

Of eggs and baskets : getting more access out of LC subject headings in online environment.

Cataloging and Classification Quarterly 13 (3-4) 1991 : 91-96.

985 Studwell, William E.

Subject access from 'if' LC to IFLA : the next logical progression.

Technicalities 21 (4) July-August 2001 : 5.

986 Studwell, William E.

Subject access on-line in academic libraries of the future : will intermediaries be an essential component?

Western Association of Map Libraries Information Bulletin 24 (2) March 1993 : 107-8 and 114.

987 Studwell, William E.

Subject suggestions 1 : Some concerns relating to geographic areas.

Cataloging and Classification Quarterly 8 (2) 1987-1988 : 91-98.

988 Studwell, William E.

Subject suggestions 2 : some concerns relating to science.

Cataloging and Classification Quarterly 9 (1) 1988 : 121-127.

989 Studwell, William E.

Subject suggestions 3 : the form of name for literatures.

Cataloging and Classification Quarterly 9 (2) 1988 : 93-100.

990 Studwell, William E.

Subject suggestions 4 : some concerns relating to iiterature and language.

Cataloging and Classification Quarterly 9 (4) 1989 : 109-114.

991 Studwell, William E.

Subject suggestions 5 : some concerns relating to art.

Cataloging and Classification Quarterly 10 (3) 1990 : 91-95.

992 Studwell, William E.

Subject suggestions 6 : some concerns relating to quantity of subjects.

Cataloging and Classification Quarterly 10 (4) 1990 : 99-104.

993 Studwell, William E.

Subject suggestions 7 : some concerns relating to the social sciences.

Cataloging and Classification Quarterly 11 (2) 1990 : 95-101.

994 Studwell, William E.

Ten years after the question : has there been an answer?

Cataloging and Classification Quarterly 20 (3) 1995 : 95-98.

995 Studwell, William E.

The 1990s : decade of subject access.

American Libraries 18 (11) Dec. 1987 : 958-960.

996 Studwell, William E.

The rocky road to a subject code.

Western Association of Map Libraries Information Bulletin 22 (2) March 1991 : 110-114.

997 Studwell, William E.

The three camps : the present and possible future status of subject access in online catalogues.

Behavioral and Social Sciences Librarian 14 (2) 1996 : 61-64.

998 Studwell, William E.

Universal subject environment : aspirations for a multinational, multicultural, and multilingual subject access system.

Technical Services Quarterly 16 (3) 1999 : 21-30.

999 Studwell, William E.

Who killed the subject code?

Technical Services Quarterly 12 (1) 1994 : 35-41.

1000 Studwell, William E. and Aggarwal, Narindar K.

Library of Congress Subject Headings period subdivisions for East Asia, South Asia, and Asia in general : some proposed additions.

Cataloging and Classification Quarterly 3 (4) Summer 1983 : 65-78.

1001 Studwell, William E. and Ericksen, D. A.

Music libraries and a subject heading code.

Music Reference Services Quarterly 1 (1) 1992 : 73-75.

1002 Studwell, William E. and Hamilton, David A.

LC Subject Headings for career materials : a critique and some suggestions.

Reference Librarian (36) 1992 : 33-39.

1003 Studwell, William E. and Hamilton, David A.

Library of Congress subject heading period subdivision for

Eastern Europe excluding the Soviet Union : some proposed additions.

Cataloging and Classification Quarterly 6 (1) Fall 1985 : 39-60.

1004 Studwell, William E. and Hamilton, David A.

Library of Congress subject heading period subdivisions for Latin America : some proposed additions.

Cataloging and Classification Quarterly 4 (3) Spring 1984 : 39-74.

1005 Studwell, William E. and Hamilton, David A.

Library of Congress subject heading period subdivisions for the Soviet Union : some proposed additions.

Cataloging and Classification Quarterly 6 (3) Spring 1986 : 63-83.

1006 Studwell, William E., Roland-Thomas, Paule and Roland-Thomas, P.

The form and structure of a subject heading code.

Library Resources and Technical Services 32 (2) April 1988 : 167-169.

1007 Subramanyam, K.

Comparison of four thesauri in education.

Herald of Library Science 13 (3-4) July-Oct. 1974 : 242-253.

1008 Sutter, E.

International dissemination of standards information-tools needed to operate the network : the ISO Thesaurus and the ISONET Manual.

Indexer 11 (3) April 1979 : 157-159.

Describes the ISO thesaurus and the ISONET Manual that are used by the ISO's network.

1009 Svenonius, E.

LCSH : semantics, syntax and specificity.

Cataloging and Classification Quarterly 29 (1-2) 2000 : 17-30.

1010 Sykes, Philippa.

If in doubt ask an expert : the GCHQ story continues.

Catalogue & Index (141) Autumn 2001 : 8-9.

Explains the Corporate Keyword Hierarchy- a taxonomy of the UK Government Communications Headquarters corporate intranet called GCWeb.

1011 Szrajber, T.

The British Museum materials thesaurus.

Indexer 21 (1) April 1998 : 52-53.

1012 Tahirkheli, Sharon N.

Thesaurus problem and solutions : the language of geology develops steadily.

Collections for the future : archivists, curators, historians. Ed. by Jean T. Eaglesfield. Alexandria, VA : Geoscience Information Society, 1988.

Describes the 5th edition of the GeoRef Thesaurus, which covers geologic and geographic terms.

1013 Takeda, N.

Problems in hierarchical structures of thesauri : their influences on the results of information retrieval.

Online Kensaku 15 (4) 1994 : 183-186.

1014 Thomas, Alan R.

British councellors' views of ERIC terms.

Catalogue and Index (95) Winter 1989 : 1-3.

1015 Thomson, Mollie.

Library of Congress and Australian subject headings.

Cataloguing Australia 6 (2) April- June 1980 : 13-19.

1016 Thurlow, H.

LCSH online at the State Library of Queensland.

Cataloguing Australia 19 (3-4) Sept.-Dec. 1993 : 253-258.

1017 Tidbury, G. E.

The CAB thesaurus.

Quarterly Bulletin of the International Association of Agricultural Information Specialists 27 (3) 1982 : 67-73.

Describes the CAB thesaurus and compares it with AGROVOC descriptors.

1018 Toma, E.

A statistical approach to the structure of thesauri : a comparative study.

Studii si Cercetari de Documentare 14 (3) Sept. 1972 : 217-229.

1019 Toma, E.

The structure of the EURATOM-thesaurus.

Journal of Documentation 27 (4) Dec. 1971 : 267-272.

1020 Tonta, Yasar.

LCSH and PRECIS in library and information science : a comparative study.

Occasional Papers (194) May 1992 : 1-68.

1021 Trendler, A. E.

The rules have changed : Library of Congress Subject Headings for Art and Architecture.

Art Documentation 20 (2) Fall 2001 : 24-29.

1022 Uhlmann, A.

Mining thesaurus : a thesaurus with UDC notations.

Tudomanyos es Muszaki Tajekoztatas 18 (10) Oct. 1971 : 763-783.

1023 Ulmann, W.

A thesaurus of nuclear science and technology : principles of design.

Teknisk-Veteskapling Forsking (TVF) 38, 1967 : 46-52.

1024 Unesco Thesaurus.

Journal of Librarianship and Information Science 29 (3) Sept. 1997 : 165-166.

1025 UNESCO thesaurus : a structured list of descriptors for indexing and retrieving literature in the fields of education, science, social and human science, culture, communication and information.

Indexer 20 (2) Oct. 1996 : 108.

1026 van Hamersveld, Ineke.

Information services in the fields of art and architecture.

Art Libraries Journal 12 (1) 1987 : 8-11.

Describes MARCDOC- a thesaurus constructed to facilitate automated access to museum collections.

1027 Vizine-Goetz, D.

Popular LCSH with Dewey numbers : subject headings for everyone.

Journal of Library Administration 34 (3- 4) 2001 : 293-300.

1028 Vizine-Goetz, D.

Subject headings for everyone : popular Library of Congress subject headings with Dewey numbers.

OCLC Newsletter (233) May -June 1998 : 29-33.

1029 Vizine-Goetz, Diane and Drabenstott, Karen Markey

Computer and manual analysis of subject terms entered by online catalog users.

ASIS '91. Systems understanding people. Proceedings of the 54th Annual Meeting of the American Society for Information Science. Washington, D.C., 27-31 October 1991. Volume 28. Ed. by Jose-Marie Griffiths. Medford : Learned Information, Inc., for American Society for Information Science, 1991 : 156-161.

Examines the differences of computer and manual analysis of the subject terms entered by users in OPAC.

1030 Vizine-Goetz, Diane and Markey, Karen.

Characteristics of subject heading records in the machine-readable Library of Congress Subject Headings.

Information Technology and Libraries 8 (2) June 1989 : 203-209.

1031 Voorbiji, H. J.

Title keywords and subject descriptors : a comparison of the subject search entries of books in the humanities and social sciences.

Journal of Documentation 54(4) 1998 : 466-476.

1032 Wake, S. and Nicholson, D.

HILT : High-Level Thesaurus Project - building consensus for interoperable subject access across communities.

D-Lib Magazine 7 (9) Sept. 2001. No page numbers.

Also available at : http://www.dlib.org/dlib/september01/wake/09wake.html

1033 Wake, S. and Nicholson, D.

HILT : subject access across domains.

SCONUL Newsletter (23) Summer-Autumn 2001 : 14-18.

Briefs and discusses the findings of the High-Level Thesaurus (HILT) project.

Also available at : http://hilt.cdlr.strath.ac.uk/

1034 Walden, C. B. and Cooke, Deborah M.

A personal on-line reference retrieval program for microcomputers.

Journal of Information Science 4 (4) July 1982 : 155-160.

Describes a thesaurus based online bibliographic reference retrieval system developed for the use of research workers at St. Thomas' Hospital, London.

1035 Walker, A. and Mulholland, S. N.

The thesaurus of psychological index terms : a historical

review.

Behavioral and Social Sciences Librarian 11 (2) 1992 : 39-57.

1036 Walker, Richard D.

GeoArchive : a brief review.

On-line 2 (4) Oct. 1978 : 40-43.

Describes GeoArchive – a geoscience database and its thesaurus called 'Geosaurus'.

1037 Wall, E.

Information retrieval thesauri.

New York : Engineer's Joint Council, 1962. 17p.

1038 Wall, R. A.

Indexing language structure for automated retrieval.

Information Storage and Retrieval 9 (11) Nov. 1973 : 607-617.

1039 Wang, S. T.

The structure of Library of Congress subject headings for belles lettres in Chinese literature.

Library Resources and Technical Services 17 (2) Spring 1973 : 231-237.

1040 Weinberg, Bella Hass.

JEWS-DASH : Library of Congress Subject Headings for Judaica : a methodology for analysis.

Judaica Librarianship 2 (1-2) Spring 1985 : 20-25 and 40.

1041 Weinberg, Bella Hass.

The hidden classification in Library of Congress Subject Headings for judaica.

Library Resources and Technical Services 37 (4) Oct. 1993 : 369-379.

1042 Wepsiec, Jan.

Hierarchical structure of subject headings in the social sciences.

Cataloging and Classification Quarterly 13 (1) 1991 : 79-102.

1043 Wepsiec, Jan.

Inquiry into the syndetic structure of the Library of Congress Subject Headings in anthropology.

Library Resources and Technical Services 22 (1) Winter 1978 : 61-80.

1044 Wepsiec, Jan.

Language of the Library of Congress Subject Headings pertaining to society.

Library Resources and Technical Services 25 (2) April-June 1981 : 196-203.

1045 Wepsiec, Jan.

Library of Congress subject headings pertaining to society.

Cataloging and Classification Quarterly 2 (3-4) 1982 : 1-29.

1046 Wilk, D. et al.

Problems in the use of Library of Congress Subject Headings as the basis for Hebrew subject headings in the Bar-Ilan University Library.

International Cataloguing and Bibliographic Control 30 (3) July-Sept. 2001 : 43-46.

1047 Will, L.

Thesauri in the age of the Internet : HILT and related projects.

Catalogue and Index (146) Winter 2002 : 8-11.

Describes High Level Thesaurus development project.

Also available at : http://hilt.cdir.strath.ac.uk/

1048 Winkel, L.

Subject headings for children : a list of subject headings used by the Library of Congress with Abridged Dewey numbers added.

Canadian Journal of Information and Library Science 24 (1)

April 1999 : 41-44.

1049 Winkel, L.

Subject headings for children : a list of subject headings used by the Library of Congress with abridged Dewey numbers added.

Catalogue and Index (131) Summer 1999 : 9-10.

1050 Winkel, L.

Subject headings for children : a list of subject headings used by the Library of Congress with Abridged Dewey numbers added.

Library Review 49 (3 and 4) 2000 : 197-199.

1051 Winkel, L.

Subject headings for children : a list of subject headings used by the Library of Congress with Dewey numbers added.

School Library Media Quarterly 23 (3) Spring 1995 : 197.

1052 Winkel, L.

Subject headings for children : a list of subject headings used by the Library of Congress with Abridged Dewey Numbers Added.

Technicalities 19 (4) April 1999 : 7-8.

1053 Winkel, L.

Subject headings for children : a list of subject headings used by Library of Congress with Dewey numbers added. Volume 1: List of headings. Volume 2 : Keyword index.

Catalogue and Index (120) Summer 1996 : 12-11.

1054 Wise Fernandez, Cheryl and Wise Fernandez, C.

Semantic relationships between title phrases and LCSH.

Cataloging and Classification Quarterly 13 (1) 1991 : 51-77.

1055 Wu, G. and Li, J.

Comparing Web search engine performance in searching consumer health information : evaluation and recommendations

Bulletin of the Medical Library Association 87 (4) Oct. 1999 : 456-461.

Presents evaluation of the search engines by applying controlled vocabulary and other features.

1056 Zeng, Lei.

Achieving compatibility of indexing languages in online access environment.

Encyclopaedia of Library and Information Science. Volume 50. Ed. by Allen Kent. New York : Marcel Dekker, 1992 : 1-24.

1057 Zeng Lei.

Establishing a compatible general vocabulary in China : the capability.

International Classification 17 (2) 1990 : 91-98.

Discusses the compatible capabilities between special and general Chinese thesauri as well as Chinese and English thesauri.

1058 Zhang, Wenxian.

The development and structure of the Chinese Thesaurus for subject indexing.

International Information and Library Review 36 (1) March 2004 : 47-54.

1059 Zhou, L.

Characteristics of material organization and classification in the Kinsey Institute Library.

Cataloging and Classification Quarterly 35 (3-4) 2003 : 335-353.

Describes the Sexual Nomenclature : a thesaurus used for cataloguing collection at the Kinsey Institute Library, Indiana University.

1060 Zijlstra, B. H. A.

History of US STI and subject categories.

Proceedings of the 1st International Conference on Grey Literature held at the RAI Congress Centre, Amsterdam, The Netherlands, 13-15 December 1993. Compiled by D. J. Farace. Amsterdam : TransAtlantic, 1994 : 269-290.

Describes the development of the TEST Thesaurus and subject categories of the COSATI for Scientific and Technical Information (STI).

Section N

Actual thesauri – monolingual

Thesauri are constructed for almost all major branches of knowledge. This section lists actual thesauri (monolingual).

1061 Aitchison, Jean.

International thesaurus of refugee terminology. 2nd ed.

New York : United Nations High Commissioner for Refugees, 1996.

1062 Aitchison, Jean.

Unesco thesaurus.

Paris : UNESCO, 1977.

1063 Aitchison, Jean; Brewin, P. R. and Cotton, J. E.

DHSS-DATA thesaurus : the thesaurus of the Department of Health and Social Security library : working edition.

London : Department of Health and Social Security, 1985.

1064 Aitchison, Jean et al.

The Royal Institute of International Affairs library thesaurus. 2 Vols.

London, Royal Institute of International Affairs, 1992.

1065 Aitchison, Jean. et al.

Thesaurofacet : a thesaurus and faceted classification for engineering and related subjects.

Whetstone (Leics) : English Electric Company Ltd., 1969. 491p.

1066 Aitchison Jean et al.

Thesaurus on youth : an integrated classification and thesaurus on youth affairs and related topics.

Leicester, England : National Youth Bureau, 1982.

1067 American Institute of Chemical Engineers.

Chemical engineering thesaurus.

New York : American Institute of Chemical Engineers, 1961.

1068 American Petroleum Institute.

Information retrieval system subject authority list. 7th ed.

New York : American Petroleum Institute, 1970, 455p.

1069 American Psychological Association.

Thesaurus of psychological terms. 2nd ed.

Washington, DC : The Association, 1977. 282p.

1070 American Society for Information Science.

ASIS thesaurus of information science and librarianship. 2nd ed.

Medford, NJ : Learned Information Inc 1998. 169p.

Also available at : http://www.asis.org/publications/thesaurus/tnhome.htm

Includes over thirteen hundred preferred terms, 691 nonpreferred terms, and 37 facet indicators. Scope notes and definitions of ambiguous terms are given. Contains an alphabetical listing, a hierarchical listing, and a rotated (KWIC) listing.

1071 American Society for Metals.

Thesaurus of metallurgical terms.

Ohio : American Society for Metals, 1968.

1072 Armed Services Technical Information Agency.

Thesaurus of ASTIA descriptors.

Arlington, VA : Armed Services Technical Information Agency, 1960.

1073 *Art and architecture thesaurus.* 2nd ed. 5 Volumes.

Oxford : Oxford University Press, 1994.

The thesaurus can be browsed online at :

http://www.getty.edu/research/conducting_research/vocabularies/aat/

1074 Askew, Colin.

Thesaurus of consumer affairs. 2 Vols.

The Hague : International Organization for Consumer's Union, 1979.

1075 *Austrialian pictorial thesaurus (APT).*

Sydney : State Library of New South Wales, 2000.

The thesaurus lists 15000 terms related with pictures of objects and images.

Information about this thesaurus can be found at : http://www.picturethesaurus.gov.au/

1076 Backer, S.

Thesaurus of textile terms covering fibrous materials and processes.

Cambridge, Mass. : M.I.T. Press, 1969. 448p.

1077 Barhydt, C. and Schmidt, T.

Information retrieval thesaurus of educational terms.

Cleveland : Case Western Reserve University, 1968.

1078 Bioethics Information Retrieval Project.

Bioethics thesaurus.

Wahington, DC : Georgetown University, Kennedy Institute of Ethics, Bioethics Information Retrieval Project, 1987.

1079 *Biomedical subject headings : a reconciliation of National Library of Medicine (MeSH) and Library of Congress subject headings.* 2nd ed.

Hamden, Conn : Shoe String, 1979.

1080 Black, W. T.

Thesaurus of terms on copper technology. 7th ed.

New York : Copper Development Association, 1981.

1081 Blagden, J. F.

Management information retrieval : a new indexing language.

London : British Institute of Management, 1969. 153p.

1082 British Standards Institution.

BSI ROOT thesaurus.

Hemel Hempstead : British Standards Institution, 1981.

1083 British Standards Institution.

BSI ROOT thesaurus. 2nd ed.

Milton Keynes, England : British Standards Institution. 1985.

1084 British Standards Institution.

BSI ROOT thesaurus. 3rd ed. 2 vols.

Milton Keynes, England : British Standards Institution. 1988.

1085 Burrell, James P.

Source header list. Supplement 2.

Alexandria, VA : Defense Documentation Center, 1979. 208p.

1086 *CAB Thesaurus.*

Wallingford (UK) : CAB International, 1999.

1086a Charles, R.; Lea, G. and Shearer, J.

Geosaurus : Geosystems' thesaurus for geoscience and guide to Geotitles Weekly.

London, Westminster : Geosystems Publications, 1973. 61p.

1087 Coombes, Judith.

Collection thesaurus - alphabetical and hierarchical. 2 vols.

Sydney : Powerhouse Publishing, 1996. [Vol.1 62p.; Vol.2 296p.]

This thesaurus, developed by the Powerhouse Museum's Registration Department, Australia contains over 5000 entries. Deals with museum collection.

1088 Cote, Roger.

Systematized nomenclature of medicine.

Skokie, Illinois : College of American Pathologists, 1979.

1089 Croghan, A.

A thesaurus-classification for non-book media.

London : The Author, 1970 : 46p.

1090 Dahlberg, I. A

General thesaurus for the German Library : pilot study.

Frankfurt am Main (West Germany) : Deutsche Bibliothek, 1980. 74p.

1091 Defense Documentation Center.

DDC retrieval and indexing terminology posting terms with hierarchy and KWOC.

Alexandria, VA : Defense Documentation Center, 1979. 376p.

Displays DDC's controlled posting vocabulary.

1092 Defriez, Philip.

The ISDD thesaurus, keywords relating to non-medical use of drugs and drug dependence. 2nd ed.

London : Institute for the study of drug Dependence, 1993.

1093 Department of Energy, Technical Information Center.

Energy Information Data Base, Subject Thesaurus.

Oak Ridge, TN : Department of Energy, Technical Information Center, 1979. 864p.

1094 Department of Energy, Technical Information Center.

Subject thesaurus permutated listing.

Oak Ridge, TN : Department of Energy, Technical Information Center, 1981. 240p.

1095 European Commission.

Thesaurus guide : an analytical directory of selected vocabularies for information retrieval. 2nd ed. Prepared for the Commission of the European Communities by Eurobrokers.

Luxembourg : Office for Official Publication of the European

Commission, 1992. 1033p.

Describes over 600 structured vocabularies which have appeared in at least one of the official languages of the European Communities

1096 *European Education Thesaurus.*

Luxembourg : Office for the Official Publication of the European Communities. (produced by the Council of Europe), 1991.

1097 European Energy Community.

EURATOM thesaurus. 2nd ed. 2 vols.

Brussels : European Energy Community, 1966-1970.

1098 Food and Agricultural Organization.

Thesaurus of terms for aquatic sciences and fisheries.

Paris : Unesco, 1976.

1099 Foskett, D. J. and Foskett, J.

The London Education Classification : a thesaurus classification of British educational terms. Second edition.

London : University of London Institute of Education Library, 1974. 165p.

1100 Gilchrist, Alan et al.

A compressed term index for library and information science.

London : Aslib, 1973 : 123p.

1101 Houston, James E.

Thesaurus of ERIC descriptors. 13th ed.

Phoenix, Arizona : Oryx, 1995.

1102 *Information Retrieval Thesaurus of Education terms.*

Cleveland, Ohio : Case Western Reserve University, 1968.

1103 Institution of Electrical Engineers.

INSPEC thesaurus.

London : Institution of Electrical Engineers, 1979.

1104 *Intelligent Transportation System thesaurus.*

California : US Transportation Research Board, 2000.

1105 International Atomic Energy Agency.

INIS Thesaurus and guidelines for the development and maintenance of the INIS thesaurus.

Vienna : International Atomic Energy Agency, 1971.

1106 International Atomic Energy Agency.

Thesaurus : terminology charts.

Vienna : International Atomic Energy Agency, 1970.

1107 International Bureau of Education.

Unesco : IBE Education Thesaurus : a list of terms for indexing and retrieving documents and data in the field of education with French and Spanish equivalents. 4th revised ed.

Paris : UNESCO, 1994.

1108 International Labour Organization.

ILO thesaurus : Labour, employment and training terminology. Ed. 5.

Geneva, ILO, 1998

1109 *International road research documentation (IRRD) thesaurus.* 2nd ed. 2 vols.

Paris : OECD, 1985.

1110 *International thesaurus of cultural development.*

Paris : UNESCO, 1981. 222p.

1111 Kumbhar, Rajendra.

Thesaurus of library and information science terms.

New Delhi : Ess Ess Publications, 2004.

1112 Lyne-Browne, R. C.

Thesaurus of terms : a list of terms and their relationships used in the library as a vocabulary reference in indexing and retrieving information.

Melbourne : Library of the Commonwealth Bureau of Roads, 1972.

1113 *Macrothesaurus for information processing in the field of economic and social development.* 5th ed.

Paris : OECD, 1998.

1114 *Medical and health related sciences thesaurus.*

Washington, DC : U. S. Department of Health Education and Welfare. Public Health Service, 1969. 460p.

1115 Merwe, C. van der.

Thesaurus of sociological research terminology.

Netherlands : Rotterdam University Press, 1974. 471p.

1116 National Aeronautic and Space Administration.

The NASA thesaurus.

Washington DC : National Aeronautic and Space Administration, 1967.

1117 National Institute on Alcohol Abuse and Alcoholism.

Alcohol and other drugs thesaurus : a guide to concepts and terminology in substance abuse and addiction. 3rd ed. 4 vols.

Rockville, MD : National Institute on Alcohol Abuse and Alcoholism, 2000.

1118 National Technical Information Services.

Computer science microthesaurus : a hierarchical list of indexing terms used by NTIS.

Springfield, VA : National Technical Information Services, 1980. 69p.

1119 National Technical Information Services.

Health care microthesaurus : a hierarchical list of indexing terms used by NTIS.

Springfield, VA. : National Technical Information Service, 1982. 64p.

1120 National Technical Information Services.

Integrated energy vocabulary.

Springfield, VA : National Technical Information Services, 1976.

1121 National Technical Information Services.

Social science and business microthesaurus : a hierarchical list of indexing terms used by NTIS.

Springfield, VA : National Technical Information Services, 1982.

1122 Radiation Chemistry Data Center.

Thesaurus for radiation chemistry.

Notre Dame, Ind. : Notre Dame University Radiation Chemistry Data Center, 1969. 55p.

1123 Roberts, M. J. et al.

Construction industry thesaurus.

London : The department of environment, Directorate of Development (housing and construction), 1972.

1124 Roberts, M. J. et al.

Construction industry thesaurus. 2nd ed.

London : The department of the environment, Property Services Agency, 1976.

1125 Royal Pharmaceutical Society of Great Britain.

Martindale online : drug information thesaurus. 2nd ed.

London : Pharmaceutical Press, 1990.

1126 Ruth, Daniel and Mills, J.

A classification and thesaurus of library and information science.

London : North London Polytechnic, School of Librarianship, 1973. 63p.

1127 Schultz, C. K.

Thesaurus of information science terminology.

Washington, D.C. : Communication Service Corporation, 1968. 246p.

1128 *SPINES thesaurus : A controlled vocabulary and structured vocabulary of science and technology for policy making, management and development.*

Paris: Unesco, 1976.

1129 *Thesaurus for graphic materials. TGM I: Subject Terms. TGM II: Genre and Physical Characteristic Terms.*

Washington, D.C. : Library of Congress, Cataloging Distribution Service, 1995. 556p.

This is the revised edition of two works : LC thesaurus for graphic materials / compiled by Elisabeth Betz Parker. LC, 1987. Descriptive terms for graphic materials / compiled and edited by Helena Zinkham and Elisabeth Betz Parker. LC, 1986.

1130 *Thesaurus of Engineering and Scientific Terms : a list of scientific and engineering terms and their relationships for use as a vocabulary in indexing and retrieving technical information - TEST.*

New York : Engineers Joint Council and US Department of Defense, 1967.

1131 *Thesaurus of ERIC descriptors.* 13th ed.

Houston, Arizona : Oryx, 1995.

1132 *Thesaurus of paint and allied technology.*

Philadelphia : Federation of the societies for paint technology, 1968.

1133 *Thesaurus of paper and pulp terms.*

Pointe Claire, Quebec : Paper and pulp research Institute, 1965.

1134 *Unesco thesaurus: a structured list of descriptors for indexing and retrieving literature in the fields of education, science, social and human science culture, communication and information.* 2nd ed.

Paris : UNESCO, 1995.

1135 United States. Department of Transportation. Federal Aviation Administration.

FAA thesaurus of technical descriptors.

Washington, DC : Federal Aviation Administration, 1969. 60p.

1136 Viet, Jean.

Thesaurus for information processing in sociology.

The Hague : Mouton, 1971. 336p.

1137 Williams, B. J. S.

Thesaurus of microform terms.

Hatfield : National Reprographic Centre for Documentation, DTL Services, 1969. 38p.

Section O
Multilingual thesauri

Multilingualism is the most common feature of many libraries in the modern world. Many users are interested in having literature in more than one language. Accordingly information professionals too have interest in collecting and organizing reading material in more than one language.

Multilingual thesauri are needed for preparing and searching subject entries of literature in more than one language.

The literature dealing with various aspects of multilingual and bilingual thesauri is grouped under following five sub-categories.

O1 Construction and use of multilingual thesauri

O2 Standards for multilingual thesaurus

O3 Softwares for multilingual thesauri

O4 Actual multilingual thesauri

O5 Bilingual thesauri

Section O1
Construction and use of multilingual thesaurus

1138 Adler, E.

Multilingual and multiscript subject access : the case of Israel.

International Cataloguing and Bibliographic Control 30 (2) April-June 2001 : 32-33.

1139 Aitchison, Jean.

The EUDISED thesaurus : a preliminary appraisal.

Education Libraries Bulletin 18 (3) Autumn 1975 : 12-25.

Describes purpose, scope and method of compilation of a multilingual thesaurus for European Documentation and

Information System for Education.

1140 Alanen, P.

Sami literature on the World Wide Web.

Scandinavian Public Library Quarterly 35 (2) 2002 : 4-7.

Describes a project that aims to offer unified access to the bibliographies of Sami literature on the World Wide Web and to develop a multilingual thesaurus of Sami terminology alongside the web literature search facility.

1141 Appleyard, R. K.; Neumeister, H. and Anderla, G. J.

Third European congress on information systems and networks : overcoming the language barrier. Luxembourg, 3-6 May 1977. Organized by the Commission of the European Communities. 2 Volumes.

Munich : Verlag Dokumentation, 1977. 675p. and 213p.

A conference proceeding, one of the themes of the conference was multilingual thesaurus.

1142 Austin, Derek.

Linguistic principles.

Report of a workshop on multingual systems edited by Verina Horsnell.

London, British Library Research and Development Department, 1976 : 6-7.

Discusses thesaurus construction and indexing grammar's role in multilingual systems.

1143 Austin, Derek.

Progress towards standard guidelines for the construction of multilingual thesauri.

Third European congress on information systems and networks : overcoming the language barrier. Luxembourg, 3-6 May 1977. Organized by the Commission of the European Communities. Volume 1. Munich, Verlag Dokumentation, 1977 : 341-402.

Reviews the proposed Unesco / ISO Draft Standard.

1144 Barrett, Jack.

ICSU AB-growth of an abstract idea.

Chemistry in Britain 12 (2) Feb. 1976 : 59-60.

Reports on works in progress about construction of multilingual thesauri.

1145 Baumgartner, Robert.

Problems and opportunities in thesaurus development for numeric databases.

Information interaction. Proceedings of the 45th ASIS Annual Meeting, 1982. Columbus, Ohio, 17-21 October 1982. Volume 19. Ed. by A. E. Petrarca, C. I. Taylor and R. S. Kohn. White Plains, New York : Knowledge Industry Publications, Inc., 1982 : 26-28.

Development of multilingual thesaurus for numeric databases is explained.

1146 Beling, Gerd.

The use of EDP in terminological work.

Third European congress on information systems and networks : overcoming the language barrier. Luxembourg, 3-6 May 1977. Organized by the Commission of the European Communities. Volume 1. Munich : Verlag Dokumentation, 1977 : 101-121.

Discusses specific problems of multilingual terminological work and proposes an interchange format for terminological data.

1147 Bivins, Kathleen T.

An approach to an atomic theory of indexing.

New trends in documentation and information. Proceedings of the 39th FID Congress, University of Edinburgh, 25-28 September 1978. Ed. by Peter J. Taylor. London : Aslib, 1980 : 55-60.

Explains the automatic theory of indexing and the applicability of multilingual thesauri.

1148 Bollmann, P. and Konrad, E.

Automatic association methods in the construction of inter-lingual thesauri.

Eurim II : a European conference on the application of research in information services and libraries; *presented by Aslib*. Ed. by W. E. Batten. London : Aslib, 1977 : 152-155.

1149 Brendler, G.

The multilingual thesaurus : a tool for rationalising information flow.

Informatika 17 (4) 1970 : 19-24.

1150 Clavel-Merrin, G.

Multilingual access to libraries' databases.

Towards a worldwide library : a ten year forecast. Proceedings of the 19th International Essen Symposium 23-26 September 1996. Ed. by Ahmed H. Helal and Joachim W. Weiss. Essen, Germany : Universitatsbibliothek Essen, 1997 : 168-179.

Discusses the need of multilingual thesauri for multilingual access.

1151 Clavel-Merrin, G.

The need for co-operation in creating and maintaining multilingual subject authority files.

International Cataloguing and Bibliographic Control 29 (3) July –Sept. 2000 : 43-45.

Also available at : http://www.bl.uk.gabriel//cobra/finrap3.html

1152 Crofts, B. A.

Problems associated with the development and maintenance of a multilingual thesaurus.

Report of a workshop on multilingual systems. Ed. by Verina Horsnell. London : British Library Research and Development

Department, 1976 : 8-9.

1153 Delbos, L.

International Union of Geological Sciences Committee on Geological Documentation.

Proceedings of the full board meetings, Brussels, Belgium, June 1975. Paris : International Council of Scientific Unions Abstracting Board, 1975 : 23-24.

Describes the activities of a special Working Group engaged in the compilation of a multilingual thesaurus for the earth sciences.

1154 Dextre Clarke, Stella G.

The construction of a multilingual thesaurus based on classified structure.

Knowledge organization for information retrieval. Proceedings of the 6th International Study Conference on Classification Research, University College London, 16-18 June 1997. The Hague, Netherlands : International Federation for Information and Documentation, 1997 : 120-128.

1155 Doerr, Martin and Fundulaki, Irini.

SIS – TMS : a thesaurus management system for distributed digital collections.

Research and Advanced Technology for Digital Libraries : Second European Conference, ECDL'98, Heraklion, Crete, Greece, September 21-23, 1998, Proceedings. Ed. By C. Nikolaou & C. Stephanidis. Heidelberg : Springer, 1998. - (Lecture Notes on Computer Science ; 1513). : 215-234.

Also available at : http://zeus.ics.forth.gr/forth/ics/isl/publications/paperlink/edl_98_springer.ps.gz

Preseents a system for managing multilingual thesauri.

1156 Dorst, L.

Restoring the Tower of Babel : building a multilingual thesaurus on health promotion.

Health Libraries Review 15 (1) March 1998 : 33-39.

1157 Dubois, C. P. R.

Multilingual information systems : some criteria for the choice of specific techniques.

Journal of Information Science 1 (1) April 1979 : 5-12.

Discusses techniques including multilingual thesauri to be applied in selecting multilingual systems.

1158 European Cooperation in Social Science Information and Documentation, Working Group 3.

ECSSID Working Group 3 meets in Bonn.

ECSSID Bulletin 6 (1) 1984 : 6-8.

Lists articles presented and recommendations made regarding multilingual thesauri by the meeting of Working Group 3 of European Cooperation in Social Science Information and Documentation.

1159 Failla, D.

Japanese lacquer art and lacquered furniture : two multilingual facetted microthesauri.

Proceedings of the 3rd International Society for Knowledge Organization (ISKO) Conference : Knowledge organization and quality management. Copenhagen, Denmark, 20-24 June 1994. Ed. by Hanne Albrechtsen and Susan Oernager, Frankfurt/Main : INDEKS Verlag, 1994 : 233-241.

1160 Felber, Helmut.

UDC and terminology.

International Forum on Information and Documentation 8 (2) April 1983 : 7-9.

States the need for a common ordering scheme applicable in multilingual thesauri.

1161 Field, B. J.

Automatic indexing for multilingual systems.

Third European congress on information systems and networks

: overcoming the language barrier. Luxembourg, 3-6 May 1977. Organized by the Commission of the European Communities. Volume 1. Munich : Verlag Dokumentation, 1977 : 469-492.

Describes techniques for automatic assignment of subject headings from English and French language thesauri.

1162 Fluhr, C.

Lexical knowledge and general public online search.

Information Studies 4 (4) Oct. 1998 : 208-211.

Discusses issues of vocabulary control related with cross-lingual searching.

1163 Francu, Victoria.

The impact of specificity on the retrieval power of a UDC-based multilingual thesaurus.

Cataloging and Classification Quarterly 37 (1-2) 2004 : 49-64.

Discusses issues of harmonizing a classificatory structure with a thesaurus structure.

1164 Geuns, A.

From ecclesiastic to theological libraries : how religious libraries cope with diversity in Europe.

Bulletin of the Association of British Theological and Philosophical Libraries 7 (3) Nov. 2000 : 13-22.

Discusses the ETHERELI project aimed to develop a Multilingual Thesaurus for Religion and other aspects of religious libraries in Europe.

1165 Geuns, A. and Hall, P. R.

Partners with Europe.

Bulletin of the Association of British Theological and Philosophical Libraries 5 (3) Nov. 1998 : 9-15.

Discusses issues related with theological libraries in Europe and the ETHERELI project, which seeks to develop a multilingual thesaurus.

1166 Gray, D. E.

Veterinary information : the current situation and future trends.

Veterinary Record 98 (14) 3 April 1976 : 271-274.

Describes the activities of the Commission of the European Community's 'veterinary round table' one of which is the compilation of a multi-lingual thesaurus.

1167 Hall, P. R.

International librarianship and the advance of global communication.

Bulletin of the Association of British Theological and Philosophical Libraries 6 (3) Nov. 1999 : 14-16.

Proposes creation of a multilingual thesaurus for theological libraries.

1168 Hargreaves, Peter.

On-line information retrieval from foreign language data bases.

Loughborough : Loughborough University of Technology, 1980. 160p.

Highlights importance of multilingual thesauri for multilingual searching.

1169 Hood, Martha W. and Ebermann, Christine.

Reconciling the CAB Thesaurus and AGROVOC.

Quarterly Bulletin of the International Association of Agricultural Information Specialists 35 (4) 1990 : 181-185.

Discusses issues encountered in reconciling descriptors from the CAB thesaurus into Agricola's AGROVOC (a multilingual thesaurus) descriptors.

1170 Hudon, M.

Compatibility and identity are not synonyms : conceptual structures in multilingual thesauri.

Information Studies 4 (4) Oct. 1998 : 202-207.

Discusses the representation of non-hierarchic associative relations in multilingual (and multicultural) thesauri.

1171 Hudon, M.

Multilingual thesaurus construction - integrating the views of different cultures in one gateway to knowledge and concepts.

Information Services and Use 17 (2-3) 1997 : 111-123.

1172 Hudon, M.

Multilingual thesaurus construction : integrating the views of different cultures in one gateway to knowledge and concepts.

Knowledge Organization 24 (2) 1997 : 84-91.

1173 Iljon, A.

Creation of thesauri for EURONET.

Third European congress on information systems and networks : overcoming the language barrier. Luxembourg, 3-6 May 1977. Organized by the Commission of the European Communities. Volume 1. Munich : Verlag Dokumentation, 1977 : 417-437.

Describes the method followed for the compilation of multilingual thesauri in three fields i.e. veterinary science; food science and technology; agricultural management and rural sociology.

1174 Jorna, K. and Davies, S.

Multilingual thesauri for the modern world - no ideal solution?

Journal of Documentation 57 (2) March 2001 : 284-295.

Describes methodology for development of a multilingual thesauri and introduces InfoDEFT- a pilot thesaurus.

1175 Krieger, C. and Schmid, H.

The thesaurus implementation for AGRIS on CD-ROM.

Quarterly Bulletin of the International Association of Agricultural Information Specialists 38 (4) 1993 : 185-189.

Describes the implementation of AGROVOC - a multilingual thesaurus of agriculture to CD-ROM database of AGRIS.

1176 Lebowitz, Abraham I.; Zwart, Robert Portegies and Schmid, Helga.

Multilingual indexing and retrieval in bibliographic systems : the AGRIS experience.

Quarterly Bulletin of the International Association of Agricultural Information Specialists 36 (3) 1991 : 187-192.

Describes the development and maintenance of AGROVOC – a multilingual thesaurus of agriculture.

1177 Li, Kar Wing and Yang, Christopher C.

Automatic crosslingual thesaurus generated from the Hong Kong SAR police department web corpus for crime analysis.

Journal of the American Society for Information Science and Technology 56 (3) Feb. 2005 : 272-282.

1178 Li, Kar Wing and Yang, Christopher C.

Building parallel corpora by automatic title alignment using length-based and text-based approaches.

Information Processing and Management 40 (6) Nov. 2004 : 939-955.

States the need to overcome limitations of controlled vocabulary while cross-lingual IR and explains methods for developing parallel corpora.

1179 Mack, R.

Creation of the veterinary multilingual thesaurus of 1979.

Quarterly Bulletin of the International Association of Agricultural Information Specialists 27 (3) 1982 : 87-89.

Describes stages and processes through which the multilingual thesaurus of veterinary science was constructed.

1180 Molster, H. C.

A proposal for an AGRIS Level Two system applied to forestry

Quarterly Bulletin of the International Association of Agricultural Information Specialists 23 (1-2) 1978 : 5-9.

Proposes a structure for an AGRIS forestry databases which includes the development of a multilingual thesaurus.

1181 Musso, V. and Zangrando, R.

The Fiat Thesaurus : an experiment by a multinational company.

Third European congress on information systems and networks : overcoming the language barrier. Luxembourg, 3-6 May 1977. Organized by the Commission of the European Communities. Volume 1. Munich : Verlag Dokumentation, 1977 : 57-70.

Describes the Fiat company's thesaurus which mainly contains vocabulary in the Italian languages, however terms from other language are also represented.

1182 Neelameghan, A.

Lateral relations and links in multicultural, multimedia databases in the spiritual and religious domains : some observations.

Information Studies 4 (4) Oct. 1998 : 221-246.

Suggests ways to identify various types of relationships among concepts for constructing multilingual thesauri.

1183 Neelameghan, A.

Lateral relations and links in multicultural, multimedia databases in the spiritual and religious domains : some observations.

Knowledge Organization 26 (2) 1999 : 74-79.

Suggests ways to identify various types of relationships among concepts for constructing multilingual thesauri.

1184 Neelameghan, A. and Prasad, K. N.

Lateral relations among concepts.

Information Studies 7 (2) April 2001 : 75-100.

1185 Neumann Duscha, I. and Ulenberg, G.

The thesaurus of the European Brewery Convention.

Third European congress on information systems and networks: overcoming the language barrier. Luxembourg, 3-6 May 1977. Organized by the Commission of the European Communities. Volume 1. Munich : Verlag Dokumentation, 1977 : 439-446.

Reports methods used for the compilation of a multilingual thesaurus, in English, French, German and Dutch.

1186 Neville, H. H.

Alternatives to conventional multilingual thesauri.

Report of a workshop on multilingual systems. Ed by Verina Horsnell. London : British Library Research and Development Department, 1976 : 10-12.

Describes 4 alternatives to or unconventional uses of multilingual thesauri.

1187 Raghavan, K. S. and Chandrakumar, V.

Databases in Indian languages : some issues.

Information management in academic and research libraries. Proceedings of the 5th National Convention for Automation of Libraries in Education and Research (CALIBER-98), Bhubaneswar, India, 4-5 March 1998. Ed. by M. Mahapatra et.al. Ahmedabad : INFLIBNET 1998 : 233-243.

Asserts the need for developing multilingual thesauri in Indian languages.

1188 Retti, Gregor and Stehno, Birgit.

The Laurin thesaurus : a large, multilingual, electronic thesaurus for newspaper clipping archives.

Journal of Documentation 60 (3) 2004 : 289-301.

1189 Rolling, Loll.

Computer management of multilingual thesauri.

Aslib Proceedings 23(11) November 1971 : 591-594.

1190 Rolling, Loll.

Multilingual systems : survey of the European scene.

Report of a workshop on multilingual systems. Ed by Verina Horsnell. London : British Library Research and Development Department, 1976 : 4-5.

Discusses the problems of multilingual thesauri, and the machine translation of abstracts and natural language text.

1191 Sager, J. C.; Sommers, H. L. and McNaught, J.

Guidelines for the establishment of comparison and compatibility matrices between thesauri in the social sciences.

Manchester : University of Manchester Institute of Science and Technology, Centre for Computational Linguistics, 1981.

Examines various thesauri in the social sciences and compares them with standards and guidelines for the development of multi-lingual thesauri.

1192 Sager, J. C.; Somers, H. L. and McNaught, J.

Thesaurus integration in the social sciences. Part I : comparison of thesauri.

International Classification 8 (3) 1981 : 133-138.

First part of a 3 part article compares thesauri as a part of creation of an integrated multilingual thesaurus for the social sciences.

1193 Sager, J. C.; Somers, H. L. and McNaught, J.

Thesaurus integration in the social sciences. Part II : stages towards integration.

International Classification 9 (1) 1982 : 19-26.

Second part of a 3 part article explains steps in the creation of an integrated multilingual thesaurus for the social sciences.

1194 Sager, J. C.; Somers, H. L. and McNaught, J.

Thesaurus integration in the social sciences. Part III : Guidelines for the integration of thesauri.

International Classification 9 (2) 1982 : 64-70.

Last part of a 3 part article provides guidelines for the creation of an integrated multilingual thesaurus for the social sciences.

1195 Schmitz-Esser, W.

Thesaurus and beyond : an advanced formula for linguistic engineering and information retrieval.

Knowledge Organization 26 (1) 1999 : 10-22.

Suggests a new method for construction and integration of multilingual thesauri.

1196 Schrader, Siegfried and Molster, H. C.

Strategies for the development of AGRIS Forestry-comments on a proposal of H. C. Molster.

Quarterly Bulletin of the International Association of Agricultural Information Specialists 24 (1) Winter-Spring 1979 : 14-16.

Comments on H. C. Molster's proposals for the structure of an AGRIS forestry database and suggests that a multilingual system using a multilingual controlled vocabulary would be the most suitable option.

1197 Schubert, K.

Parameters for the design of an intermediate language for multilingual thesauri.

Knowledge Organization 22 (3-4) 1995 : 136-140.

1198 Semturs, F.

Information retrieval from documents in multilingual textual data banks.

Third European congress on information systems and networks: overcoming the language barrier. Luxembourg, 3-6 May 1977. Organized by the Commission of the European Communities. Volume 1. Munich : Verlag Dokumentation, 1977 : 463-467.

Illustrates the use of multilingual thesaurus in searching multilingual textual databank.

1199 Stern, Alice and Rischette, Norbert.

On the construction of a super thesaurus based on existing

thesauri.

Tools for knowledge organisation and the human interface. Proceedings of the 1st International ISKO Conference, Darmstadt, (Germany) *14-17 August 1990. Advances in knowledge organization, no. 1/2.* Ed. by R. Fugmann. Part II. Frankfurt/Main : Indeks. 1990 : 134-144.

Reports an ongoing project aimed to create a multilingual thesaurus from several existing thesauri in different subject fields.

1200 Szilard, Paula.

AGROVOC : a multilingual agricultural thesaurus.

Journal of Agricultural and Food Information 2 (1) 1994 : 119.

1201 Van Slype, G.

The qualitative and quantitative characteristics of monolingual and multilingual thesauri.

Third European congress on information systems and networks : overcoming the language barrier. Luxembourg, 3-6 May 1977. Organized by the Commission of the European Communities. Volume 1. Munich : Verlag Dokumentation, 1977 : 403-415.

Compares 20 recently compiled monolingual / multilingual thesauri.

1202 Wolff Terroine, M.

Multilingual systems.

Second European congress on information systems and networks, Luxembourg, 27-30 May 1975. Organised by the Commission of the European Communities. Munich : Verlag Dokumentation, 1976 : 149-158.

Discusses compilation of multilingual thesaurus as one of the important aspect of developing multilingual systems.

1203 Wolpert, Samuel A.

A command language for the executive.

Information Services and Use 3 (5) Oct. 1983 : 261-272.

Describes the Predicasts program, which has multilingual thesaurus and other features.

1204 Wu, Guang-wei.

Survey of term equivalence between English, Japanese and Chinese.

*Tools for knowledge organisation and the human interface. Proceedings of the 1st International ISKO Conference, Darmstadt, (*Germany) *14-17 August 1990. Advances in knowledge organization, no. 1/2.* Ed. by R. Fugmann. Part I. Frankfurt/Main : Indeks. 1990 : 108 - 111.

Presents results of a survey of term equivalence between English and German, Japanese and Chinese, which is useful in constructing multilingual thesauri.

1205 Zingel, Hermann Josef.

Experiences with TITUS II.

International Classification 5 (1) March 1978 : 33-37.

Describes TITUS i.e. Textile Information Treatment Users' Service which uses a automatic vocabulary translation software so as to enable multilingual retrieval.

Section O2

Standards for multilingual thesaurus

1206 British Standards Institution.

BS 6723 : Guidelines for the establishment and development of multilingual thesauri. 2nd ed.

London : British Standards Institution, 1985.

1207 International Organization for Standardization.

ISO 5964 : Guidelines for the establishment and development of multilingual thesauri.

Geneva : International Organization for Standardization, 1985.

1208 UNESCO.

Guidelines for the establishment and development of multilingual thesauri.

Paris : UNESCO, 1980.

Section O3
Softwares for multilingual thesauri

1209 Hauer, M.

Building a multilingual company thesaurus : distributed development based on IC INDEX : the Deutsche Post World Net project.

Online information 2001. Proceedings of the International Online Information Meeting, London, 4-6 December 2001. Oxford : Learned Information Europe Ltd, 2001 : 41-47.

Describes methodology adopted for developing a multilingual company thesaurus by using the thesaurus development software named IC INDEX.

Also available at :

http://www.online-information.co.uk/proceedings/online/2001/hauer_m.asp

Section O4
Actual multilingual thesauri

1210 Commission of the European Communities.

Food : Multilingual thesaurus. 2nd ed.

London : Clive Bingley, K. G. Saur, 1979.

1211 Viet, Jean.

EUDISED multilingual thesaurus for information processing in the field of education. 1st English edition.

Paris : Documentation Centre for Education in Europe, 1973. 391p.

Section O5
Bilingual thesauri

1212 Abdoulaye, K.

Perceptions of cataloguers and end-users towards bilingual authority files.

Electronic Library 20 (3) 2002 : 202-210.

1213 Bykova, L. N. et al.

Creation of a bilingual thesaurus for indexing documents and inquiries in the field of nuclear science and technology.

Information Systems, their interconnection and compatibility. Proceedings of a symposium. Vienna : International Atomic Energy Agency, 1975 : 167-174.

1214 Jiun Wu, Wan et al.

AGRI-THESAURUS : a Chinese thesaurus for the Agricultural Science and Technology Information Management System.

Information interaction: proceedings of the 45th ASIS Annual Meeting, 1982. Columbus, Ohio, 17-21 October 1982. Volume 19. Ed. by A. E. Petrarca, C. I. Taylor and R. S. Kohn. White Plains, New York : Knowledge Industry Publications, Inc., 1982 : 342-344.

Describes the AGRI THESAURUS – a Chinese and English bilingual thesaurus.

1215 Merilainen, O.

Descriptor equivalence in the context of bilingual indexing.

Libri 47 (2) June 1997 : 107-113.

Explains the concept of descriptor equivalence through a study of the compatibility of the Finnish language sports thesaurus with the Canadian Sport Thesauri.

1216 Rolland-Thomas, Paul and Mercure, Gerard.

Subject access in a bilingual online catalogue.

Cataloging and Classification Quarterly 10 (1-2) 1989 : 141-163.

Describes use of online bilingual thesaurus in a bilingual OPAC.

1217 Salem, Shawky.

Computerized bilingual thesauri : problems of thesauri construction and development in Arabic languages - case studies.

Microcomputers for Information Management 8 (1) March 1991 : 27-44.

1218 Schuck, H. J.

Linguistic aspects in the translation of thesauri.

Third European congress on information systems and networks: overcoming the language barrier. Luxembourg, 3-6 May 1977. Organized by the Commission of the European Communities. Volume 1. Munich : Verlag Dokumentation, 1977 : 447-462.

Discusses linguistic difficulties in translating the English TEST into German.

1219 Vesenyi, Paul E.

An experiment with bilingual subject headings.

Indexer 10 (2) Oct. 1976 : 73-74.

Section P
Switching vocabulary

Some times a variety of controlled languages such as thesauri, subject headings, classification schemes are produced on one and the same subject. Efforts are made to bring compatibility between these languages through thesaurus mapping. Thesaurus mapping creates link between two or more controlled languages. Another way of thesaurus reconciliation is creating a system for switching vocabulary. This is a system which enables reconciliation of terms from number of thesauri through intermediate language. A fair amount of literature is published on this aspect of thesaurus. This section lists literature dealing with thesaurus mapping, intermediate and switching vocabularies.

1220 Beling, Gerd and Wersig, Gernot.

The new concept of an intermediary language system for information networks.

Eurim II : a European conference on the application of research in information services and libraries ; presented by Aslib. Ed. by W. E. Batten. London : Aslib, 1977 : 117-121.

1221 Chamis, Alice Yanosko.

Selection of online databases using switching vocabularies.

Journal of the American Society for Information Science 39 (3) May 1988 : 217-218.

Describes the use of Vocabulary Switching System (VSS), and a thesaural relationship model developed to measure the degree of compatibility and switching capability of thesauri and other vocabularies.

1222 Chamis, Alice Yanosko.

The usefulness of switching vocabularies for online databases.

ASIS '85. Proceedings of the 48th ASIS Annual Meeting 1985. Las Vegas, Nevada, 20-24 October 1985. Volume 22. Ed. by Carol A. Parkhurst. White Plains, New York : Knowledge Industry Publications Inc. for the American Society for Information Science, 1985 : 311-314.

1223 Chaplan, M. A.

Mapping Laborline Thesaurus terms to Library of Congress Subject Headings : implications for vocabulary switching.

Library Quarterly 65 (1) Jan. 1995 : 39-61.

Examines the feasibility of automatic vocabulary switching from the Laborline Thesaurus to LCSH.

1224 Coates, E. J.

Third European congress on information systems and networks : overcoming the language barrier; report, and critical appraisal of some interlingual conversion problems in documentation.

London : British Library, 1977. 21p. BLRD report 5380.

1225 Dahlberg, Ingetraut.

Conceptual compatibility of ordering systems.

International Classification 10 (1) 1983 : 5-8.

1226 Dahlberg, Ingetraut.

Towards establishment of compatibility between indexing languages.

International Classification 8(2) 1981 : 86-91.

1227 Fidel, Raya and Efthimiadis, E. N.

Terminological knowledge structure for intermediary expert systems.

Information Processing and Management 31 (1) Jan.-Feb. 1995 : 15-27.

Explains the need of an intermediary expert system containing terminological knowledge structure for term selection and query expansion.

1228 Gilchrist, Alan.

Intermediate languages for switching and control.

Aslib Proceedings 24, 1972 : 387-399.

1229 Halpern, Jacques and Sargent, Heather Anne.

A new end-user interface for bilingual searching of MEDLINE.

Online Information 88. Proceedings of the 12th International Online Information Meeting, London, 6-8 December 1988. Oxford : Learned Information (Europe) Ltd, 1988 : 427-443.

1230 Hammond, William and Staffen Rosenbord.

Experimental study of convertibility between large technical indexing vocabularies – with table of indexing equivalents.

Silver Spring, MD : Datatrol Corp. 1962.

1231 Horsnell, V.

The intermediate lexicon : an aid to international cooperation.

Aslib Proceedings 27(2) February 1975 : 57-66.

1232 Landry, Patrice.

Multilingual subject access : the linking approach of MACS.

Cataloging and Classification Quarterly 37 (3-4) 2004 : 177-191.

Explains the MACS (Multilingual access to subjects) project, which is exploring solutions to multilingual subject access to online catalogs by developing Web-based link and search interface through which equivalents between three Subject Heading Languages-SWD/RSWK (Schlagwortnormdatei/ Regeln fur den Schlagwortkatalog) for German, RAMEAU (Repertoire d'Autorite-Matiere Encyclopedique et Alphabetique Unific) for French, and LCSH (Library of Congress Subject Headings) for English-can be created and maintained.

1233 Muraszkiewicz, H. et al.

Software problems of merging thesauri.

Compatibility and integration of order systems : Research Seminar Proceedings of the TPI/ISKO Meeting, Warsaw, 13-15 September, 1996. Warsaw, Wydawnictwo, SPB, 1996 : 58-67.

1234 Niehoff, R. T.

Development of an integrated energy vocabulary and the possibilities for on-line subject switching.

Journal of the American Society for Information Science 27 (1) Jan.-Feb. 1976 : 3-17.

Explains the development of an integrated vocabulary of energy terminology and explores the possibility for a fully developed vocabulary switching system.

1235 Niehoff, Robert and Mack, Greg.

The vocabulary switching system.

International Classification 12(1) 1985 : 2-6.

1236 Silvester, J. P. and Klingbiel, P. H.

An operational systems for subject switching between controlled vocabularies.

Information Processing and Management 29(1) 1993 : 47-59.

1237 Soergel, Dagobert.

Data model for an integrated thesaurus database.

Compatability and integration of order system. Research Seminar Proceedings of the TIP/ISKO meeting, Warwaw, 13-15 September 1996. Warwaw : Wydawnictwo SBP, 1996 : 47-57.

1238 Vilenskaya, S. K.

On the compatibility of different information retrieval languages within the integrated information system.

New trends in documentation and information. Proceedings of the 39th FID Congress, University of Edinburgh, 25-28 September 1978. Ed. by Peter J. Taylor. London : Aslib, 1980 : 315-325.

Section Q
Thesaurus and classification

Thesaurus and classification schemes share many common features. As such for constructing both, the thesaurus and a classification scheme an analogous methodology is adopted. Many a time a thesaurus is constructed by using an existing or specially constructed classification scheme. Also in many thesauri entries are arranged in a systematic way (following classificatory structure) apart from alphabetical order. So there exists literature discussing the symbiotic relationship between the classification scheme and the thesaurus. This section lists literature on thesaurus and classification.

1239 Abell, A.

Business services thesaurus for Business Link.

Information Management Report June 1994 : 16-19.

Reports the work of 'Business Link project (UK)', which has constructed controlled subject structure i. e. a combination of thesaurus and classification scheme for business services information.

1240 Aitchison, Jean.

A classification as a source for thesaurus : the Bibliographic Classification of H. E. Bliss as a source of thesaurus terms and structure.

Journal of Documentation 42 (3) Sept. 1986 : 160-181.

Difficulties, advantages and the future of using the 2nd ed. of Bliss Bibliographic Classification for thesaurus construction is discussed.

1241 Aitchison, Jean.

A thesaurus for LCBS.

London Classification of Business Studies : report of the 3rd

Seminar held at Oxford Management Centre 11 June 1976. London : London Business School, 1976 : 16-18.

Describes the thesaurus, which supplements the LCBS as its index.

1242 Araghi, Gholamreza Fadaie.

A new scheme for library classification.

Cataloging & Classification Quarterly 38 (2) 2004 : 75-99.

Proposes a hierarchism and binary theory based classification scheme and explains its usefulness in thesaurus construction.

1243 Bakewell, K. G. B.; Lang, Valerie and Vernon, K. D. C.

The London Classification of Business Studies : further progress towards a revised edition.

Aslib Proceedings 29 (2) Feb. 1977 : 104-109.

Discusses the proposed revisions to the London Classification of Business Studies, converting the index into an index-thesaurus is one of the proposal.

1244 Benediktsson, Daniel.

Problems of subject access to Icelandic collections throughout OPACs.

Scandinavian Public Library Quarterly 23 (4) 1990 : 24-27.

Discusses problems of Iceland's OPAC system. These are lack of compatibility among computer systems adopted by the major libraries, the differing classification schemes, and the lack of controlled indexing vocabulary.

1245 Blanken, R. R. and Stern, B. T.

Structuring the Excerpta Medica thesaurus via a poly-hierarchic decimal classification system.

Eurim II : a European conference on the application of research in information services and libraries 23-25 March 1976, RAI International Congrescentrum, Amsterdam, Netherlands. Presented by Aslib. Ed. by W. E. Batten. London : Aslib, 1977 : 148-150.

1246 Broughton, V.

Faceted classification as a basis for knowledge organization in a digital environment : the Bliss Bibliographic Classification and the creation of multi-dimensional knowledge structures.

New Review of Hypermedia and Multimedia 7, 2001 : 67-102.

Describes the philosophy and function of BC2 and the process of building a knowledge structure based on it, which can function as thesaurus, subject headings list.

1247 Chan, Lois Mai and Zeng, Marcia Lei.

Trends and issues in establishing interoperability among knowledge organization systems.

Journal of the American Society for Information Science and Technology 55 (5) March 2004 : 377-395.

Discusses the methodologies used in establishing interoperability among knowledge organization systems (KOS) such as controlled vocabularies and classification schemes that present the organized interpretation of knowledge structures.

1248 Dahlberg, Ingetraut.

The Broad System of Ordering (BSO) as a basis for an Integrated Social Science Thesauri?

International Classification 7 (2) 1980 : 66-72.

Examines the feasibility of using the BSO as the basis for generating an integrated thesaurus of the social sciences.

1249 Elizabeth Moys awarded MBE.

Catalogue and Index (135) Spring 2000 : 3.

Reports about the award given to Elizabeth ('Betty') Moys and describes how Betty Moys developed the Moys classification and thesaurus for legal materials.

1250 Gilchrist, Alan.

Classification and subject indexing.

British librarianship and information work. Ed. by H. A. Whatley. London : Library Association, 1977 : 57-64.

Describes the INSPEC thesaurus, the Construction Industry Thesaurus and the London Classification of Business Studies.

1251 Gilchrist, Alan.

Classification and thesauri.

Fifty years of information progress : a Journal of Documentation review. Ed. by B. C. Vickery.

London : Aslib, 1994 : 85-118.

1252 Godby, C. J. and Reighart, R.

Terminology identification in a collection of Web resources.

Journal of Internet Cataloging 4 (1-2) 2001 : 49-65.

Describes the Cooperative Online Resource Catalogue programme which identifies terms for classification schemes and thesaurus

1253 Godby, J. and Vizine-Goetz, D.

ISKO participants discuss ways librarianship can improve responsiveness of the Web.

OCLC Newsletter (247) Sept.-Oct. 2000 : 22-25.

Reports an ISKO conference, which discussed shortcomings of knowledge organization schemes such as thesaurus developed for the Web without input from the classification research.

1254 Gopinath, M. A.

Lexicographic approach to classification and thesaurus construction.

International Information Communication and Education 20 (1) March 2001 : 13-24.

Describes thesaurus construction method based on classification.

1255 Gopinath, M. A.

Symbiosis between classification and thesaurus.

Library Science with a Slant to Documentation 24 (4) Dec. 1987 : 211-225.

Discusses the symbiotic relations in the procedure for the construction of a classification scheme and a thesaurus.

1256 Gopinath, M. A. and Prasad, K. N.

Compatibility of the principles for design of thesaurus and classification scheme.

Library Science with a Slant to Documentation 13 (2) June 1976 : 56-66.

Discusses the compatibility of ISO guidelines for thesaurus construction with classification scheme construction.

1257 Gopinath, M. A. and Prasad, K. N.

Thesaurus and classification scheme : a study of compatibility of principles for construction of thesaurus and classification schemes.

Seminar on thesaurus in information systems. Banglore : DRTC, 1975 : Paper AF.

1258 Konig, E.

Application of an expert system to assist retrieval from agricultural databases (AGRIRES).

Quarterly Bulletin of the International Association of Agricultural Information Specialists 37 (1-2) 1992 : 31-34.

Describes AGRIRES - an agricultural expert system based on various agricultural thesauri and classification schemes.

1259 Korevaar, J. D.

Thesaurus problems : UDC and legal literature.

International Journal of Law Libraries 2 (1) March 1974 : 20-21.

1260 Kumbhar Rajendra and Vaishnav A. A.

Depth classification's application in thesaurus construction : a case study.

Information management : trends and issues. Ed. by Ramesh Babu, A. A. Vaishnav, and S. Gopalkrishan, New Delhi, Researchco Book Centre, 2003 : 227-235.

1261 Kumbhar Rajendra.

Speciator based faceted depth classification's application in thesaurus construction.

Annals of Library and Information Studies, 52(1) March 2005 : 15-24.

1262 Lansky, R.

Resolution to create a uniform legal thesaurus and a uniform legal classification system for the German Federal Republic.

Zeitschrift fur Bibliothekswesen und Bibliographie 20 (4) July-August 1973 : 285-287.

1263 Maltby, Arthur.

Dewey Decimal Classification : a liability?

Catalogue and Index (72) Spring 1984 : 4-5.

Describes features of DDC and the Curriculum thesaurus being developed at Aberdeen University, Scotland, as alternatives to DDC.

1264 McIlwaine, I. C. and Williamson, N. J.

A feasibility study on the restructuring of the Universal Decimal Classification into a full-faceted classification system.

Proceedings of the 3rd International Society for Knowledge Organization (ISKO) Conference : Knowledge organization and quality management, Copenhagen, Denmark, 20-24 June 1994. Ed. by Hanne Albrechtsen and Susan Oernager. Frankfurt/Main : INDEKS Verlag, 1994 : 406-413.

Proposes a methodology for restructuring of UDC and a thesaurus derived from the restructured scheme, which will act as an index to it.

1265 Neelameghan, A. and Prasad, K. N.

Digitized schemes for subject classification and thesauri :

complementary roles.

Information Studies 8 (1) Jan. 2002 : 25-42.

1266 Neil, A. G.

The new London Education Classification and Thesaurus : a critique.

Education Libraries Bulletin 17 (3) Autumn 1974 : 11-20.

1267 Pickles, Stephen.

Using LEC2 to index a pilot study of the computer generation of catalogues to a thesis collection.

Education Libraries Bulletin 19 (3) Autumn 1976 : 22-25.

Reports an indexing pilot study which used the second edition of the London education classification : a thesaurus / classification of British education terms.

1268 Riesthuis, Gerhard J. A. and Bliedung, Steffi.

Thesaurification of the UDC.

*Tools for knowledge organisation and the human interface. Proceedings of the 1st International ISKO Conference, Darmstadt, (*Germany) *14-17 August 1990. Advances in knowledge organization, no. 1/2.* Ed. by R. Fugmann. Part II. Frankfurt/Main : Indeks. 1990 : 109-117.

Describes an experiment to construct a thesaurus of UDC class 314-Demography

1269 Riesthuis, Gerhard J. A. and Storm, R.

GOO : the Dutch National System for subject indexing.

International Cataloguing and Bibliographic Control 28 (4) Oct.–Dec. 1999 : 91-93.

Describes Dutch Basic Classification (BC) and a national thesaural system, the GOO Subject Headings Thesaurus (GTT) used for maintaining and searching the NCC (Dutch Union Catalogue) is an integrated catalogue of about 400 Dutch libraries.

1270 Rixon, J. P.

A comparison between the INSPEC Classification and Thesaurus.

London : City University, 1983. 71p.

1271 Robinson, C.

Records control and disposal using functional analysis

Archives and Manuscripts 25 (2) Nov. 1997 : 288-303.

Explains use of functional analysis for developing a business thesaurus and classification scheme.

1272 Scibor, Eugeniusz.

UDC in relation to thesauri : a state-of-the-art report.

New trends in documentation and information: proceedings of the 39th FID Congress, University of Edinburgh, 25-28 September 1978. Ed. by Peter J. Taylor. London : Aslib, 1980 : 248-258.

Compares UDC and thesauri and explains a method to bring the UDC structure nearer to the structure of thesauri.

1273 Wang, Jun.

A knowledge network constructed by integrating classification, thesaurus, and metadata in digital library.

International Information and Library Review 35 (2-4) June-Dec. 2003 : 383-397.

Describes the procedure adopted in creating a knowledge network by integrating Chinese classification and thesaurus.

1274 Weinberg, B. H.

Library classification and information retrieval thesauri : comparison and contrast.

Cataloging and Classification Quarterly 19 (3-4) 1995 : 23-44.

Discusses the complementary roles of classification and thesauri.

1275 Whitehead, Cathleen.

Faceted classification in the Art and Architecture Thesaurus.

Art Documentation 8 (4) Winter 1989 : 175-177.

Describes how the ATT's faceted hierarchies function as a classification system for subject cataloguing.

1276 Will, L.

The indexing of museum objects.

Indexer 18 (3) April 1993 : 157-160.

Describes a project of developing comprehensive data standards for indexing museum objects and the role of thesaurus-controlled indexing, classification schemes and free-text indexing.

1277 Yoshida, S.

Construction of library and information science thesaurus.

International Information Communication and Education 12 (2) Sept. 1993 : 166-172.

Reports development of a Japanese thesaurus based on faceted classification.

Section R
Thesaurofacet and classaurus

By using the classification schemes as a basis, two types of thesauri are constructed. They are thesaurofacet and classaurus.

The literature listed under each of these categories deals with construction and use of thesaurofacet and classaurus respectively. Section R1 lists literature on thesaurofacet and Section R2 lists literature on classaurus.

Section R1
Thesaurofacet

1278 Aitchison, Jean.

The thesaurofacet : a multipurpose retrieval language tool.

Journal of Documentation 26 (3) Sept. 1970 : 187-203.

1279 Aitchison, Jean; Gomersall, A. and Ireland, R.

Thesaurofacet : a thesaurus and faceted classification for engineering and related subjects.

Whetstone : English Electric Company, 1969. 491p.

1280 Ciganik, M.

Thesaurus on the basis of facet classification.

Kniznice a Vedecke Informacie 2 (1) 1970 : 3-18.

1281 Negrini, G.

CLASTHES : a thesaurofacet creator.

Library Science with a Slant to Documentation 31 (1) March 1994 : 1-12.

Describes CLASTHES- a software meant for creating a thesaurofacet.

1282 Popowska, H.

A 'Thesaurofacet'-an example of combining a facet classification with a thesaurus.

Aktualne Problemy Informacji Dokumentacji 17 (4) 1972 : 6-12.

Section R2
Classaurus

1283 Bhattacharyya, G.

Classaurus : its fundamentals, design and use.

Proceedings of 4th International Study Conference on Classification Research. Augsburg, 28th June – 2nd July 1982. Indeks Verlag : Frankfurt, 1982 : 139-148.

1284 Biswas, Subal C. and Smith, Fred.

Classed thesauri in indexing and retrieval : a literature review and critical evaluation of online alphabetic classaurus.

Library and Information Science Research 11 (2) April-June 1989 : 109-141.

1285 Biswas, Subal C. and Smith, Fred

Computerised Deep Structure Indexing System-a critical appraisal

International Classification 15 (1) 1988 : 2-12.

Explains the DSIS - a version of POPSI. DSIS uses vocabulary control tool such as classaurus and other useful components like syntax rules and a set of postulated Elementary Categories.

1286 Dasgupta, S.

Financial economics : a classaurus. (Guided research project submitted in partial fulfillment of the course leading to the award of Associateship in Documentation of Information Science.

Banglore : DRTC, 1988.

1287 Devadason, Francis Jawahar.

Computer based system for generating different types of subject indexes and alphabetical classaurus based on the "deep structure" subject indexing language. (Ph. D. thesis).

Dharwad, Karnataka University, 1984.

1288 Devadason, Francis Jawahar.

Computer generation of different types of subject index entries based on deep structure of subject indexing languages : deep structure indexing system

ASIS '85. Proceedings of the 48th ASIS Annual Meeting 1985. Las Vegas, Nevada, 20-24 October 1985. Volume 22. Ed. by Carol A. Parkhurst. White Plains, New York : Knowledge Industry Publications Inc. for the American Society for Information Science, 1985 : 88-96.

Describes DSIS – an indexing system based on classaurus.

1289 Devadason, Francis Jawahar.

Computerization of deep structure based indexes.

International Classification 12 (2) 1985 : 87-94.

Explains the computerization of Deep Structure Indexing System, which uses classaurus along-with other elements.

1390 Devadason, Francis Jawahar.

Online construction of alphabetic classaurus : a vocabulary control and indexing tool.

Information Processing and Management 21 (1) 1985 : 111-126.

Defines classaurus and explains methodology online construction of classaurus.

1291 Fugmann, Robert.

An interactive classaurus on the PC.

International Classification 17 (3-4) 1990 : 133-137.

Describes the construction and use of classauri during computer aided indexing.

Section S

Lists of subject headings

The subject heading lists too help in the vocabulary control. They are similar to thesaurus in their structure. Due to this reason other sections of the bibliography also have literature dealing with various aspects of subject headings lists. So this Section lists 'subject heading lists'.

1292 American Library Association.
List of subject headings for use in dictionary catalogue.
Boston, Mass. : Library Bureau, 1895.

1293 Charen, Thelma.
Medical Subject Headings : Tree Annotations, 1980.
Bethesda, MD : National Library of Medicine, 1979. 126p.

1294 Charen, Thelma.
Medical Subject Headings : Tree Annotations, 1983.
Bethesda, MD : National Library of Medicine, 1982. 125p.

1295 Foster, Nancy.
Subject headings listing for small instructional materials centers.
Arlington, VA : Educational Resources Information Center, 1980. 29p.

1296 Library of Congress.
Free-floating sub-divisions : an alphabetical index.
Washington DC : Cataloguing Distribution Services, Library of Congress, 1989.

1297 Library of Congress.
Library of Congress subject headings.
Washington DC : Cataloguing Distribution Services, Library

of Congress, 1910-1914.

1298 Library of Congress.

Revised Library of Congress subject headings : cross references from former to current subject headings, compiled from the online subject authority file of the Library of Congress, 1st ed.

Washington DC : Cataloguing Distribution Services, Library of Congress, 1991.

1299 Mason, B. M. and Thompson, A.

List of subject headings on architecture and related subjects. Revised ed.

London, Royal Institute of British Architects, 1968, 208p.

1300 Miller, J. *Ed.*

Sears list of subject headings. 15th Ed.

New York : H. W. Wilson, 1994.

1301 National Library of Medicine.

Medical Subject Headings (MeSH)

Bethesda, MD : National Library of Medicine Annual update.

Also available at : http://www.nlm.nih.gov/mesh

http://www.nlm.nih/gov/mesh/changes2000.html

Section T
Metadata and thesaurus

Metadata are data about the data. The metadata like a catalogue describes the electronic document. As such the metadata record, along with other bibliographic details includes the subject representing terms. To control these terms the thesaurus is useful. Thus there exists a relationship between the metadata and thesaurus. This section lists literature dealing with metadata and thesaurus.

1302 Armstrong, C. J.

Why metadata could offer an answer to the quality question.

Assignation 16 (2) Jan. 1999 : 1-3.

Recommends that metadata is the WWW's equivalent of controlled vocabulary and it will help to search quality information.

1303 Baca, Murtha.

Practical issues in applying metadata schemas and controlled vocabularies to cultural heritage information.

Cataloging and Classification Quarterly 36 (3-4) 2003 : 47-55.

Explains the use of metadata schemas and thesaurus for organizing the cultural heritage information.

1304 Banski, E.

Implementation of the Dublin Core at the University of Alberta libraries.

OCLC Systems and Services 18 (3) 2002 : 130-138.

Explains the implementation of DC metadata and controlled vocabulary.

1305 Boyle, J. M. et al.

Sentence-based metadata : an approach and tool for viewing database designs.

Journal of Information Science 28 (2) 2002 : 143-156.

Explains how the Museum Archive Retrieval System (MARS) through a common thesaurus structure enables organizations to exchange digital images.

1306 Buckland, M. et al.

Mapping entry vocabulary to unfamiliar metadata vocabularies.

D-Lib Magazine 5 (1) Jan. 1999. No page numbers.

Describes California University's (Berkeley) activities regarding the design and development of English language indexes to metadata vocabularies.

Also available at : http://www.dlib.org/dlib/january99/buckland/01buckland.html

1307 Darmoni, S. J. et al.

The use of Dublin Core metadata in a structured health resource guide on the Internet.

Bulletin of the Medical Library Association 89 (3) July 2001 : 297-301.

Describes the Catalogue et Index des Sites Medicaux Francophones (CISMeF) project which uses MeSH and the DC metadata format.

1308 Dextre Clarke, Stella G.

Interoperability : love it or loathe it?

Legal Information Management 3 (3-4) Winter 2003 : 185-187.

Identifies the need for the development of thesaurus and application of the e-government metadata standards for the e-Government Interoperability Framework (e-GIF), which is a collection of standards aimed at improving the UK citizen's access to government information.

1309 Dunn, H.

Collection level description : the museum perspective.

D-Lib Magazine 6 (9) Sept. 2000. No page numbers.

Explains the use of ATT and metadata in describing museum collections on the web.

Also available at : http://www.dlib.org/dlib/september00/dunn/09dunn.html

1310 Graham, S. R. and Ross, D. D.

Metadata and authority control in the Civil Rights in Mississippi Digital Archive.

Journal of Internet Cataloging 6 (1) 2003 : 33-42.

1311 Hearn, S. S.

Metadata structures and authority control.

Technicalities 19 (6) June-July 1999 : 7-9.

1312 Hughes, Baden and Kamat, Amol.

A metadata search engine for digital language archives.

D-Lib Magazine; 11 (2) Feb. 2005. No page numbers.

Describes a metadata search engine for digital archives, which includes a thesaurus of alternate language names and other features.

1313 Mackenzie, Maureen.

A quest for knowledge : the goal of future researchers. Abstracts from the Connections 8 Conference of the Canadian Association for Information Science (Abstracts only)

Canadian Journal of Information and Library Science 27 (4) Dec. 2003 : 55-91.

Gives abstracts of papers presented at Connections 8 conference – one of the themes of the conference was metadata and thesaurus.

1314 Mao, Jun.

Research on the RDF-based thesaurus.

Journal of the China Society for Scientific and Technical Information 22 (2) 2003 : 163-168.

1315 Mathys, Tony.

Metadata matters in the UK.

Burisa (156) June 2003 : 9-12.

Describes thesaurus construction and other areas of cooperation between EDINA (Data Library, Edinburgh University) and the Association for Geographic Information for creation of metadata for geographic information systems.

1316 Rand, R Y. et al.

Libraries, global change data, and information management.

Library Hi Tech 13 (1-2) 1995 : 26-42.

Reports on GCDIS Thesaurus project which includes evaluation of the thesaurus, metadata description and other aspects of the US Global Change Research Program.

1317 Rowlatt, M.

A new profile for citizens' (or community) information?

Ariadne (19) March 1999. No page numbers.

Explains thesaurus development, metadata formats and other efforts towards the development of citizens' information database.

Also available at : http://www.ariadne.ac.uk/issue19/rowlatt/

1318 Rowlatt, M. et al.

SEAMLESS : an organisational and technical model for seamless access to distributed citizens' information.

British Library. Library and Information Commission Research Report (37) 2000 : 127.

Explains thesaurus development, metadata formats and other efforts towards the development of citizens' information database.

1319 Smith, Terence R. and Zeng, Marcia L.

Building semantic tools for concept-based learning spaces :

knowledge bases of strongly-structured models for scientific concepts in advanced digital libraries.

Journal of Digital Information 4 (4) 2003. No page numbers.

Also available at : http://jodi.ecs.soton.ac.uk/Articles/v04/i04/Smith/

Explains the role of thesaurus, metadata and other tools in knowledge management.

1320 Steemson, M.

State of Australasian records management. Cricket, rugby and records management . . . we've set the standard.

Records Management Bulletin (96) April 2000 : 26-31.

Describes various advancements and tools including thesauri and metadata standards developed for records management in Australia.

1321 Wang, Jun.

VISION : a conceptual network integrated classification, thesaurus and semantic metadata.

Journal of the China Society for Scientific and Technical Information 22 (4) 2003 : 412-418.

1322 Westcott, S.

Modernising government : the cataloguing and indexing contribution.

Catalogue and Index (138) Winter 2000 : 1-3.

Explains the need of departmental thesaurus and standard metadata indexing of documents in government departments.

Section U
Uses of thesaurus

Thesauri are primarily used to get standard vocabulary for information storage and retrieval. However thesauri are also useful for getting a map of a given field of knowledge, for locating new concepts in a scheme of relationships.

The literature in this section deals with these and other uses of thesauri. The literature listed in this section also deals with need, importance and functions of thesaurus.

1323 Abbott, R.

'Aboutness' and other problems of text retrieval in the pharmaceutical industry.

Drug Information Journal 31 (1) Jan.-March 1997 : 125-135.

Reports problems in the text retrieval and asserts the need for controlled vocabulary for enhancing the precision.

1324 Adams, Audrey.

Indexing of a computerized bibliography for London's archaeology.

Indexer 14 (4) Oct. 1985 : 235-240.

Explains the importance of controlled vocabulary in indexing a computerized bibliography.

1325 Aitchison, T. M. and Peter, Harding.

Automatic indexing and classification for mechanized information retrieval.

Information management research in Europe : Proceedings of the EURIM 5 conference, Versailles, France May 1982. London : Aslib, 1983 : 47-55.

1326 Alexander, A. and Meehleib, T.

The Thesaurus for Graphic Materials : its history, use and future.

Cataloging and Classification Quarterly 31 (3-4) 2001 : 189-212.

1327 Allen, Lynn.

Alphabetical subject access ; LCSH and a non-traditional approach.

Cataloguing Australia 7 (4) Oct.-Dec. 1981 : 32-41.

1328 Allen, Lynn.

The subject catalogue of the University of Western Australia : some problems and solutions in relation to subject heading practice using LCSH as a base.

Cataloguing Australia 5 (1) Jan.-March 1979 : 38-49.

1329 Aloman, Ileana and Ionescu, Adriana.

Utilization of SPINES thesaurus as an indexing language in the computerized information and documentation system for science policy [in English and Rumanian].

Probleme de Informare si Documentare 17 (4) Dec. 1983 : 218-231.

1330 Aloman, Ileana; Ionescu, Adriana and Ialomiteanu, Alexandra.

Utilization of the SPINES thesaurus as an indexing language in the automated information and documentation system for the field of science policy [in English and Rumanian].

Probleme de Informare si Documentare 17 (1) Jan.-March 1983 : 37-58.

1331 Anholt, Elizabeth and Hurt, Howard.

Undergraduate access to bibliographic databases : a comparison of descriptor-dependent batch searching and online searching of ERIC.

Canadian Journal of Information Science 13 (3-4) Dec. 1988 : 34-39.

1332 ARLIS / NA in Phoenix, Arizona.

Art Documentation 8 (3) Fall 1989 : 115-142.

Reports a conference, which discussed implementation of the AAT's controlled vocabulary in the extended MARC format.

1333 Atherton Cochrane, Pauline et al.

Modern subject access in the online age.

American Libraries 15 (5) May 1984 : 336-339.

1334 Automatic subject lookup.

Silverplatter Exchange 6 (1) Oct. 1993 : 28-29.

Discusses the problems faced by end users while using controlled vocabulary during database searches.

1335 Bainbridge, William Sims.

Massive questionnaires for personality capture.

Social Science Computer Review 21 (3) Fall 2003 : 267-280.

Describes use of thesauri in designing lengthy questionnaires for knowing user's characteristics.

1336 Baird, B. and Sheridan, S.

Indexing the Australian Women's Weekly.

Australian Library Journal 41 (2) May 1992 : 145-150.

Discusses specialties of indexing a women's magazine and the issues related with the choice of a thesaurus for preparing such an index.

1337 Bakewell, K. G. B. et al.

A study of indexers' reactions to the PRECIS indexing system.

Liverpool : Liverpool Polytechnic, Department of Library and Information Studies, 1978. 63p.

Presents a survey that aimed to know British indexers' reactions to PRECIS where some respondents have expressed urgent need for a thesaurus of PRECIS terms.

1338 Baldacchini, Lorenzo.

Authority control of printers, publishers, and booksellers.

Cataloging & Classification Quarterly 38 (3-4) 2004 : 269-280.

Traces the evolution of access points for printers, publishers, and booksellers from eighteenth century to modern bibliographical databases and catalogs of early printed materials, and asserts the need for an authority file covering activities of these agencies.

1339 Ballard, T.

Keyword / Subject : finding the middle path.

Information Today 15 (6) June 1998 : 58.

Suggests a hybrid approach that uses keywords and controlled vocabulary for effective search results.

1340 Banks, B.

Oracle Libraries - multimedia and Windows OPAC.

Vine (90) March 1993 : 14-23.

Describes a OPAC based on Oracle relational database management system and a thesaurus.

1341 Barnes, C. I.; Costantini, L. and Perschke, S.

Automatic indexing using the SLC-II system.

Information Processing and Management 14 (2) 1978 : 107-119.

Compares automatic indexing using a pre-existent thesaurus as it stands, with automatic indexing using the same thesaurus 'enriched', i.e. augmented with terms selected from the texts being indexed.

1342 Barnett, P. J. and Petersen, Toni.

Implementing the Art and Architecture Thesaurus : controlled vocabulary in the extended MARC format.

Art Documentation 8 (4) Winter 1989 : 171-190.

1343 Barratt, A.

Minorities and the MFECANE : adapting Library of Congress Subject Headings for use in a South African Library.

Innovation (10) June 1995 : 21-27.

1344 Bastow, Stan.

ORACLE digests LC subject authorities at State Library of Queensland.

LASIE 14 (5) March-April 1984 : 22.

1345 Bates, Marcia J.

How to use controlled vocabularies more effectively in online searching.

Online '88. Proceedings of the Conference, New York, 11-12 October 1988. Weston, Connecticut, Online Inc., 1988 : 1-6.

1346 Bates, Marcia J.

Integrating the machine-readable LCSH into online catalogs.

Information Technology and Libraries; 7 (3) Sept. 1988 : 299-312.

1347 Bates, Marcia J.

Optimal use of controlled vocabularies in online searching.

Online '87, Proceedings of the Conference, Anaheim, California. Part 1. Weston, CT : Online Inc., 1987 : 14-19.

1348 Bates, Marcia. J.

Subject access in online catalogs : a design model.

Journal of American Society for Information Science 37(6) 1986 : 357-376.

1349 Bates, Marcia J.; Wilde, D. N. and Siegfried, S.

An analysis of search terminology used by humanities scholars : The Getty online searching project report : Number 1.

Library Quarterly 63(1) 1993 : 1-39.

1350 Batty, David.

WWW — wealth, weariness or waste : controlled vocabulary and thesauri in support of online information access.

D-Lib Magazine November 1998. No page numbers.

Also available at : http://www.dlib.org/dlib/november98/11batty.html

1351 Bauer, Gerd.

Knowledge structures promoting problem solutions : possibilities of graphic representation of knowledge in thesaurus-like fashion.

International Classification 16 (2) 1989 : 73-81.

1352 Bauer, Gerd.

Promoting creative processes by a thesaurus-like representation of knowledge structure.

*Tools for knowledge organisation and the human interface. Proceedings of the 1st International ISKO Conference, Darmstadt, (*Germany) *14-17 August 1990. Advances in knowledge organization, no. 1/2.* Ed. by R. Fugmann. Part II. Frankfurt/Main : Indeks. 1990 : 62-69.

Illustrates how graphic representation of knowledge as in thesaurus can promote the creativity in knowledge processing for the purpose of solving scientific problems.

1353 Bawden, David.

Chemical toxicology searching.

Database 2 (2) June 1979 : 11-18.

Describes the procedure, databases and controlled vocabulary used for searching information on chemical toxicology.

1354 Baxter, G. and Anderson, D.

Image indexing and retrieval : some problems and proposed solutions.

New Library World 96 (1123) 1995 : 4-13.

Discusses role of thesauri in image indexing and retrieval.

1355 Benedetti, J. M.

Words, words, words : folk art terminology - why it (still) matters.

Art Documentation 19 (1) 2000 : 14-21.

Explains the importance of standard folk art terminology.

1356 Berger, F. C. and Huibers, T. W. C.

A framework based on situation theory for searching in a thesaurus.

New Review of Document and Text Management 1, 1995 : 253-276.

1357 Berkovich, Simon Ya and Shneiderman, Ben.

Lexical problems in large distributed information systems.

Information Processing and Management 16 (6) 1980 : 259-267.

Describes a lexical subsystem in an information system architecture which deals with linguistic and control functions concerning lexical problems in local and network environments.

1358 Bernier, C. L.

Correlative indexes II : correlative trope indexes.

American Documentation 8 (1) 1957 : 47-50.

1359 Bernier, C. L. and Heumann, K. F.

Correlative indexes III : semantic relations among semantemes – the technical thesaurus.

American Documentation 8 (2) 1957 : 211-220.

1360 Berta, E.

Inter- and intrabibliographical relationships : a concept for a hypercatalog.

Proceedings of the 15th International Essen Symposium : Opportunity 2000 : understanding and serving users in an electronic library. 12-15 October 1992. Ed. by Ahmed H. Helal and Joachim W. Weiss Essen, Germany : Universitatsbibliothek Essen, 1993 : 211-223.

Explains how the thesaurus handling concepts and practices can be applied to create links between bibliographic units in a catalogue.

1361 Bethel, K. E.

Culture keepers : cataloguing the Afrocentric way.

Reference Librarian (45-46) 1994 : 221-240.

Explains the use of controlled vocabulary for the cataloguing of Afrocentricity.

1362 Bielicka, L.

The problem of choice of a descriptor language for use in a system of scientific technical and economic information.

Aktualne Problemy Informacji Dokumentacji 19 (5) 1974 : 8-14.

1363 Binding, Ceri and Tudhope, Douglas.

KOS at your service : programmatic access to knowledge organisation systems.

Journal of Digital Information 4 (4) 2003.

Also available at : http://jodi.ecs.soton.ac.uk/Articles/v04/i04/Binding/

Describes thesaurus as a browsing and search tools.

1364 Blake, P. and Nelson, M.

Ovid unveils Java search client.

Information World Review (120) Dec. 1996 : 31-32.

Thesaurus is described as interface tool in Ovid Technologies Java client.

1365 Bonzi, Susan.

Terminological consistency in abstract and concrete disciplines.

Journal of Documentation 40(4) 1984 : 247-263.

1366 Booth, Pat F.

Thesauri-their uses for indexers.

Indexer 15 (3) April 1987 : 141-144.

1367 Boughanem, Mohand; Loiseau, Yannick and Prade, Henri.

Qualitative pattern matching with linguistic terms.

AI Communications 17 (1) 2004 : 25-34.

Presents the qualitative pattern matching system to match request and data expressed in words with the help of thesaurus or ontology.

1368 Bower, J.

Vocabulary control and the virtual database.

Knowledge Organization 20 (1) 1993 : 4-7.

Describes controlled vocabulary used for indexing virtual databases.

1369 Boyce, Bert R. and McLain, John P.

Entry point depth and online search using a controlled vocabulary.

Journal of the American Society for Information Science 40 (4) July 1989 : 273-276.

Highlights the importance of controlled vocabulary in online search.

1370 Brenner, E. and Lunin, L. F.

Change : the NFAIS 1993 annual conference.

Information Today 10 (5) May 1993 : 52-53.

Reports a conference discussions in the context of changes in various aspects of librarianships including the changes in the context of thesaurus.

1371 Brenner, E. H. et al.

American Petroleum Institute's machine-aided indexing and searching project.

Science and Technology Libraries 5 (1) Fall 1984 : 49-62.

Reports the development of an automated indexing system which will convert words in an abstract and user's query to controlled keywords of the thesaurus for effective retrieval.

1372 Bretney, Nel.

Building a Caribbean bibliographic database : a view from a cataloguer's desk.

Cataloging and Classification Quarterly 8 (3-4) 1988 : 187-197.

Examines the comparative merits of printed and on-line thesauri in the light of building the Caribbean bibliographic database.

1373 Brewin, Paul.

Use of STATUS for housekeeping at the DHSS.

Vine (58) March 1985 : 3-9.

Describes STATUS – a library automation system of Department of Health and Social Security, UK, which links a thesaurus of terms to Bliss Classification numbers.

1374 Briggs, Anne.

Keep it simple : the key to (almost) instant cataloguing.

ASSIGnation 7 (4) July 1990 : 21-22.

Describes the computerized cataloguing system based on classification scheme and a thesaurus.

1375 Brisner, Odd.

A system for automatic indexing and keyword translation as the basis for international co-operation

Information revolution. Proceedings *of the 38th ASIS Annual Meeting*. Volume 12. Ed. by Charles W. Husbands, Ruth L. Tighe. Washington, DC : American Society for Information Science, 1975 : 75-76.

Describes a system that generates descriptors from document titles, abstracts, list of forbidden words, and a thesaurus.

1376 Buchan, Ronald L.

The NASA STI facility.

Sci-Tech News 40 (4) Oct. 1986 : 111-113.

Describes how the NASA Scientific and Technical Information (STI) Facility provides access to aerospace documents by using the NASA thesaurus.

1377 Buchinski, Edwin J.; Newman, William L. and Dunn, Mary Joan.

The automated authority subsystem at the National Library of Canada.

Journal of Library Automation 9 (4) Dec. 1976 : 279-298.

1378 Buckland, Michael.

Vocabulary as a central concept in library and information science.

Digital libraries : interdisciplinary concepts, challenges, and cpportunities. Proceedings of the 3rd International Conference on Conceptions of Library and Information Science. CoLIS3, Dubrovnik, Croatia, 23-26 May 1999. Ed. by T. Arpanac et al. Zagreb : Lokve, 1999 : 3-12.

Also available at : http://www.sims.berkeley.edu/~buckland/colisvoc.htm

Examines the nature and role of vocabulary in information systems.

1379 Burnett, J. E. et al.

Document retrieval experiments using indexing vocabularies of varying size : I - variety generation symbols assigned to the fronts of index terms.

Journal of documentation 35(3) 1979 : 197-206.

1380 Burress, Elaine P.

Automated indexing versus KWOC : a performance comparison.

Journal of the American Society for Information Science 31 (1) Jan. 1980 : 60-61.

Compares the retrieval performance of automated indexing based on controlled vocabulary with KWOC indexing.

1381 Busch, J. A. and Petersen, T.

Automated mapping to topical subject headings into faceted index strings using the 'Art and Architecture Thesaurus' as a machine-readable dictionary.

Proceedings of the 3rd International Society for Knowledge Organization (ISKO) Conference : Knowledge organization and quality management. Copenhagen, Denmark, 20-24 June 1994. Ed. by Hanne Albrechtsen and Susan Oernager, Frankfurt/Main : INDEKS Verlag, 1994 : 390-397.

1382 Cain, A. M.

Thesaural problems in an on-line system.

Bulletin of the Medical Library Association 57 (3) July 1969 : 250-259.

1383 Calabretta, Nancy et al.

Watch your language : a CAI approach to teaching MeSH.

Medical Reference Services Quarterly 9 (4) Winter 1990 : 1-16.

1384 Calderon, Federman.

Library of Congress Subject Headings : vested interest versus the real needs of the information society.

Cataloging and Classification Quarterly 11 (2) 1990 : 85-94.

1385 Callihan, John C. and Stepp, Dena F.

Finding geoscience information in the Chemical Abstracts Service data base.

The user and geoscience information : Proceedings of the 21st meeting of the Geoscience Information Society, San Antonio, Texas, 10-13 November 1986. Volume 17. Ed. by Robert A. Bier. Alexandria, VA : Geoscience Information Society, 1987 : 77-95.

Illustrates searching of geoscience information from CAS and the use of controlled vocabulary.

1386 Campbell, T.

Possibilities for the international sharing of retroconverted map files.

IFLA Journal 20 (1) 1994 : 46-52.

Asserts the need of geographical name and subject thesauri for providing international access to cartographic materials.

1387 Caplan, Priscilla Louise.

Thesaurus-based automatic indexing : a study of indexing failure.

Chapel Hl : North Carolina University, 1978. 129p.

Reports on the use of a manually constructed thesaurus for automatic indexing.

1388 Carlyle, Allyson.

Matching LCSH and user vocabulary in the library catalog.

Cataloging and Classification Quarterly 10 (1-2) 1989 : 37-63.

1389 Cawkell, A. E.

Imaging systems and picture collection management : a review.

Information Services and Use 12 (4) 1992 : 301-325.

Presents review of image storage and retrieval technology and the use of thesauri, picture description languages and visual thesauri.

1390 Cerchez, Claudia et al.

Testing the pertinence of the SPINES thesaurus as an indexing language in the field of information and documentation [in English and Rumanian].

Probleme de Informare si Documentare 17 (1) Jan.-March 1983 : 3-36.

1391 Chambers, J.

Authorities and more authorities! Loading LCSH at Griffith University Library.

Cataloguing Australia 25 (1-4) March-Dec. 1999 : 99-104.

1392 Chamis, A. Y.

Vocabulary control and search strategies in online searching.

Westport, CT : Greenwood, 1991.

1393 Chammou, Eliezer.

Near or Middle East? Choice of name.

Cataloging and Classification Quarterly 7 (3) Spring 1987 : 105-120.

1394 Chaplin, M. F.

Quality and quantity of information.

Aslib Proceedings 32 (2) Feb. 1980 : 62-67.

Describes use of information by construction industry and the Construction Industry Thesaurus.

1395 Chatterjee, Amitabha.

Thesaurus : an aid to information retrieval.

Information science and libraries. Ed. by Pushpa Dhyani. New Delhi, Atlantic Publishers, 1990 : 43-65.

1396 Chau, Michael et al.

HelpfulMed : intelligent searching for medical information over the Internet.

Journal of the American Society for Information Science and Technology 54 (7) May 2003 : 683-694.

Illustrates use of automatic thesaurus in searching medical information on the web.

1397 Chen, H. and Ng, T.

An algorithmic approach to concept exploration in a large knowledge network (automatic thesaurus consultation) : symbolic branch-and-bound search versus connectionist Hopfield Net Activation.

Journal of the American Society for Information Science 46 (5) June 1995 : 348-369.

1398 Chen, H. et al.

Alleviating search uncertainty through concept associations : automatic indexing, co-occurrence analysis, and parallel computing.

Journal of the American Society for Information Science 49 (3) March 1998 : 206-216.

Compares automatic indexing based on thesauri generated through combined object filtering method and manually generated INSPEC thesaurus.

1399 Chen, H. et al.

Internet browsing and searching : user evaluations of category map and concept-space techniques.

Journal of the American Society for Information Science 49 (7) May 1998 : 582-603.

Discusses the implementation of an automatically generated thesaurus and other aspects of the Internet browsing.

1400 Chen, H. L. and Rasmussen, E. M.

Intellectual access to images.

Library Trends 48 (2) Fall 1999 : 291-302.

Discusses and compares the two approaches of indexing images i.e. concept based indexing which uses controlled vocabulary or natural language and content based indexing which uses pixel levels.

1401 Chen, K. H. and Wu, C. T.

The automatic indexing with controlled vocabulary.

Bulletin of the Library Association of China (61) Dec. 1998 : 81-102.

Presents an indexing model, which automatically uses controlled vocabulary based on word frequency and semantics.

1402 Chishti, S. H.

CD-ROM vs. online : a comparison of PsycLIT (CD-ROM) and PsycINFO (DIALOG).

Reference Librarian (40) 1993 : 131-155.

Reports a comparative study of controlled vocabulary used for retrieval from the two databases of psychology i.e. PsycINFO and PsycLIT.

1403 Chute, C. G. and Yang, Y.

An overview of statistical methods for the classification and retrieval of patient events.

Methods of Information in Medicine 34 (1-2) March 1995 : 104-110.

Describes text retrieval technique, which does not depend upon elaborate knowledge bases, lexicons, or thesauri.

1404 Cimino, J. J.

Distributed cognition and knowledge-based controlled medical terminologies.

Artificial Intelligence in Medicine : 12 (2) Feb. 1998 : 153-168.

Asserts the need for controlled medical terminologies and efforts required to control and maintain the same.

1405 Cimino, J. J.

Use of the Unified Medical Language System in patient care at the Columbia-Presbyterian Medical Center.

Methods of Information in Medicine 34 (1-2) March 1995 : 158-164.

Examines the suitability of the UMLS for representing patient care information at the CPMC.

1406 Cimino, James J. and Robert V. Sideli.

Using the UMLS to bring the library to the bedside.

Medical Decision Making 11. Supplement. Oct.-Dec. 1991 : 116-120.

1407 Cochrane, Pauline A.

Indexing and searching thesauri, the Janus or Proteus of information retrieval.

Classification research for knowledge representation and organization. Proceedings of the 5th International Study Conference on Classification Research, Toronto, Canada, 24-28 June 1991. Ed. By N. J. Williamson and H. Hudon.

Amsterdam : Elsevier Science Publishers BV and FID, 1992 : 161-177.

1408 Cochrane, Pauline A. and Johnson, E. H. *Eds.*

Visualizing subject access for Twenty first Century information resources. Proceedings of the 1997 Clinic on Library Applications of Data Processing, Urbana-Champaign, Illinois 2-4 March 1997. Urbana-Champaign, Illinois : Illinois University at Urbana-Champaign, Graduate School of Library and Information Science, 1998. 176p.

Discusses the growth of Internet and the role of thesauri.

Also available at : http://www.lis.uiuc.edu/puboff/

1409 Colby, M.

Nailing Jell-O to a tree : improving access to Twentieth Century music.

Cataloging and Classification Quarterly 26 (3) 1998 : 31-39.

Discusses the problems in the use of LCSH for indexing music and suggests use of music thesaurus as a substitute.

1410 Collins, Kenneth Alan.

The CRISP system : an untapped resource for biomedical research project information.

Bulletin of the Medical Library Association 77 (1) Jan. 1989 : 8-14.

Describes the Computer Retrieval of Information on Scientific Projects programme, which has developed its own controlled vocabulary.

1411 Collison, Robert L.

The future of indexes and indexing.

Indexer 12(4) Oct. 1981 : 171-173.

States the need for the compilation of thesauri for the use of indexers.

1412 Condron, L.

Management by action : how we're embracing new cataloging work at Tufts.

Cataloging and Classification Quarterly 30 (2-3) 2000 : 299-313.

Reports new cataloguing tools such as metadata as substitute to thesauri.

1413 Congreve, Juliet.

Problems of subject access : (i) automatic generation of printed indexes and online thesaural control.

Program 20 (2) April 1986 : 204-210.

Reports an ongoing research at Middlesex Polytechnic aimed to test the PRECIS RIN file as a basis for online thesaural control.

1414 Connaway, L. S.; Johnson, D. W. and Searing, S. E.

Online catalogs from the users' perspective : the use of focus group interviews.

College and Research Libraries 58 (5) Sept. 1997 : 403-420.

Reports a study of search capabilities of different types of users, which indicated that users have confusion between keyword searching and searching with controlled vocabulary.

1415 Connell, T. H.

Use of the LCSH system : realities.

Cataloging and Classification Quarterly 23 (1) 1996 : 73-98.

1416 Conturbia, S. D.; Miller, J. P. and Yang, Z. Y.

NOTIS and statistical masterfile as sources for international information.

Technical Services Quarterly 14 (4) 1997 : 27-35.

Compares transactions from NOTIS and Statistical Masterfile databases, which used controlled vocabulary for determining possible correlations between the two.

1417 Cortez, E. M.

Use of metadata vocabularies in data retrieval.

Journal of the American Society for Information Science 50 (13) Nov. 1999 : 1218-1223.

1418 Crafts Lighty, A. et al.

The use of ADLIB and the root thesaurus to manage a special library.

Seventh International Online Information Meeting London 6-8 December 1983. Oxford and New Jersey : Learned Information, 1983 : 465-469.

1419 Craig, A. and Schriar, S.

The 'Find-It! Illinois' controlled vocabulary : improving access to government information through the Jessica subject tree.

Government Information Quarterly 18 (3) 2001 : 195-208.

Describes controlled vocabulary as one of the essential component for searching government information.

1420 Craven, T. C.

A thesaurus for use in a computer-aided abstracting tool kit.

Proceedings of the 56th Annual Meeting of the American Society for Information Science, Columbus, Ohio, 24-28 October 1993. Ed. by Susan Bonzi. Medford, New Jersey : Learned Information, Inc., 1993 : 178-184.

Explains the role of thesaurus in computer-aided abstracting.

1421 Crawford, R. G. and Macleod, I. A.

A relational approach to modular information retrieval systems design.

The information age in perspective. Proceedings of the 41st Annual Meeting, New York, 13-17 November 1978. Volume 15. Compiled by Everett H. Brenner, White Plains, New York : Knowledge Industry Publications for American Society for Information Science, 1978 : 83-85.

Illustrates how flexible vocabularies can be easily incorporated in bibliographic databases.

1422 Dack, D.

Authority control in ABN and NLA.

Cataloguing Australia 8 (3) Sept. 1982 : 25-31.

1423 Dahamna, Badisse et.al.

Enhancing the MeSH thesaurus to retrieve French online health resources in a quality-controlled gateway.

Health Information and Libraries Journal 21 (4) Dec. 2004 : 253-261.

Describe the various enhancements made to the MeSH thesaurus by the CISMeF (Catalogue and Index of Health Resources in French) team to adapt this terminology to the health resources on the Internet.

1424 Dahlberg, I.

A general thesaurus for the German Library. Pilot study.

Frankfurt am Main (West Germany) : Deutsche Bibliothek, 1980. 74p.

Describes the kind and form of the terms used by the Deutsche Bibliothe for subject description and discusses their use as elements of a general library thesaurus.

1425 Daniels, P. C.

The thesaurus in action: background information for a thesaurus.

Washington, DC : Department of the Army, Information Systems Office, 1969. 33p.

1426 Danskin, A.

A world turned upside down.

An Leabharlann 10 (2) 1993 : 35-6 and 38-40.

Asserts the importance of controlled vocabulary and authority control.

1427 Dassa, Rebecca.

LC Subject Headings of interest to Judaica librarians.

Judaica Librarianship 4 (1) Fall 1987-Winter 1988 : 40-45.

1428 Dassa, Rebecca.

LC Subject Headings of interest to Judaica librarians.

Judaica Librarianship 4 (2) Spring 1988-Winter 1989 : 157-162.

1429 Davies, Ron.

Thesaurus-aided searching in search and retrieval protocols.

Knowledge organization and change. Proceedings of the 4th International ISKO Conference 5-18 July 1996. Advances in knowledge organization. Volume 5. Ed. by Rebecca Green Washington DC : Indeks Verlag, 1996 : 137-143.

1430 Davis, M. A.

Tackle box strategy : using a matrix to facilitate library research strategy.

Research Strategies 14 (4) Fall 1996 : 205-213.

Describes uses of controlled vocabulary.

1431 Davison, Keith.

Future of subject headings in an increasingly computerised catalogue.

Cataloguing Australia 5 (3) July-Sept. 1979 : 47-53.

1432 DeHart, Florence E.

Topic relevance and retrieval effectiveness.

International Classification 10 (1) 1983 : 9-14.

Examines the role of thesauri in the context of topic relevance.

1433 DeHart, Florence E. and Matthews, Karen.

French fiction : LCSH applications.

Cataloging and Classification Quarterly 9 (2) 1988 : 3-24.

1434 DeHart, Florence E. and Matthews, Karen.

Subject enhancements and OPACs : planning ahead.

Technical Services Quarterly 7 (4) 1990 : 35-52.

1435 Delozier, E. P.

Personal information accessories on the Internet.

Medical Reference Services Quarterly 16 (4) Winter 1997 : 63-67.

Describes thesauri and other tools which help to find personal information of the web.

1436 Delozier, E. P. and Lingle, V. A.

MEDLINE and MeSH : challenges for end users.

Medical Reference Services Quarterly 11 (3) Fall 1992 : 29-46.

1437 Desmousseaux, S.

Two experiments in automatic documentation at Compagnie Generale d'Electricite.

ANRT Information et Documentation (2) June 1969 : 47-49.

Describes experiments in automatic documentation along with the use thesauri.

1438 Despres-Lonnet, M.; Aubry, M. and Briatte, K.

The LIB. R. I. S. project : from heritage conservation to user-oriented concerns.

Vine (107) 1998 : 8-15.

Describes a project aimed at the creation of an archive of digitized images and the use of specially prepared thesauri for the same.

1439 Detant, M.

The mechanized documentation system of Euratom.

Revue Universelle des Mines 112 (2) June 1969 : 75-93.

Discusses the role of thesauri in managing mechanized documentation system of Euratom.

1440 DeZelar-Tiedman, C.

Subject access to fiction : an application of the Guidelines.

Library Resources and Technical Services 40 (3) July 1996 :

203-8 and 210.

1441 Diaz, K. R.

The invisible Web : navigating the Web outside traditional search engines.

Reference and User Services Quarterly 40 (2) Winter 2000 : 131-134.

Considers the importance of thesauri for effective use of databases.

1442 Dillon, Martin.

An experiment in superficial indexing.

Information Storage and Retrieval 10 (2) Feb. 1974 : 63-71.

Explains the role of thesauri in automatic indexing.

1443 Dillon, Martin.

Thesaurus-based automatic book indexing.

Information Processing and Management 18 (4) 1982 : 167-178.

1444 Dillon, Martin et al.

The use of automatic indexing for authority control.

Journal of Library Automation 14 (4) Dec. 1981 : 268-277.

1445 Ding, Y.; Chowdhury, G. G. and Foo, S.

Bibliometric cartography of information retrieval research by using co-word analysis.

Information Processing and Management 37 (6) Nov. 2001 : 817-842.

Explains the use of co-word analysis for studying patterns and trends in IR for which it used keywords from SSI and SSCI and other vocabulary control tools.

1446 Ding, Y.; Chowdhury, G. G. and Foo, S.

Incorporating the results of co-word analyses to increase search variety for information retrieval.

Journal of Information Science 26 (6) 2000 : 429-451.

Compares results of Co-word analysis in IR domain with similar data obtained from three thesauri i.e. LISA thesaurus, LCSH and Thesaurus of Information Technology Terms.

1447 Diodato, Virgil and Henty, G.

The rates of assignment of narrower terms at the Thesaurus of ERIC Descriptors.

Journal of Information Science 19 (2) 1993 : 137-141.

Examines the link between the use of an indexing term and its similarity to its narrower terms.

1448 Diodato, Virgil and Pearson, Karen.

Source indexing in science journals and indexing services : a survey of current practices

Science and Technology Libraries 6 (1-2) Fall-Winter 1985-1986 : 103-118.

Presents a survey of source indexing and discusses the use of controlled vocabulary for source indexing.

1449 Dodd, Nancy G. and Hubbard, Abigail.

An analysis of effective management information searching : a comparison of the three major bibliographic databases.

National Online Meeting. Proceedings 1981. Compiled by Martha E. Wliams and Thomas H. Hogan. Medford, New Jersey : Learned Information, Inc., 1981 : 167-177.

Compares bibliographic databases of management considering various criteria including thesauri.

1450 Dolan, Donna R.

How to write for retrieval.

Database 5 (2) June 1982 : 82-83.

Suggests use of controlled vocabulary for writing searchable articles.

1451 Donati, Robert.

Spanning the social sciences and humanities through DIALOG : part 1.

Online 1 (4) Oct. 1977 : 48-54.

Reviews various social science databases available with DIALOG and the use of controlled vocabulary.

1452 Donati, Robert.

Spanning the social sciences : searching techniques when online : Part 2.

Online 2 (1) Jan. 1978 : 41-52.

Use of on-line thesauri; direct thesaurus display are explained.

1453 Dorsch, J. L.

BIOETHICSLINE use by medical students : curriculum-integrated instruction and collection development implications.

Bulletin of the Medical Library Association 85 (2) April 1997 : 147-153.

Reports a study that examined online uselogs of medical students, which indicated that many students used controlled vocabularies.

1454 Doupi, P. and van der Lei, J.

Towards personalized Internet health information : the STEPPS architecture.

Medical Informatics and The Internet in Medicine 27 (3) 1 Sept. 2002 : 139-151.

Describes STructured Evaluated Personalized Patient Support (STEPPS) system, which uses UMLS based thesaurus to manage burnt patient's record in electronic format.

1455 Dow, E. H.

EAD and the small repository.

American Archivist 60 (4) Fall 1997 : 446-455.

Explains use of controlled vocabulary control and other finding aids so as to have intellectual access to manuscript collection.

1456 Dozier, Marshall and Haig, Alex.

BEME Guide No. 3 : Systematic searching for evidence in

medical education - Part 2 : Constructing searches.

Medical Teacher 25 (5) Sept. 2003 : 463-484.

Explains how controlled vocabularies can be used to search information on evidence in medical education.

1457 Drabenstott, Karen Markey.

Facilitating geographic subdivision assignment in subject headings.

Library Resources and Technical Services 36 (4) Oct. 1992 : 411-425.

1458 Drabenstott, Karen Markey.

The need for machine-readable authority records for topical subdivisions.

Information Technology and Libraries 11 (2) June 1992 : 91-104.

1459 Drabenstott, Karen Markey and Vizine-Goetz, Diane.

Search trees for subject searching in online catalogs.

Library Hi Tech 8 (3) 1990 : 7-20.

Explains the matching of user's queries with the catalogue's controlled vocabulary by using computers.

1460 Drabenstott, Karen Markey and Vizine-Goetz, Diane.

Using subject headings for online retrieval : theory, practice, and potential.

Information Processing and Management 31 (3) May-June 1995 : 450-451.

1461 Drabenstott, Karen Markey and Vizine-Goetz, Diane.

Using subject headings for online retrieval : theory, practice, and potential.

Information Technology and Libraries 14 (1) March 1995 : 59-60.

1462 Drabenstott, Karen Markey and Vizine-Goetz, Diane.

Using subject headings for online retrieval : theory, practice and potential.

Journal of the American Society for Information Science 46 (5) June 1995 : 396.

1463 Drabenstott, Karen Markey and Vizine-Goetz, Diane.

Using subject headings for online retrieval: theory, practice and potential.

Library Resources and Technical Services 41 (1) Jan. 1997 : 60-67.

1464 Dubois, C. P. R.

The use of thesauri in online retrieval.

Journal of Information Science 8 (2) March 1984 : 63-66.

1465 Duckitt, Pauline.

The value of controlled indexing systems in online text databases.

Fifth International Online Information Meeting, London, 8-10 December 1981. Oxford : Learned Information, 1980 : 447-453.

Explains the value of controlled vocabulary in managing and searching full-text databases.

1466 Dueltgen, Ronald R.

Chemical information in non-chemical databases. 4 :forest and paper databases.

Database 6 (2) June 1983 : 80-82.

Explains the use of thesaurus in retrieving chemical information from non-chemical databases.

1467 Dueltgen, Ronald R.

Chemical information in non-chemical databases. V : textiles databases.

Database 6 (4) Dec. 1983 : 96-97.

Asserts importance of thesauri in retrieving complete chemical information from non-chemical databases.

1468 Dunsire, Gordon.

SCOTLOC.

Scottish Libraries (19) Jan.-Feb. 1990 : 14-15.

Describes 'SCOTLOC' - a ISRS based on a structured thesaurus.

1469 Durr, W. Frederick.

CD-ROM and information precision.

National Online Meeting Proceedings 1987. New York, 5-7 May 1987. Ed. by Martha E. Wliams and Thomas H. Hogan. Medford, New Jersey : Learned Information Inc., 1987 : 119-120.

Explains the use of controlled vocabulary and hierarchical thesauri in searching information from CDROM databases.

1470 Dykstra, Mary.

PRECIS in the online catalog.

Cataloging and Classification Quarterly 10 (1-2) 1989 : 81-94.

Discusses subject control in PRECIS in the context of online catalogue.

1471 Dykstra, Mary.

Subject analysis and thesauri : a background.

Art Documentation 8 (4) Winter 1989 : 173-174.

1472 Ebinuma, Y.

The process and method for determination of final query formations and their statistical characteristics in the Euratom Nuclear Documentation System.

Dokumentesyon Kenkyu 20 (4) April 1970 : 97-107.

Discusses role of thesauri in query formulation.

1473 Ebinuma, Y. et al.

Promotion of keyword assignment to scientific literature by contributors.

International Forum on Information and Documentation 8 (3) July 1983 : 16-20.

Explains the effect of the keyword assignment scheme in free terms on effective dissemination of scientific literature.

1474 Edstrom, M. E. and Wallin, Marie A.

Implementation of a new interactive on-line information retrieval system : 3RIP.

First International Online Information Meeting. London, 13-15 December 1977. Oxford : Learned Information, 1977 : 83-93.

Explains advantages of using online thesauri in online searching.

1475 El Hadi, M.

CAFRAD Information Retrieval System (CAFRADIRS) with particular emphasis on CAFRAD Thesaurus of Administrative Information Descriptors.

Official report of the African seminar for librarians and documentalists of administrative information services, 31st March 7th April 1975. Achimota : Ghana Institute of Management and Public Administration, 1975 : 211-228.

1476 Eriksen, L.

NOVAGate : Nova Information Gateway; Nordic Gateway to forestry, veterinary and agricultural information.

Synopsis 29 (1) Feb. 1998 : 37-38.

Describes usefulness of AGROVOC and national thesauri in developing subject-based Internet gateway.

1477 Fagan, J. C.

Searching for E-business information in online databases.

Behavioral and Social Sciences Librarian 20 (1) 2001 : 45-53.

Discusses terms to be used in framing search strategies for searching e-business information in online databases.

1478 Falk, M. W.

Full-text Arctic databases : the tool, the methodology, the research potential.

Proceedings of the 15th Polar Libraries Colloquy, Bipolar information initiatives : the needs of polar research. Cambridge, 3-8 July 1994. Ed. by D. W. H. Walton, W. Mls and C. M. Phlips. Bluntisham, UK : Bluntisham Books for Polar Libraries Colloquy Steering Committee, 1995 : 134-137.

Discusses controlled vocabulary as one of the tools in the use of full-text databases.

1479 Fangmeyer, H. and Lustig, G.

The Euratom automatic indexing project. Information Processing Congress, Edinburgh, 5-10 August 1968.

Edinburgh : Information Processing Congress, 1970.

Describes the thesaurus based Euratom, an automatic indexing project.

1480 Farrell, Deborah R. and Compton, Anne W.

POPLINE : An overview for searchers.

Medical Reference Services Quarterly 2 (4) Winter 1983 : 1-20.

Describes search techniques based on the POPLINE Thesaurus.

1481 Fawcett, Trevor.

Control of text and images : tradition and innovation.

Art Libraries Journal 7 (2) Summer 1982 : 7-16.

Discusses problems of subject control of both textual and visual art and identifies ATT and other agencies role in providing access to art material.

1482 Fawcett, Trevor

Subject indexing in the visual arts.

Art Libraries Journal 4 (1) Spring 1979 : 5-17.

Explains the use of controlled vocabulary in indexing visual arts documents.

1483 Ferrari, R. C.

Art on the 'Net : enhanced research for art and architecture.

Journal of Library Administration 30 (1-2) 2000 : 39-62.

Highlights the usefulness of ATT for searching Art information on the Internet.

1484 Fidel, Raya.

Who needs controlled vocabulary?

Special Libraries 83 (1) Winter 1992 : 1-9.

Discusses the various factors that affected the selection of search terms for database searches.

1485 Field, B. J.

A thesaurus-based indexing and classification system development for INSPEC products and services.

Journal of Documentation 30 (1) 1974 : 1-17.

1486 Field, B. J.

Towards automatic indexing : automatic assignment of controlled-language indexing and classification from free indexing.

Journal of Documentation 31 (4) Dec. 1975 : 246-265.

1487 Figueira, N. M.

Globo TV Documentation Center : news, communication and engineering.

IASA Journal (5) May 1995 : 44-47.

Describes the use of name dictionaries subject thesauri by Globo TV Documentation Center, Brazil.

1488 Figueroa-Servin, R. D. and Encisco, B.

Subject authority control at El Colegio de Mexico's Library : the whats and hows of a project.

Cataloging and Classification Quarterly 32 (1) 2001 : 65-80.

1489 Filliatre, B.

Use of a thesaurus of analogical links between concepts in a documentation system.

Information Processing and Management 11 (3-4) August 1975 : 107-113.

1490 Fischer, Dietrich H.

Consistency rules and triggers for thesauri.

International Classification 18 (4) 1991 : 212-225.

Discusses desirable functions of thesauri.

1491 Fisseha, Frehiwot et el.

Reengineering thesauri for new applications : the AGROVOC example.

Journal of Digital Information 4 (4) 2003. No page numbers.

Also available at : http://jodi.ecs.soton.ac.uk/Articles/v04/i04/Soergel/

Presents a case study using a traditional thesaurus for developing a full-fledged ontology.

1492 Fletcher, L.

The language of communication (summary).

CIIG Bulletin 2 (3) July 1972 : 8-14.

Discusses use of construction industry thesaurus.

1493 Flint, J. and Franklin, A.

Local studies collections : guidelines and subject headings for organizing and indexing resources.

Sydney (New South Wales) : Library Association of Australia, 1982. 203p.

1494 Foster, W. R.; Beckhard, E. J. and Hart, C. S.

The coordinated development of health-related clearinghouse vocabularies : a proposed technique.

Information choices and policies. Proceedings *of the 1979 ASIS Annual Meeting.* Volume 16. Ed. by Roy D. Tally and Ronald R. Deultgen. White Plains, New York : Knowledge Industry Publications for American Society for Information Science, 1979 : 159-167.

Suggests that individualized vocabularies are to be avoided to search health related databases as these confuse users.

1495 Fott, D. L.

Adding another file or why the MARC records shouldn't be enhanced.

Cataloguing Australia 17 (3/4) Sept.–Dec. 1991 : 21-30.

Explains the usefulness of thesauri in enhancing access.

1496 Franklin, Rosemary Aud.

Re-inventing subject access for the semantic web.

Online Information Review 27 (2) 2003 : 94-101.

Highlights importance of controlled vocabularies in subject access.

1497 Freedman, B.

Thesauri for vocabulary control.

Drexel Library Quarterly 9, 1972 : 125-128.

1498 Fugmann, R.

Limitations of the thesaurus method for rendering concept relationships.

Nachrichten fur Dokumentation 26 (1) Feb. 1975 : 2-7.

1499 Fugmann, R.

The glamour and the misery of the thesaurus approach : treatise IV on information retrieval theory.

International Classification 1 (2) Nov. 1974 : 76-86.

1500 Fujiwara, Y.

The model for self-structured semantic relationships of information and its advanced utilization.

International Forum on Information and Documentation 19 (2) April 1994 : 8-10.

Describe a model of semantic relationship that uses thesauri and taxonomies.

1501 Fujiwara, Y. and Liu, Y.

The Homogenized Bipartite Model : HBM for self organization of knowledge and Organization.

International Forum on Information and Documentation 23 (1) Jan.-March 1998 : 13-17.

Describes the use of the HBM in representing the meaning of terms as well as relationships among terms.

1502 Furniss, K. and Gabel, L.

Forms / genre headings : challenges for catalog management. A report of the meeting of the ACLTS Catalog Management Discussion Group. American Library Association midwinter meeting, San Antonio, January, 2000.

Technical Services Quarterly 18 (2) 2000 : 57-60.

Reports libraries responses to LC's 1999 introduction of coding form subdivisions by $v and the incorporation of multiple thesauri.

1503 Garrod, P.

Use of the UNESCO Thesaurus for archival subject indexing at UK NDAD.

Journal of the Society of Archivists 21 (1) April 2000 : 37-54.

Explains the use of the 2nd edn. of the UNESCO Thesaurus at the UK National Digital Archive of Datasets.

1504 Garshol, Lars Marius.

Metadata? Thesauri? Taxonomies? Topic maps! Making sense of it all.

Journal of Information Science 30 (4) 2004 : 378-391.

Reviews topic maps as a terminological tool.

1505 Gatenby, J.

Fulfilling promises : authority control today.

Cataloguing Australia 16 (2) June 1990 : 35-38.

1506 Gavrych, Jacquelyn A.

Teaching concept identification through the use of the thesaurus of ERIC descriptors.

Online 4 (1) Jan. 1980 : 31-34.

1507 Gerhan, David R.

LCSH in vivo : subject searching performance and strategy in the OPAC era.

Journal of Academic Librarianship 15 (2) May 1989 : 83-89.

1508 Gilchrist, Alan.

The role of thesauri in mechanized systems.

Indexer 9 (4) Oct. 1975 : 146-154

1509 Gilchrist, Alan.

The subject approach in managing information.

Handbook of special librarianship and information work. 7th ed. Ed. by A. Scammell. London : Aslib 1997 : 51-79.

1510 Gillespie, Roy and Kean, Doreen.

The experimental use of on-line terminals in public libraries. Phase 2 (Scotland). Final report Oct. 79-Sept. 81.

Glasgow : Glasgow District Libraries, Mitchell Library, 1982.

Reports difficulties faced in obtaining thesauri for online search in public libraries.

1511 Gillman, P.

ConQuest : retrieval on a large scale.

TIP Applications 9 (3) Sept. 1995 : 4-6.

Describes thesaurus-based retrieval of ConQuest - a text retrieval software.

1512 Gitisetan, D.

Subjects of concern : selected examples illustrating problems affecting information retrieval on Iran and related subjects using LCSH.

Cataloging and Classification Quarterly 20 (3) 1995 : 43-55.

1513 Godert, Winfried.

Subject headings for mathematical literature.

Journal of Documentation 36 (1) March 1980 : 11-23.

1514 Gomez, L. M.; Lochbaum, C. L. and Landauer, T. K.

All the right words - finding what you want as a function of richness of indexing vocabulary.

Journal of American Society for Information Science 41(8) 1990 : 547-559.

1515 Gordon, B. L.

Terminology and content of the medical record.

Computers and Biomedical Research 3, 1970 : 436-444.

1516 Gordon, I.

Terminology management is not an option - it's essential.

Online and CD Notes 11 (10) Dec. 1998 : 3-4.

States importance of controlled vocabulary and describes Multiterm - standard terminology of industry and multiterm web interface.

1517 Gordon, M. D.

User-based document clustering by re-describing subject description with a genetic algorithm.

Journal of American Society for Information Science 41(5) 1991 : 311-322.

1518 Gorman, Michael

Authority control in the context of bibliographic control in the electronic environment.

Cataloging & Classification Quarterly 38 (3-4) 2004 : 11-22.

Examines the importance of authority control for UBC.

1519 Gorman, Michael.

Fate, time, occasion, chance, and change; or how the machine may yet save LCSH.

American Libraries 11 (9) Oct. 1980 : 557-558.

1520 Graves, R. W. and Helander, D. P.

A feasibility study of automatic indexing and information retrieval.

IEEE Transactions on Engineering Writing and Speech 13 (2) Sept. 1970 : 58-59.

Discusses feasibility of automatic indexing along with the use of thesauri.

1521 Greaves, Monica A.

A comparative study of verbal subject data in information retrieval systems in education.

Education Libraries Bulletin 21 (2) Summer 1978 : 1-19.

Analyses the differences between terms used in various computerized education information retrieval systems.

1522 Greenberg, Jane.

Automatic query expansion via lexical-semantic relationships.

Journal of the American Society for Information Science 52 (5) March 2001 : 402-415.

Describes methodology and advantages of automatic query expansion by using thesauri.

1523 Greenberg, Jane.

Intellectual control of visual archives : a comparison between the Art and Architecture Thesaurus and the Library of Congress Thesaurus for Graphic Materials.

Cataloging and Classification Quarterly 16 (1) 1993 : 85-117.

1524 Greenberg, Jane.

Optimal query expansion (QE) processing methods with semantically encoded structured thesauri terminology.

Journal of the American Society for Information Science 52 (6) April 2001 : 487-498.

Discusses comparative advantages of using thesauri for automatic and interactive QE.

1525 Greenberg, Jane.

User comprehension and searching with information retrieval thesauri.

Cataloging and Classification Quarterly 37 (3/4) 2004 : 103-120.

Presents results of a research that aimed to know user's understanding of the thesauri.

1526 Hainebach, R.

European Community databases - a subject analysis.

Online Information 92. Proceedings of the 16th International Online Information Meeting, London, 8-10 December 1992. Ed. by David I. Raitt. Oxford : Learned Information (Europe) Ltd, 1992 : 509-526.

Discusses problems of using multiple thesauri for EC databases and suggests solutions.

1527 Hall, Audrey and Hounsell, D.

British Education Index and PRECIS : a rejoinder to Dai Hounsell.

Education Libraries Bulletin 26 (1) Spring 1983 : 61-63.

Notes lacunae in the BEI and suggests that the provision of a thesaurus, extensive cross-referencing, or a classified arrangement could help to improve the system.

1528 Hallet, K. S.

Separate but equal? a system comparison study of MEDLINE's controlled vocabulary MeSH.

Bulletin of the Medical Library Association 86 (4) Oct. 1998 : 491-495.

Reports an experiment that tested the effects of implementation of MeSH vocabulary in DIALOG and Ovid's database searches.

1529 Hammond, R.

Negotiating the medical maze.

Library Association Record 103 (4) April 2001 : 218-220.

Discusses problems of cross searching in medical databases and the need for SignPost, a substitute for super thesauri.

1530 Haravu, L. J. and Neelameghan, A.

Text mining and data mining in knowledge organization and discovery : the making of knowledge-based products.

Cataloging and Classification Quarterly 37 (1-2) 2004 : 97-113.

Highlights the importance of thesaurus and other structured vocabulary tools in text and data mining.

1531 Harrison, L. D.

Implementing the MALIMET thesaurus on TRIP / TDBS.

Information Services and Use 12 (4) 1992 : 327-343.

Implementation of Mini-MALIMET - a conventional thesaurus available on magnetic tape is described.

1532 Hass, S. W.

Covering the vocabulary of technical abstracts using standard and specialized dictionaries.

Interlending and Document Supply 18 (5) 1992 : 363-373.

1533 Hass Weinberg, Bella.

Compilations of Library of Congress Subject Headings for Judaica : comparison, evaluation, and recommendations.

Judaica Librarianship 5 (1) Spring 1989-Winter 1990 : 36-40.

1534 Hass Weinberg, Bella and Cunningham, Julie A.

Term specificity and online postings : inverse relationship?

1984 : Challenges to an information society proceedings of the 47th ASIS annual meeting. Compiled by Barbara Flood, Joanne Witiak and Thomas Hogan. White Plains, New York :

Knowledge Industry Publications, 1984 : 144-147.

Reports an experiment aimed at testing the hypothesis that the inverse relationship holds only for peripheral terms of a discipline rather than for central terms.

1535 Hatano, H.

The image processing and database system in the National Museum of Western Art, Tokyo : an integrated system for art research.

Art Libraries Journal 21 (1) 1996 : 18-22.

Describes an art research ISRS based on machine-readable thesauri.

1536 Hearn, S.

Machine-assisted validation of LC Subject Headings : implications for authority file structure.

Cataloging and Classification Quarterly 29 (1-2) 2000 : 107-115.

1537 Heiner-Freiling, M.

Survey on subject heading languages used in national libraries and bibliographies.

Cataloging and Classification Quarterly 29 (1- 2) 2000 : 189-198.

1538 Henry, Georgianna.

The rates of assignment of thesaurus terms in the ERIC information retrieval system : an analysis of hierarchies and levels.

Journal of Documentation 47 (3) Sept. 1991 : 276-283.

1539 Hertzum, M.; Soes, H. and Frokjoer, E.

Information retrieval systems for professionals : a case study of computer supported legal research.

European Journal of Information Systems 2 (4) Oct. 1993 : 296-303.

Suggests the development of an ISRS for legal professionals based on dynamic thesaurus.

1540 Hewison, Nancy S.

Descriptions and reviews of software packages : online sources.

Medical Reference Services Quarterly 5 (4) Winter 1986 : 47-59.

Describes controlled vocabulary and other aspects of online software packages.

1541 Hewison, Nancy S.

Online documentation : keeping up and keeping track.

Database 11 (3) June 1988 : 67-71.

Suggests methods and tools including thesauri for handling on-line documentation.

1542 Hildreth, Charles R.

To Boolean or not to Boolean.

Information Technology and Libraries 2 (3) Sept. 1983 : 235-237.

Discusses the advantages and disadvantages of using Boolean search and its integration with controlled vocabulary.

1543 Hines, Theodore C. and Winkel, Lois.

A new information access tool for children's media.

Library Resources and Technical Services 27 (1) Jan.-March 1983 : 94-104.

Explains the need of a thesaurus in ISRS.

1544 Hjerppe, Roland.

The role of classification in hypertext : issues in implementing Roget's Thesaurus as a hypertext.

*Tools for knowledge organisation and the human interface. Proceedings of the 1st International ISKO Conference, Darmstadt, (*Germany) *14-17 August 1990. Advances in knowledge organization, no. 1/2.* Ed. by R. Fugmann. Part I.

Frankfurt/Main : Indeks. 1990 : 206-215.

1545 Hjorland, B.

Domain analysis in information science : eleven approaches - traditional as well as innovative.

Journal of Documentation 58 (4) 2002 : 422-462.

Discusses the production of special classification and thesauri as one of the approaches to domain analysis.

1546 Hlava, M. M. K.

Machine-Aided Indexing (MAI) in a multilingual environment.

Online Information 92. Proceedings of the 16th International Online Information Meeting, London, 8-10 December 1992. Ed. by David I. Raitt. Oxford : Learned Information (Europe) Ltd, 1992 : 297-300.

Asserts that use of MAI across several languages with controlled vocabularies for each language provides a consistency in indexing.

1547 Hoffmann, G.

Notes on the compatibility of subject thesauri for patent documentation.

Informatika 16 (4) 1969 : 27-32.

1548 Hubbard, Abigail.

Managing reprint files-decisions.

Medical Reference Services Quarterly 5 (1) Spring 1986 : 1-15.

Describes controlled vocabulary and other pre-requisites for managing reprints files.

1549 Huber, J. T. and Gillaspy, M. L.

Social constructs and disease : implications for a controlled vocabulary for HIV / AIDS.

Library Trends 47 (2) Fall 1998 : 190-208.

1550 Hudon, Michele.

True and tested products : thesauri on the Web.

Indexer 23 (3) April 2003 : 115-119.

1551 Humphrey, Susanne M. and Miller, Nancy E.

The NLM Indexing Aid project.

ASIS '86. Proceedings of the 49th ASIS Annual Meeting. Chicago, Illinois, 28 September –2 October 1986. Volume 23. Ed. by Julie M. Hurd and Charles H. Davis. Medford, New Jersey : Learned Information Inc. for the American Society for Information Science, 1987 : 106-112.

Reports controlled vocabulary based Indexing Aid project of the NLM.

1552 Hyams, E. and Maclachlan, L.

All change at the DTI.

Library + Information Update 1 (9) Dec. 2002 : 46- 47.

Describes implementation of document and records management system of the UK Department of Trade and Industry and explains the need of thesaurus for the same.

1553 Irving, H.

cait : Computer-Assisted Indexing Tutor : implemented for training at NAL.

Agricultural Libraries and Information Notes 21 (4-6) April-June 1995 : 1-5.

Describes 'cait' - computer-Assisted Indexing Tutor which directs novice indexers to existing information sources in agriculture and guides them through the selection and application of CAB Thesaurus terms, AGRICOLA Subject Category Codes, uncontrolled terms and geographic terms.

1554 Jackson, Philip.

A thesaurus for enhanced geographic access.

LASIE 22 (3) Nov.-Dec. 1991 : 49-60.

Explains that geographic access in on-line catalogues could be improved by organizing and structuring geographic data through the hierarchies of a thesaurus.

1555 Jacso, P.

Information Science Abstracts.

Link-Up (USA) 14 (3) May-June 1997 : 3 and 11.

Compares the ISA with LISA and criticizes the ISA for lack of controlled vocabulary.

1556 Jacso, P.

KnowledgeCite.

Database 21 (6) Dec. 1998 : 71-72.

Describes how search terms are selected through subject matching across the thesauri for searching KnowledgeCite-website.

1557 Jamieson, A. J.; Dolan, E. and Declerck, L.

Keyword searching vs. authority control in an online catalog.

Journal of Academic Librarianship 12(5) 1986 : 277-283.

1558 Jarvelin, K. et al.

A deductive data model for thesaurus navigation and query expansion.

Finland, Tampere, Abo, Oulu : Tampere University, 1996. 69p.

1559 Jizba, L. and McDonald, R. F.

Innovation on campus : Robert F. McDonald on the NYU School of Medicine's project to catalog the research interests of faculty members.

Journal of Internet Cataloging 5 (1) 2002 : 3-16

Describes the creation MeSH based Faculty Research Catalogue at the Yew York University School of Medicine.

1560 Johnson, Eric H.

Distributed thesaurus web services.

Cataloging and Classification Quarterly 37 (3-4) 2004 : 121-153.

Discusses the concept of thesaurus-web i.e. a proposed network of thesaurus access and navigation.

1561 Johnston, S. M.

Effect of thesaurus indexing on retrieval from machine-readable databases.

Quarterly Bulletin of the International Association of Agricultural Information Specialists 27 (3) 1982 : 90-96.

Discusses the advantages and disadvantages of using free language and thesaurus in indexing and retrieval of information from machine-readable databases.

1562 Jolley, J. L.

Progress in documentation : Punched feature cards.

Journal of Documentation 31 (3) Sept. 1975 : 199-215.

Traces the history of punched cards used for ISR and highlights the importance of thesaurus.

1563 Jones, D. R.

The Shropshire's Past Unfolded Project, 1998-2001.

Journal of the Society of Archivists 22 (2) Oct. 2001 : 149-160.

Describes use of thesauri in cataloguing the Shropshire County Council, UK office records.

1564 Jones, S.

A thesaurus data model for an intelligent retrieval system.

Journal of Information Science 19 (3) 1993 : 167-178.

1565 Jones, S.

Interactive thesaurus navigation : intelligence rules OK?

Journal of the American Society for Information Science 46 (1) Jan. 1995 : 52-59.

Examines feasibility of building an intelligent rule or weight-based algorithms for interactive thesaurus navigation.

1566 Jones, S. and Hancock-Beaulieu, M.

Support strategies for interactive thesaurus navigation.

Proceedings of the 3rd International Society for Knowledge Organization (ISKO) Conference : Knowledge organization and quality management. Copenhagen, Denmark, 20-24 June 1994. Ed. by Hanne Albrechtsen and Susan Oernager, Frankfurt/Main : INDEKS Verlag, 1994 : 366-373.

The need of support in direct interactive use of thesauri is asserted.

1567 Joshi, P. G.

Utilization of a specific subject thesaurus in computer-based IR systems : a case study.

Seminar on thesaurus in information system. Banglore : DRTC, 1975 : Paper CD.

1568 Jouguelet, Suzanne.

A network of subject headings : the Repertoire of Laval University adapted by the Bibliotheque Nationale, Paris.

International Cataloguing 12 (2) April-June 1983 : 17-19.

Describes indexing at the Bibliotheque Nationale, Paris, based on Laval University's Repertoire de Vedettes-Matiere as an authority list.

1569 Joyce, T. and Needham, R. M.

The thesaurus approach to information retrieval.

American Documentation 9, 1958 : 92-197.

1570 Kaiser, D.

Integrated online access to databases.

Quarterly Bulletin of the International Association of Agricultural Information Specialists 39 (1-2) 1994 : 93-97.

States the importance of thesauri in integrating online access.

1571 Kasiviswanadham, S.

Thesaurus approach in profile construction.

Lucknow Librarian 22 (3-4) Sept.–Dec. 1990 : 68-74.

Discusses the use of thesauri in developing user profile for SDI.

1572 Keen, M.

Using channels, topics, keywords and other metadata in an electronic alerting service.

Vine (117) 2000 : 3-12.

Describes an electronic CAS designed using controlled vocabulary based on channels, topics and keywords.

1573 Kendereski, D.; Matejka, L. and Hack, R.

A thesaurus to supplement the International Patent Classification in the field of biomedical engineering.

World Patent Information 5 (2) 1983 : 101-109.

1574 Kesselman, Martin and Iwan, Irene Perry.

Database indexes and the end-user.

Eighth International Online Information Meeting : London 4-6 December 1984. Oxford : Learned Information (Europe), 1984 : 283-288.

Discusses vocabulary problems faced by the end-users.

1575 Killion, V. J.

RNdex Top 100 : a quality-filtered database for nursing research.

Medical Reference Services Quarterly 14 (3) Fall 1995 : 1-11.

Describes a thesaurus based 'RNdex Top 100' i.e. a CD-ROM abstracting database of nursing periodicals.

1576 King, M. J.

Excerpta Medica on-line-an evaluation.

London : City University, Centre for Information Science, 1979. 113p.

Presents the evaluation of online Excerpta Medica in the context of its use of Malimet thesaurus.

1577 King, N. S.

End-user errors : a content analysis of PaperChase transaction logs.

Bulletin of the Medical Library Association 81 (4) Oct. 1993 : 439-441.

Presents analysis of use of PaperChase - a software developed for searching MEDLINE and discusses the misuses and failures in the use of controlled vocabulary while using this software.

1578 Knapp, S. D.; Cohen, L. B. and Juedes, D. R.

A natural language thesaurus for the humanities : the need for a database search aid.

Library Quarterly 68 (4) Oct. 1998 : 406-430.

1579 Kopp, C.

Searching online : tips and strategies.

Nebraska Library Association Quarterly 25 (1) Spring 1994 : 40-45.

Provides guidance in online search including the use of thesauri.

1580 Kreider, L. J.

LCSH works! Subject searching effectiveness at the Cleveland Public Library and the growth of Library of Congress Subject Headings through cooperation.

Cataloging and Classification Quarterly 29 (1-2) 2000 : 127-134.

1581 Kristensen, Joana.

Expanding end-users' query statements for free text searching with a search-aid thesaurus.

Information Processing and Management 29 (6) Nov.-Dec. 1993 : 733-744.

1582 Kristensen, Joana and Jarvelin, Kalervo.

The effectiveness of a searching thesaurus in free-text searching in a full-text database.

International Classification 17 (2) 1990 : 77-84.

1583 Kumar, S. K.; Raghavendra Rao, M. K. and Kamath, V. A.

Thesaurus : an ideal tool for vocabulary control in post-coordinate systems : INIS Thesaurus - a case study.

Seminar on thesaurus in information systems. Banglore : DRTC, 1957 : Paper CA.

1584 Kuranz, John.

Management Contents : a brand new file for business and public administration.

Online 1 (3) July 1977 : 30-34.

Describes the 'management contents' database, which is created and searched by using a thesaurus.

1585 Lambert, Maureen and Brody, Fern.

Tailoring search strategy for a highly specialised topic ... Proof once again of the necessity of using file documentation to the fullest.

Database 8 (1) Feb. 1985 : 58-61.

Explains the usefulness of thesauri for tailoring search strategy for tree-text searching.

1586 Lambert, Nancy.

How to search the IFI Comprehensive Database Online : tips and techniques.

Database 10 (6) Dec. 1987 : 46-59.

Provides tips for searching IFI Comprehensive Database of US Chemical Patents and the use of controlled vocabulary in searching the database.

1587 Lambert, Nancy.

Of thesauri and computers : reflections on the need for thesauri.

Searcher 3 (8) Sept. 1995 : 18-22.

Examines the need of thesauri.

1588 Lambert, Nancy.

Online statistical techniques patent search tools : not for patent searchers only.

Database 19 (1) Feb.-March 1996 : 74-78.

Explains the use of online statistical techniques to find and judge the relevance of controlled vocabulary indexing and subject coding.

1589 Lancaster, F. W.

Vocabulary control in information retrieval systems.

Advances in librarianship. Volume 7. Ed. by M. J. Voigt, M. H. Harris. New York : Academic Press, 1977 : 1-40.

Describes the role of controlled vocabulary in ISRS.

1590 Landau, Herbert B.; Byer, Wendy L. and Neufeld, M Lynne.

Applications of information storage and retrieval techniques to the development of product safety databases.

Information revolution. Proceedings of the 38th ASIS Annual Meeting. Boston, Massachusetts, October 26-30, 1975. Volume 12. Ed. by Charles W. Husbands, Ruth L. Tighe. Washington (DC) : American Society for Information Science, 1975 : 116-117.

Reports a survey, which used thesaurus for vocabulary control of trade name product ingredient information.

1591 Larson, Ray R.

Evaluation of advanced retrieval techniques in an experimental online catalog.

Journal of the American Society for Information Science 43 (1) Jan. 1992 : 34-53.

Describes retrieval tests of using thesauri, authority file and various IR techniques.

1592 Lee, J. H. and Kim, M. H.

Ranking documents in thesaurus-based Boolean retrieval systems.

Information Processing and Management 30 (1) Jan.-Feb. 1994 : 79-91.

Describes Extended Relevance algorithm – a thesaurus based document ranking system.

1593 Lee-Smeltzer, K. H.

Finding the needle : controlled vocabularies, resource discovery, and Dublin Core.

Library Collections, Acquisitions, and Technical Services 24 (2) Summer 2000 : 205-215.

Asserts that use of DC with controlled vocabularies will enhance the retrieval performance of the Internet searches.

1594 Leitmeyer, J. and Gillum, T.

Consistency in adverse event terminology : Merck's modified CLINTERM.

Drug Information Journal 27 (2) April-June 1993 : 431-435.

1595 Leska, M. and Leski, K.

The thesaurus for scientific information (informatics) of VINITI.

Aktualne Problemy Informacji Dokumentacji 19 (6) 1974 : 26-30.

1596 Leung, C. H. and Kan, W. K.

A statistical learning approach to automatic indexing of controlled index terms.

Journal of the American Society for Information Science 48 (1) Jan. 1997 : 55-66.

Describes the learning and indexing processes used to assign controlled index terms.

1597 Lincicum, S.

Critical appraisal of the use of classification in the future : non traditional uses of classification - report of a panel discussion.

Cataloging and Classification Quarterly 21 (2) 1995 : 87-89.

Compares uses of thesauri and classification schemes.

1598 Linford, John E.

Effective subject control of administrative materials.

Official report of the African seminar for librarians and documentalists of administrative information services. 31 March – 7 April 1975. Achimota : Ghana Institute of Management and Public Administration, 1975 : 200-210.

Describes thesaurus and various other methods of subject control.

1599 Linnarsson, R.

Decision support for drug prescription integrated with computer-based patient records in primary care.

Medical Informatics 18 (2) April-June 1993 : 131-142.

Describes a decision support system consisting of controlled vocabulary, a patient database, and a knowledge base.

1600 Litkowski, K. C.

Category development based on semantic principles.

Social Science Computer Review 15 (4) Winter 1997 : 394-409.

Explains the role of thesauri in computerized IR and text analysis.

1601 Llorens, Juan; Martinez, Vicente and Moreiro, Jose A.

Automatic generation of domain representations using thesaurus structures.

Journal of the American Society for Information Science and Technology 55 (10) August 2004 : 846-858.

Presents mathematical, statistical and neural techniques that enables domain representation in thesaurus.

1602 Loguinov, B.

SOYUZMEDINFORM computer technology and Soviet medical databases.

Resource Sharing and Information Networks 9 (1) 1993 : 115-124.

Describes SOYUZMEDINFORM – a MeSH based medical database of the All-Union branch medical information centre, which is a part of Russian Ministry of Public Health.

1603 Lorence, Daniel P. and Spink, Amanda.

Semantics and the medical web : a review of barriers and breakthroughs in effective healthcare query.

Health Information and Libraries Journal 21 (2) June 2004 : 109-116.

Examines current medical vocabularies and their impact on searching healthcare information on the web.

1604 Louis Gavet, G.

Reduction of a thesaurus in a documentary system.

TA Informations (1) 1973 : 27-37.

Explains the role of thesaurus in managing a documentary retrieval system.

1605 Lussier, Y. A.; Rothwell, D. J. and Cote, R. A.

The SNOMED model : a knowledge source for the controlled terminology of the computerized patient record.

Methods of Information in Medicine 37 (2) June 1998 : 161-164.

1606 MacEwan, A.

LCSH and the British Library : an international subject authority database?

Catalogue and Index (120) Summer 1996 : 1-6.

1607 MacEwan, A.

Working with LCSH : the cost of cooperation and the achievement of access - a perspective from the British Library.

International Cataloguing and Bibliographic Control 28.(4) Oct.-Dec. 1999 : 94-97.

Reports on the use of LSCH for the BNB and suggests the need for development of fully automated authority control.

1608 Machovec, George S.

Expert systems in libraries.

Online Libraries and Microcomputers 2 (12) Dec. 1984 : 1-4.

Describes thesaurus as one of the essential component for developing an expert system for libraries.

1609 MacNeil, H.

Subject access to archival fonds : balancing provenance and pertinence.

Fontes Artis Musicae 43 (3) July-Sept. 1996 : 242-258.

Discusses issues related with translating indexing concepts into the terms of a controlled vocabulary and other issues related with subject access to archives.

1610 Madkour, Mohamed A.

Linguistic impediments on information transfer for and from the Arab states : towards an automated solution.

Proceedings of the symposium on scientific and engineering secondary information transfer for the developing countries: sponsored by ICSU Abstracting Board and the World Federation of Engineering Organizations Committee on Engineering Information in association with UNISIST; held at the Bibliotheque Royale Albert Ier Brussels 23-24 June 1975. Paris : International Council of Scientific Unions Abstracting Board, 1975 : 47-59.

Describes how the OECD Macrothesaurus can be used to retrieve documents indexed by one of the language versions of this thesaurus by searches in any of the other languages.

1611 Maguire, J. T.

Metadata Unravelled Seminar, Canberra, August 26-27 1998 convened by Federal Libraries Information Network.

Cataloguing Australia 24 (3-4) Sept.-Dec. 1998 : 121-128.

Reports the seminar discussions, which included various aspects of metadata and also the use of controlled vocabulary.

1612 Mai Chan, Lois.

Inter-indexer consistency in subject cataloging.

Information Technology and Libraries 8 (4) Dec. 1989 : 349-357.

Compares indexing consistency of cataloguers who used the same controlled vocabulary.

1613 Malvad, N. M.

Query formulation and feedback study for a thesaurus-based information system.

Seminar on thesaurus in information system. Banglore : DRTC, 1975 : Paper CB.

1614 Mandala, R.; Tokunaga, T. and Tanaka, H.

Query expansion using heterogeneous thesauri.

Information Processing and Management 36 (3) May 2000 : 361-378.

1615 Mandersloot, W. G. B.; Douglas, E. M. B. and Spicer, N.

Thesaurus control - the selection, grouping, and cross-referencing of terms for inclusion in a coordinate index word list.

Journal of the American Society for Information Science 21 (1) Jan.-Feb. 1970 : 49-57.

1616 Mannix, M. K.

The automation of the Frances Louise Day postcard collection of the Howard County Historical Society (Ellicott City, MD).

Popular Culture in Libraries 3 (2) 1995 : 187-197.

Described thesauri and authority file used for cataloguing of postcard collection.

1617 Marchetti, Pier Giorgio and Belkin, Nicholas J.

Interactive online search formulation support.

National Online Meeting 1991 : Proceedings of the 12th National Online Meeting, New York, 7-9 May 1991. Edited by Martha E. Wliams. Medford, New Jersey : Learned Information, Inc., 1991 : 237-243.

Reports a research programme aimed to develop an intelligent support to the end-user interaction including a user thesaurus.

1618 Markey, Karen.

Retrieval performance of a KWOC index to the 1498 work unit summary database.

Alexandria, VA : Defense Technical Information Center, 1979. 28p.

Controlled vocabulary based automatic indexing's retrieval performance is compared with KWOC.

1619 Markey, Karen.

Visual arts resources and computers.

Annual Review of Information Science and Technology. Volume 19. Ed. by Martha E. Wliams. New York, Knowledge Industry Publications, Inc., 1984 : 271-309.

Explains the usefulness of thesauri in describing art objects with the help of computer.

1620 Marner, J. C.

Measuring the success of keyword search strategy in an online catalog.

Technical Services Quarterly 11 (2) 1993 : 1-11.

Presents a study that investigated sufficiency of keywords for searching the OPAC and asserts the need for controlled vocabulary.

1621 Marosi, A.

Euratom thesaurus and UDC combined use for the subject organization of a small information service.

Journal of Documentation 25 (3) Sept. 1969 : 197-213.

1622 Masaric, Fred E. and Miller, Randolph A.

Medical Subject Headings and medical terminology : an analysis of terminology used in hospital charts.

Bulletin of the Medical Library Association 75 (2) April 1987 : 89-94.

1623 Mauldin, Michael; Carbonell, Jaime and Thomason, Richmond.

Beyond the keyword barrier : knowledge-based information retrieval.

Information Services and Use 7 (4-5) 1987 : 103-117.

Considering the lacunae of the controlled vocabularies suggests a knowledge-based IR system.

1624 Mazur, Zygmunt.

Inverted file organization in the information retrieval system based on thesaurus with weights.

Information Processing and Management 15 (5) 1979 : 227-234.

Examines properties and operations of inverted files used in a system based on a thesaurus with weights.

1625 Mazur, Zygmunt.

Models of a distributed information retrieval system based on thesauri with weights.

Information Processing and Management 30 (1) Jan.-Feb. 1994 : 61-77.

1626 Mazur, Zygmunt.

On a model of distributed information retrieval systems based on thesauri.

Information Processing and Management 20 (4) 1984 : 499-505.

Describes a mathematical model developed for distributed on-line information retrieval system based on a single thesaurus.

1627 Mazur, Zygmunt.

Organization of the inverted files in a distributed information retrieval system based on thesauri.

Information Processing and Management 22 (3) 1986 : 243-250.

Explains the need to modify operations of local inverted files so as to use them in thesauri based distributed ISRS.

1628 Mazur, Zygmunt.

Properties of a model of information retrieval system based on thesaurus with weights.

Information Processing and Management 15 (3) 1979 : 145-154.

Illustrates the use of a thesaurus with weights in a model IR system.

1629 McAleese, Ray and Duncan, Elizabeth B.

The graphical representation of 'terrain' and 'street' knowledge in an interface to a database system.

Online information 87. Proceedings of the 11th International Online Information Meeting, London, 8-10 December 1987. Oxford : Learned Information (Europe), 1987 : 443-456.

Demonstrate the use of graphical techniques along with thesaurus to represent knowledge in databases.

1630 McKiernan, G.

Beyond bookmarks : a review of frameworks, features, and functionalities of schemes for organizing the Web.

Internet Reference Services Quarterly 3 (1) 1998 : 69-82.

Describes websites that use standard classification schemes and controlled vocabulary.

1631 McLelland, Joe.

Computers, databases and thesauri.

Aslib Proceedings 42 (7-8) July-August 1990 : 201-205.

Describes role of thesauri in maintaining databases.

1632 Mcmath, Chuck; Tamaru, Bob and Rada, Roy.

Graphical interface to thesaurus-based information retrieval systems.

International Journal of Man-Machine Studies 31, 1989 : 121-147.

1633 Micco, Mary and Smith, Irma.

Designing a workstation for information seekers.

Reference Librarian (23) 1989 : 135-152.

Describes a workstation equipped with a CD-ROM jukebox of reference books and vocabulary control tools on laser discs with keyword access.

1634 Miller, E. J.

National reports : Great Britain - Report on the activities of the Sub-committee on Cataloguing and Classification of the Executive Committee of the British and Irish Association of Law Librarians.

International Journal of Law Libraries 1 (2) July 1973 : 83-85.

Discusses issues related with application of vocabulary control in law.

1635 Miller, Peter and Roberts, Mike.

Let your keywords do the walking.

Building. 237 (39) 1979 : 59-60.

Describes use of Construction Industry Thesaurus.

1636 Miller, T.

Looking into the future : the development of Microsoft's internal library shows the way.

Information World Review (125) May 1997 : 18.

Describes the use of controlled vocabulary by the Microsoft's intranet called MSWeb.

1637 Miller, U. and Teitelbaum, R.

Pre-coordination and post-coordination : past and future.

Knowledge Organization 29 (2) 2002 : 87-93.

Explains the pre and post-coordination approaches and thesauri - the tool used by these approaches.

1638 Milstead, J. L.

Cross-file searching : how vendors help-and don't help-improve compatibility.

Searcher 7 (5) May 1999 : 44-55.

Reports a survey aimed to know how various agencies such as database producers, hosts, search facilitators, aggregators etc. manage vocabulary for cross- file search.

1639 Milstead, J. L.

Thesauri in a full text world.

Visualizing subject access for Twenty first Century information resources. Proceedings of the 1997 Clinic on Library Applications of Data Processing, 2-4 Mar 1997. Ed. by Pauline Atherton Cochrane and Eric H. Johnson (with the assistance of Sandra Roe). Urbana-Champaign, Illinois: Illinois University at Urbana-Champaign, Graduate School of Library and Information Science, 1998 : 28-38.

1640 Mitchell, J. S.

Flexible structures in the Dewey Decimal Classification.

Information Studies 4 (4) Oct. 1998 : 212-216.

Describes a method for linking entries from other thesauri to support flexible structures within the DDC.

1641 Mitchell, Kabby.

Preparing computerized ERIC search statements : a self instructional learning package.

Syracuse, New York : ERIC Clearinghouse on Information Resources, 1978. 33p.

Describes a self-instructional learning package designed to teach skills needed to improve computer searches of the ERIC database. This package is to be used with the seventh edition of the 'Thesaurus of ERIC Descriptors'.

1642 Mohjolt, Pat and Petersen, T.

The role of the 'Art and Architecture Thesaurus' in communicating about visual art.

Knowledge Organization 20 (1) 1993 : 30-34.

Examines the role of ATT in developing approaches towards visual arts.

1643 Molholt, Pat; Crouch, D. and Petersen, T.

Art and architecture thesaurus.

The information community : an alliance for progress proceedings of the 44th ASIS Annual Meeting, Washington, DC 25-30 October 1981. Volume 18. Ed. by Lois F. Lunin, Madeline Henderson and Harold Wooster. New York : Knowledge Industry Publications Inc., 1981 : 320-323.

Explains the need of Art and Architecture Thesaurus.

1644 Moorcroft, H.

The construction of silence.

Australian Library Journal 42 (1) Feb. 1993 : 27-32.

Analyses the role of the Australian Public Affairs Information Service thesaurus in controlling and interpreting history of Australian Aboriginal people.

1645 Moore, Alexandra L.

COLUG : Chicago Online Users introductory guide.

Chicago, Online Users Group, IL., 1978. 48p.

Provides guidance for selecting thesauri for online searching.

1646 Morris, Anne; Dyer, Hilary and Dowling, Rick.

Workstation design for the online searcher.

Online information 87. Proceedings of the 11th International Online Information Meeting, London, 8-10 December 1987. Oxford : Learned Information (Europe), 1987 : 227-239.

Discusses role of thesauri in increasing the efficiency of on-line workstations.

1647 Moschopoulos, Dionysis; Papatheodorou, Christos and Prokopiadou, Georgia.

Integrating knowledge management tools for government information.

Government Information Quarterly 21 (2) 2004 : 170-198.

Examines qualities of Ontologies, taxonomies, and thesauri in representing geospatial and administrative hierarchy for management, search, and retrieval of government information.

1648 Moss, Michael and Tough, Alistair.

Metadata, controlled vocabulary and directories : electronic document management and standards for records management.

Records Management Journal 13 (1) 2003 : 24-31.

1649 Moss, R.

Minimum vocabularies in information indexing.

Journal of Documentation 23(2) 1967 : 179-196.

1650 Moys, Elizabeth M.

Cataloguing and indexing

Manual of law librarianship : the use and organization of legal literature. Ed. by Elizabeth M. Moys. London : Andre Deutsch, 1976 : 509-547.

Discusses the role of thesauri and subject heading lists in cataloguing and indexing.

1651 Moys, Elizabeth M.

Legal vocabulary and the indexer.

Indexer 18 (2) Oct. 1992 : 75-78.

1652 Nair, Rajesh and Rost, Burkhard.

Annotating protein function through lexical analysis

AI Magazine 25 (1) Spring 2004 : 45-56.

Explains the use of controlled vocabularies and ontologies in annotating protein functions.

1653 Nanfito, M.

The indexed Web : engineering tools for cataloging, storing and delivering Web based documents.

Information Outlook 3 (2) Feb. 1999 : 18-22.

Describes the creation of Java based software to use controlled vocabularies for cataloguing of legal resources of the web.

1654 Nedobity, Wolfgang.

The relevance of terminologies for automatic abstracting.

Journal of Information Science 4 (4) July 1982 : 161-165.

Discusses issues related with the use of machine-readable subject terminologies for automatic abstracting.

1655 Neelameghan, A. and Prasad, K. N.

Digitized schemes for subject classification and thesauri : complementary roles.

Information Studies 8 (1) Jan. 2002 : 25-42.

Examines complementary roles of subject classification schemes and thesauri in information systems.

1656 Neubert, Gunter.

Machine-aiding of translation processes by user-controlled dictionary look-up.

International Forum on Information and Documentation 5 (2) April 1980 : 30-31.

Explains the importance and use of controlled terms for machine-aiding translation.

1657 Newton, Carl.

The thesaurus is not dead : it was never alive.

Records Management Bulletin (116) Oct. 2003 : 9-12.

Reviews Roget's thesaurus as a tool for records managers.

1658 Nicholson, Scott.

Understanding the foundation : the state of generalist search education in library schools as related to the needs of expert searchers in medical libraries.

Journal of the Medical Library Association (JMLA) 93 (1) Jan. 2005 : 61-68.

Presents report of a survey aimed at knowing focus of LIS education and needs of medical library users regarding online search capabilities based on controlled vocabulary.

1659 Nie, J. Y. and Brisebois, M.

An inferential approach to information retrieval and its implementation using a manual thesaurus.

Artificial Intelligence Review 10 (5-6) Oct. 1996 : 409-439.

Describes a method to incorporate a human defined thesaurus into inference by considering user relevance feedback.

1660 Nielson, L. M.

Tuture thesauri : what kind of conceptual knowledge do searchers need?

Advances in knowledge organization. Volume 6. Structure and relations in knowledge organization. Proceedings of the 5th International ISKO Conference, Lille, France, 25-29 August 1998. Wurzburg, Germany : Ergon, Verlag, 1998 : 153-160.

1661 Nkwenti-Azeh, B.

The use of thesaural facets and definitions for the representation of knowledge structures.

Proceedings of the 3rd International Society for Knowledge Organization (ISKO) Conference : Knowledge organization and quality management. Copenhagen, Denmark, 20-24 June 1994. Ed. by Hanne Albrechtsen and Susan Oernager. Frankfurt/Main : INDEKS Verlag, 1994 : 374-381.

1662 Nuotio, Samuli.

Helsinki Metropolitan Area Public Library Network 1989.

OPACs and the user : Proceedings of the 3rd Anglo-Nordic

Seminar, April 1990. London : British Library, 1991 : 36-37.

Describes the use of the Common Finnish Thesaurus by libraries of Helsinki Metropolitan Area Public Library Network.

1663 OCLC to release beta version of New FirstSearch this month.

Advanced Technology Libraries 28 (4) April 1999 : 2.

Describes beta version of the OCLC, which enables thesaurus aided searching.

1664 Ohlgren, Thomas H.

Image analysis and indexing in North America : a survey.

Art Libraries Journal 7 (2) Summer 1982 : 51-60.

Reports a survey of indexing process and vocabulary control tools used for managing image collections in North America.

1665 Ojala, M.

Print lives!

Business Information Alert 10 (5) May 1998 : 1-3.

Presents results of a survey conducted to know the importance of printed reference sources including thesauri.

1666 O'Leary, Mick.

GuruNet : cheap, simple, and good.

Information Today : 21 (11) Dec. 2004 : 31 and 34.

Describes GuruNet - a multidisciplinary web reference service (www.gurunet.com), which uses thesaurus and other vocabulary tools.

1667 Oppenheim, C.; Perryman, S. and Mulvihill, J.

GoeRef/GeoArchive

Database 3 (4) Dec. 1980 : 41-48.

Compares the two databases in the field of geosciences considering various aspects including the use of thesauri.

1668 Orom, Anders.

Knowledge organization in the domain of art studies - history, transition and conceptual changes.

Knowledge Organization 30 (3-4) 2003 : 128-143.

Examines the need of thesauri and other requirements for the organization of knowledge in the domain of visual art.

1669 Osigwe, C. C.

The effect of semantic and syntactic relationships in the choice of descriptor elements for precision in document indexing and information retrieval.

Quarterly Bulletin of the International Association of Agricultural Information Specialists 37 (4) 1992 : 205-208.

Identifies problems arising from the interaction between semantic and syntactic relationships and proposes the introduction of a generalized thesaurus.

1670 Ostroff, Harriet.

Subject access to archival and manuscripts material.

American Archivist 53 (1) Winter 1990 : 100-105.

Discusses problems in using existing vocabulary control tools in subject cataloguing of archival material and suggests solutions.

1671 Otradinskii, V. V.

A possible dictionary control procedure in formalized document and request indexing.

Nauchno- Tekhnicheskaya Informatsiya; Series 2 (1) 1972 : 9-12.

1672 Paice, Chris D.

A thesaural model of information retrieval.

Information Processing and Management 27 (5) 1991 : 433-447.

Examines the scope for using thesauri for representing user's queries and documents.

1673 Park, J. R.

Hindrances in semantic mapping involving thesauri and metadata : a linguistic perspective.

Journal of Internet Cataloging 5 (3) 2002 : 59-77.

1674 Pasanen-Tuomainen, I.

Monitoring online catalogues in the Nordic technological university libraries.

Nordinfo Nytt (4) 1992 : 23-27.

Reports a study aimed at discovering which terms - (thesauri, free text, title) are used by different types of users to carry out searches on OPACs.

1675 Pedley, P.

Having access to good content is not enough.

Managing Information 9 (1) Jan.-Feb. 2002 : 16-17.

Explains the need of thesauri, taxonomies and classification for efficient information search on the web.

1676 Peters, Thomas A. and Kurth, Martin.

Controlled and uncontrolled vocabulary subject searching in an academic library online catalog.

Information Technology and Libraries 10 (3) Sept. 1991 : 201-211.

1677 Petersen, Toni.

Computer-aided indexing in the arts : the case for a thesaurus of art terms.

Art Libraries Journal 6 (3) Autumn 1981 : 6-11.

Discusses the advantages of thesauri in computerized indexing.

1678 Petersen, Toni.

Information on images : the Art and Architecture Thesaurus as a front end for retrieval.

National Online Meeting. Proceedings 1989, New York, 9-11 May 1989. Ed. by Carol Nixon and Lauree Padgett . Medford,

New Jersey : Learned Information, Inc., 1989 : 335-341.

Reports an experiment carried out at DIALOG to test the AAT's effectiveness as a search tool against natural language queries.

1679 Petersen, Toni.

The AAT in the online catalog environment.

Art Documentation 1 (6) Dec. 1982 : 183-185.

1680 Petersen, Toni and Barnett, P. J.

Guide to indexing and cataloguing with the Art and Architecture.

Journal of the American Society for Information Science 46 (2) March 1995 : 152-160.

1681 Petofi, J. S.

Some aspects of a multi-purpose thesaurus.

International Classification 1 (2) Nov. 1974 : 69-76.

1682 Pickens, Keith.

Adapting ERIC to New Zealand.

Education Libraries Journal 33 (2) Summer 1990 : 8-13.

Reports on using the ERIC thesaurus to index several samples of documents on education in New Zealand Education.

1683 Pickens, Keith.

The relationship of bibliographic database design to the structure of information : a case study in education.

Journal of Documentation 50 (1) March 1994 : 36-44.

Suggests a record structure for an entry in bibliographic database, which uses controlled vocabulary.

1684 Piternick, Anne B.

Searching vocabularies : a developing category of online search tools.

Online Review 8 (5) Oct. 1984 : 441-449.

Asserts the importance of searching vocabularies.

1685 Piternick, Anne B.

Vocabularies for online subject searching.

Encyclopaedia of library and information science. Volume 45, supplement 10. Ed. by Allen Kent. New York : Marcel Dekker Inc., 1990 : 399-420.

1686 Plaunt, C. and Norgard, B. A.

An association-based method for automatic indexing with controlled vocabulary.

Journal of the American Society for Information Science 49 (10) August 1998 : 887-902.

1687 Pokras, Yu L.

Retrieval recall and precision as affected by additional indexing of requests with the aid of a thesaurus.

Nauchno- Tekhnicheskaya Informatsiya; Series 2 (4) 1970 : 32-37.

1688 Pollard, R.

A hypertext-based thesaurus as a subject browsing aid for bibliographic databases.

Information Processing and Management 29 (3) May-June 1993 : 345-357.

1689 Pollitt, Arthur Steven.

MenUSE for medicine : end-user browsing and searching of MEDLINE via the MeSH Thesaurus.

International Forum on Information and Documentation 13 (4) Oct. 1988 : 11-17.

Describes the MeSH based IR system called MenUSE -Menu-based User Search Engine used for browsing and searching MEDLINE.

1690 Pollitt, Arthur Steven.

The key role of classification and indexing in view-based searching.

International Cataloguing and Bibliographic Control 27 (2) April-June 1998 : 37-40.

Discusses the usefulness of classified arrangement in thesauri to be used for view-based searching.

1691 Pollitt, Arthur Steven and Ellis, G. P.

Improving search quality using thesauri for query specification and the presentation of search results.

Proceedings of the 3rd International Society for Knowledge Organization (ISKO) Conference : Knowledge organization and quality management. Copenhagen, Denmark, 20-24 June 1994. Ed. by Hanne Albrechtsen and Susan Oernager. Frankfurt/Main : INDEKS Verlag, 1994 : 382-389.

1692 Pollitt, Arthur Steven; Smith, M. P. and Ellis, G. P.

Peek-a-boo revived : end-user searching of bibliographic databases using filtering views.

Online Information 94. Proceedings of the 18th International Online Information Meeting, London, 6-8 December 1994. Ed. by David I. Raitt and Ben Jeapes. Oxford : Learned Information (Europe) Ltd., 1994 : 63-73.

Explains use of Boolean combinations along with thesauri for searching EPOQUE and INSPEC databases.

1693 Pollitt, Arthur Steven et al.

A common query interface for multilingual document retrieval from databases of the European Community Institutions.

Online Information 93. Proceedings of the 17th International Online Information Meeting, London, 7-9 December 1993. Ed. by David I. Raitt and Ben Jeapes, Oxford : Learned Information (Europe) Ltd, 1993 : 47-61.

Describes EuroMenUse software (Developed to improve access to EPOQUE - a document database of the European Parliament), which uses the EUROVOC thesaurus.

1694 Pollitt, Steve.

The careful choice of confusing words.

Computing 8 (30) 24 July 1980 : 22.

Describe methods, such as, use of controlled vocabulary, truncations etc. that help to improve precision.

1695 Poswick, R. F.

ETHERELI (European Thesaurus for Indexing in Religious Libraries).

Bulletin of the Association of British Theological and Philosophical Libraries 5 (2) June 1998 : 4-7.

Proposes creation of an European Thesaurus for Indexing in Religious Libraries.

1696 Preschel, Barbara M.

Encyclopedia article titles as thesauri terms in indexing.

The information age in perspective. Proceedings of the 41st Annual Meeting, New York, 13-17 November 1978. Volume 15. Compiled by Everett H. Brenner. White Plains, New York : Knowledge Industry Publications for American Society for Information Science, 1978 : 264-266.

1697 Priss, U.

Lattice based information retrieval.

Knowledge Organization 27 (3) 2000 : 132-142.

Explains the use of 'FaIR' - a lattice model of IR, which incorporates a graphical representation of a faceted thesaurus.

1698 ProQuest introduces ProQuest Smart Search.

Advanced Technology Libraries 33 (9) Sept. 2004 : 2-3.

Reports various techniques used for mapping user's search terms to Pro-Quest Smart Search system's controlled vocabulary.

1699 ProQuest launches dissertation archiving program.

Advanced Technology Libraries 32 (11) Nov. 2003 : 4.

Describes the dissertation archiving program and explains how its expert indexing based on controlled vocabulary ensure easy search.

1700 Qin, J.

Semantic similarities between a keyword database and a controlled vocabulary database : an investigation in the antibiotic resistance literature.

Journal of the American Society for Information Science 51 (2) Feb. 2000 : 166-180.

Examines similarities and dissimilarities of databases based on keywords and controlled vocabulary.

1701 Quam, E.

Informing and evaluating a metadata initiative : usability and metadata studies in Minnesota's 'Foundations' Project.

Government Information Quarterly 18 (3) 2001 : 181-194.

Examines the feasibility of using controlled vocabulary in DC metadata.

1702 Quint, B.

H. W. Wilson launches major upgrade of WilsonWeb.

Information Today 19 (11) Dec. 2002 : 24.

Describes various features of WilsonWeb including the availability of database specific subject thesaurus.

1703 Quint, B.

Out-of-the-box experiences and taxonomies.

Information Today 18 (10) Nov. 2001 : 8 and 10 and 12.

Describes thesauri as one of the content management tools.

1704 Rackmore, Marlene.

Facet analysis and thesauri for corporate information retrieval.

Tools for knowledge organisation and the human interface. Proceedings of the 1st International ISKO Conference, Darmstadt, (Germany) *14-17 August 1990. Advances in knowledge organization, no. 1/2.* Ed. by R. Fugmann. Part II. Frankfurt/Main : Indeks. 1990 : 233-238.

Discuses the advantages of facet analysis and thesauri in corporate ISRS.

1705 Rada, Roy.

Connecting and evaluating thesauri : issues and cases.

International Classification 14 (2) 1987 : 63-69.

Reports experiments in connecting the MeSH with other thesauri in medical science.

1706 Rada, Roy and Bicknell, Ellen.

Ranking documents with a thesaurus.

Journal of the American Society for Information Science 40 (5) Sept. 1989 : 304-310.

Reports on the use of a formula called DISTANCE evolved for evaluating and improving a thesaurus through studying its effect on retrieval.

1707 Rada, Ray et al.

Document ranking using an enriched thesaurus.

Journal of Documentation 47 (3) Sept. 1991 : 240-253.

1708 Rada, Roy. et al.

A vocabulary for medical informatics.

Computer and Biomedical Research 20, 1987 : 244-263.

1709 Radecki, Tadeusz.

Mathematical model of information retrieval system based on the concept of fuzzy thesaurus.

Information Processing and Management 12 (5) 1976 : 313-318.

Presents a mathematical model of IR based on Zadeh's theory of fuzzy set, which enables to use the concept of a fuzzy thesaurus to formalize relations between terms describing documents and user's requests.

1710 Rainey, L.

Experiences with the new TEST thesaurus and the new NASA

thesaurus.

Special Libraries 61 (1) Jan. 1970 : 26-32.

1711 Raitt, D. I.

Recall and precision devices in interactive bibliographic search and retrieval systems.

Aslib Proceedings 32 (7-8) July-August 1980 : 281-301.

Explains thesauri based searches and recall and precision devices.

1712 Reich, Phyllis and Biever, Erik J.

Indexing consistency : the input / output function of thesauri.

College and Research Libraries 52 (4) July 1991 : 336-342.

1713 Renford, Beverly L.

MeSH and the quality of searching.

DLA Bulletin 9 (3) Winter 1989 : 3-5.

1714 Revie, Crawford and Shiri, Ali Asghar.

The effects of topic complexity and familiarity on cognitive and physical moves in a thesaurus-enhanced search environment.

Journal of Information Science 29 (6) 2003 : 517-526.

1715 Ribeiro, F.

Subject indexing and authority control in archives : the need for subject indexing in archives and for an indexing policy using controlled language.

Journal of the Society of Archivists 17 (1) April 1996 : 27-54.

Discusses the importance of controlled vocabulary in subject indexing.

1716 Ribeiro-Neto, Berthier and Silveira, Maria L.

Concept-based ranking : a case study in the juridical domain.

Information Processing and Management 40 (5) Sept. 2004 : 791-805.

Explains how query terms are used to match concepts in thesaurus, which ultimately helped to improve precision.

1717 Richardson, R. and Smeaton, A. F.

Automatic word sense disambiguation in a KBIR application.

New Review of Document and Text Management 1, 1995 : 299-319.

Describes a Knowledge Based IR system, which used the knowledge base as a controlled vocabulary to represent documents and queries.

1718 Richmond, Phyllis A.

A thesaurus within a thesaurus : a study in ambiguity.

Towards a theory of librarianship : papers in honour of Jesse Hauk Shera. Ed. by Conrad H. Rawski Metuchen, New Jersey : Scarecrow Press, 1973 : 268-301.

1719 Richwine, P. W.

A study of MeSH and UMLS for subject searching in an online catalog.

Bulletin of the Medical Library Association 81 (2) April 1993 : 229-233.

1720 Roberts, D. and Souter, C.

The automation of controlled vocabulary subject indexing of medical journal articles.

Aslib Proceedings 52 (10) Nov.-Dec. 2000 : 384-401.

Explains the advantages of automaton of indexing based on controlled vocabulary.

1721 Roberts, G. Louis and Kenny, Carol E.

Hypertext image retrieval : the evolution of an application.

Microcomputers for Information Management 8 (3) Sept. 1991 : 167-185.

Describes the changes in interface brought about by moving from workstation platform to client server, and combining a controlled vocabulary database with a full text database.

1722 Roberts, Mike and Miller, Peter.

Information retrieval by keywords.

DOE Construction (20) Dec. 1976 : 37-38.

1723 Robinson, F.

A computer based retrieval system using a reactive thesaurus.

Information Storage and Retrieval 6 (2) June 1970 : 171-177.

1724 Robinson, M. L.

A survey of SIC code searchable databases on DIALOG.

Online Review 13 (4) August 1989 : 313-319.

Presents results of a survey of use of the Standard Industrial Classification codes as a form of controlled vocabulary by business databases.

1725 Roe, S.

Online subject access.

Journal of Internet Cataloging 2 (1) 1999 : 69-78.

Explains usefulness of thesauri in online subject access.

1726 Roe, S. K.

Subject access vocabularies in a multi-type library consortium.

Cataloging and Classification Quarterly 33 (2) 2001 : 55-67.

1727 Rogalski, Leanore.

On-line searching of the American Petroleum Institute's databases.

Journal of Chemical Information and Computer Sciences 18 (1) Feb. 1978 : 9-12.

Describes searching of the American Petroleum Institute's databases by using controlled vocabulary.

1728 Romanos, Vasso Apostolidis and Fittipaldi, John J.

The Energy Related Construction Information System ERCIS : response to a need for information on army facilities

Online Review 11 (3) June 1987 : 167-181.

Describes the ERCIS – a controlled vocabulary based bibliographic information system.

1729 Ropke, W.

Classifications of statistics used as thesauri.

Nachrichten fur Dokumentation 25 (3) June 1974 : 112-122.

1730 Ross, Johanna C.

Searching the chemical literature via three on-line vendors : a comparison.

Journal of the American Society for Information Science 30 (2) March 1979 : 103-106.

Nine chemical databases available online via vendors are compared considering various criteria including use of controlled vocabulary.

1731 Rousseau, R.

Use of an existing thesaurus in a knowledge based indexing and retrieval system.

Annals of Library Science and Documentation 38 (4) Dec. 1991 : 127-130.

1732 Rowley, J. E. and Butcher, D. R.

The Searcher / Information Interface Project 2 : manual and online searching—pilot study.

Journal of Information Science 15 (2) 1989 : 109-114.

Reports a pilot study that evaluated search success by considering the search and thesaurus terminology as some of the criteria.

1733 Roy, A. K.

Indexing vocabularies in glass technology and need for an information retrieval thesaurus : a pilot study.

Seminar on thesaurus in information system. Banglore : DRTC, 1975 : Paper CH.

1734 Roy, A. K.

Thesaurus in information system.

Indexing systems: concepts, models and techniques. Ed. by T. N. Rajan. Calcutta : IASLIC, 1981 : 164-165.

1735 Ruan, L.

Providing better subject access to nonprint fire emergency materials for Illinois firefighters.

Cataloging and Classification Quarterly 31 (3-4) 2001 : 213-235.

Describes the use of FireTalk - a Fire Service Institute's (Library) thesaurus in effective searching of the OPAC.

1736 Russell, B. M.

'Anchors aweigh!': cruise books in a military history collection.

Humanities Collections 1 (2) 1999 : 33-39.

Provides information about Cruise books collections i.e. pictorial works produced by ships' crews to document the daily life and voyages of their vessel and states that controlled vocabulary to catalogue them will help to enhance access to these collections.

1737 Sahli, Marilyn Sue.

Terminology of the social sciences : the term 'cognitive processes' in the thesauri of two discipline-based information systems.

Ann Arbor, Michigan : University Microforms International, 1981. 245p.

Analyzes the term 'cognitive processes in ERIC thesaurus and Thesaurus of Psychological Index terms.

1738 Saito, K.

The present status and the future of JICST Domestic Medical Literature File.

Journal of Information Processing and Management 25 (2) 1982 : 102-124.

Describes JICST's (Japan Information Centre for Science and Technology) file of domestic medical literature, which contains bibliographic records prepared under the descriptors taken from the JICST Thesaurus on Science and Technology.

1739 Saito, T.

Development of an interactive data base system for document retrieval and thesaurus study.

Library and Information Science (12) 1974 : 243-258.

1740 Salami, R.

Agricultural documentation-The I.A.R. Information Retrieval System.

Library Scientist 10, 1983 : 35-47.

Describes the thesaurus-based Institute for Agricultural Research information system.

1741 Saracevic, Tefko.

Intellectual organization of knowledge : the American contribution.

Bulletin of the American Society for Information Science 2 (8) March 1976 : 16-17.

Examines the use of thesauri in the intellectual organization of knowledge.

1742 Sasamori, K.

IR-Lecture series 7 : Thesaurus no. 2.

Dokumentesyon Kenkyu 20 (2) Feb. 1970 : 46-53.

1743 Scammell, A.

Use of the CAIRS' thesaurus facility at the Council of Mortgage lenders.

Managing Information 1 (2) Feb. 1994 : 35-37.

Describes use of Computer Assisted Information Retrieval System's thesaurus.

1744 Schimpfermann, M.; Pollok, K. and Gerisch, H.

On the compatibility of national thesauri as a prerequisite for the creation of an international building information system.

Informatika 18 (4) 1971 : 23-25.

1745 Schmidt, R. M.

Online public access catalogs serving users in an electronic library environment.

Proceedings of the 15th International Essen Symposium : Opportunity 2000 : understanding and serving users in an electronic library. 12-15 October 1992. Ed. by Ahmed H. Helal and Joachim W. Weiss. Essen, Germany : Universitatsbibliothek Essen, 1993 : 263-276.

Highlights importance of thesauri in online catalogues.

1746 Schmitz-Esser, Winifried.

New approaches to thesaurus application.

International Classification 18 (3) 1991 : 143-147.

Explains the scope for the use of thesauri in expert systems; interface systems; object-oriented design and programming; hypertext systems; machine translation; and computerized abstracting.

1747 Schmitz-Esser, Winfried.

Thesauri facing new challenges.

International Classification 17 (3-4) 1990 : 129-132.

Discusses various issues concerning the use of thesauri in computerized ISRS.

1748 Schuller, J. A.

Manual systems-TDCK circular thesaurus system.

Storage and retrieval of information : a user-supplier-dialogue. Proceedings. 18-30-June-1968. Neuly-sur-Seine : North Atlantic Treaty Organization, Advisory Group for Aerospace Research and Development, 1968 : 99-110.

1749 Schumacher, B.

Content integration for customer-focused applications.

Information Today 20 (1) 2003 : 58.

Explains the need of controlled vocabulary for integrating structured company data.

1750 Schutze, H. and Pederson, J. O.

A co-occurrence-based thesaurus and two applications to information retrieval.

Information Processing and Management 33 (3) May 1997 : 307-318.

1751 Sciffmann, Genevieve N.

'Hedges'... The sometimes ignored search technique that can save a lot of time.

Online 9 (6) Nov. 1985 : 40-41.

Defines hedges and explains the use of hedges.

1752 Sedlow, Walter A.

Semantics for humanities applications : context and significance of semantic 'stores'.

ASIS '85. Proceedings of the 48th ASIS Annual Meeting 1985. Las Vegas, Nevada, 20-24 October 1985. Volume 22. Ed. by Carol A. Parkhurst. White Plains, New York : Knowledge Industry Publications Inc., 1985 : 363-366.

Examines computational studies of thesauri and dictionaries as possible approaches to the study of semantic spaces in humanities.

1753 Semturs, Friedrich.

STAIRS/TLS-a system for 'free text' and 'descriptor' searching.

The information age in perspective. Proceedings of the 41st Annual Meeting, New York, 13-17 November 1978. Volume 15. Compiled by Everett H. Brenner. White Plains, New York : Knowledge Industry Publications for American Society for Information Science, 1978 : 295-298.

Describes use of thesauri in formulating query while searching the Storage and Information Retrieval System's Thesaurus and Linguistic Information System.

1754 Sengupta, Benoyendra.

Press cutting in news libraries : their arrangement and filing.

Indian Journal of Library Science 3 (1-4) Jan.-Dec. 1977 : 16-22.

Suggests the use of controlled vocabulary for arranging information in the press cutting's files.

1755 Seulowitz, Lois.

All the news that's fit to printout.

Online 1 (1) Jan. 1977 : 57-60.

Explains the use of controlled vocabulary by the York Times Information Bank and describes its other features.

1756 Shapiro, C. D. and Yan, P. F.

Generous tools : thesauri in digital libraries.

Proceedings of the 17th National Online Meeting 1996. 14-16 May 1996. Ed. by Martha E. Wliams. Medford, New Jersey : Information Today, Inc., 1996 : 323-332.

1757 Sharp, Geoffrey.

Online business information.

Online 2 (1) Jan. 1978 : 33-40.

Explains use of 3 thesauri in accessing Predicasts (database).

1758 Shaw, D.

Bibliographic database searching by graduate students in language and literature : search strategies, system interfaces, and relevance judgments.

Library and Information Science Research 17 (4) Fall 1995 : 327-345.

Reports controlled vocabulary as one of the influencing factors of searcher's behaviour of language and literature students.

1759 Shaw, D.

Undergraduate use of CD-ROM databases : observations of human-computer interaction and relevance judgments.

Library and Information Science Research 18 (3) 1996 : 261-274.

Presents results of an experiment that tested how controlled vocabulary helped the undergraduates to make relevance judgments while searching CD-ROM databases.

1760 Shekhtman, N. A.

The thesaurus : a form of presenting semantic information.

Nauchno- Tekhnicheskaya Informatsiya; Series II (2) 1973 : 25-27.

1761 Shemakin, Yu I.

Some problems relating to the development and study of a descriptive information retrieval language in the field of general technology.

Nauchno- Tekhnicheskaya Informatsiya; Series 2 (6) 1969 : 8-13

1762 Shemakin, Yu I. and Kulik, A. N.

On information retrieval system compatibility and the role of a polytechnical thesaurus in a unified information network.

Nauchno- Tekhnicheskaya Informatsiya; Series II (8) 1970 : 30-34.

1763 Sheppard, Judy and Schleffler, Diane.

Subject headings for information and referral.

California Librarian 37 (3) 1976 : 14-17.

1764 Shiri, A. A.; Revie, C. and Chowdhury, G.

Thesaurus assisted search term selection and query expansion : a review of user centered studies.

Knowledge Organization 29 (1) 2002 : 1-19.

1765 Shiri, A. A.; Revie, C. and Chowdhury, G.

Thesaurus-enhanced search interfaces.

Journal of Information Science 28 (2) 2002 : 111-122.

Also available at : http://www.ingentaselect.com/lg=eng/nw=1/rpsv/ij/sage/01655515/v28n2/s3/p111

Provides a review of a category of information retrieval interfaces that are enhanced by incorporating standard thesauri as part of their searching and browsing facilities.

1766 Shively, Daniel.

CD-ROM public access catalogs : database creation and maintenance.

Library Hi Tech 6 (1) 1988 : 67-86.

Explains use of controlled vocabulary in CD-ROM public access catalogues.

1767 Shively, Daniel.

Idea retrieval.

Technical Services Quarterly 6 (1) 1988 : 23-30.

Describes a model for idea retrieval, which includes controlled vocabulary and logical structuring.

1768 Shoham, S. and Kedar, R.

The subject cataloging of monographs with the use of keywords.

Cataloging and Classification Quarterly 33 (2) 2001 : 29-54.

Highlights the importance of thesaurus in indexing and compares indexing efficiency of library science students and expert indexers.

1769 Sievert, MaryEllen and Boyce, Bert R.

Hedge trimming and the resurrection of the controlled vocabulary in online searching.

Online Review 7 (6) Dec. 1983 : 489-494.

States the need to analyze and minimize the entry terms for effective online searching.

1770 Sihvonen, Anne and Vakkari, Pertti.

Subject knowledge improves interactive query expansion assisted by a thesaurus.

Journal of Documentation 60 (6) 2004 : 673-690.

Reports results of an experiment, which reveals that the use of thesauri by subject experts has an advantage over the non-experts.

1771 Sikorski, L.

Structure of a uniform thesaurus for various branches of industry : illustrated by the example of the thesaurus for 'Agricultural Machines and Mechanisation of Agriculture'.

Informatika 18 (6) 1971 : 23-26.

1772 Silva, W. T. and Milidiu, R. L.

Belief Function Model for information retrieval.

Journal of the American Society for Information Science 44 (1) Jan. 1993 : 10-18.

Describes the Belief Function Model – a model of automatic indexing based on controlled vocabulary.

1773 Silvester, J. P.; Genuardi, M. T. and Klingbiel, P. H.

Machine-aided indexing at NASA.

Information Processing and Management 30 (5) Sept.-Oct. 1994 : 631-645.

Describes NASA's computer assisted indexing system that automatically suggests a set of candidate terms from NASA's controlled vocabulary for any natural language text input.

1774 Simmons, Robert M.

A library user's guide to ERIC 1980 edition.

Syracuse, New York : ERIC Clearinghouse on Information Resources, 1980. 36p.

1775 Slater, Ron.

Authority control in a bilingual OPAC : MultiLIS at Laurentian.

Library Resources and Technical Services 35 (4) Oct. 1991 : 422-458.

1776 Slaton, G. and Zhang, Y.

Enhancement of text representations using related document titles.

Information Processing and Management 22 (5) 1986 : 385-394.

Explains the advantages of using titles of related documents to extract terms useful for indexing.

1777 Smit, A.

Cartographic material in the Pica Library Network : system description.

European Research Libraries Cooperation 2 (2) 1992 : 176-191.

Describes thesauri and authority files available for searching the PICA (Project for Integrated Catalogue Automation) network in the Netherlands.

1778 Smith, A. G.

Search features of digital libraries.

Information Research 5 (3) April 2000. No page numbers.

Also available at : http://www.shef.ac.uk/~is/publications/infres/paper73.html

Explains the need of controlled vocabulary for effective use of digital libraries.

1779 Smith, Aida Marissa.

An examination of PubMed's ability to disambiguate subject queries and journal title queries.

Journal of the Medical Library Association (JMLA) 92 (1) Jan. 2004 : 97-100.

Also available at : http://www.pubmedcentral.nih.gov/articlerender.fcgi?artid=314110

Evaluates PubMed's (a term mapping system available on the

MEDLINE) ability to match user's terms to controlled vocabulary.

1780 Smith, I. A. and O'Brien, A.

Signposts to information : keywords, indexes and thesauri.

Education Libraries Journal 36 (3) Autumn 1993 : 7-27.

Explains with examples the use of thesauri in effective IR.

1781 Smith, Inese A.

Development of indexing systems at the National Youth Bureau.

Catalogue and Index (73) Summer 1984 : 1-4.

Describes the development of an indexing system based on Thesaurus on youth.

1782 Smith, L. C.

Systematic searching of abstracts and indexes in interdisciplinary areas.

Journal of the American Society for Information Science 25 (6) Nov.-Dec. 1974 : 343-353.

Examines the use of thesauri in searching interdisciplinary information sources.

1783 Snow, Bonnie.

A new medical device directory online : ECRI's HEALTH DEVICES SOURCEBOOK.

Online 13 (3) May 1989 : 103-107.

Describes the HEALTH DEVICES SOURCEBOOK- a controlled vocabulary based database.

1784 Snow, Bonnie.

Why use a database thesaurus.

Online 9(6) November 1985 : 92-96.

1785 Socci, A. C. F.

A thesaurus for improving information retrieval in an integrated legal expert system.

Proceedings of the 3rd International Society for Knowledge Organization (ISKO) Conference : Knowledge organization and quality management. Copenhagen, *Denmark, 20-24 June 1994.* Ed. by Hanne Albrechtsen and Susan Oernager. Frankfurt/Main : INDEKS Verlag, 1994 : 242-250.

1786 Soergel, D.

A Universal Source Thesaurus as a classification generator.

Journal of the American Society for Information Science 23 (5) Sept.-Oct. 1972 : 299-305.

1787 Sokolov, A. V.

On the pragmatics of a descriptor language (from an analysis of empirical microthesauri).

Nauchno- Tekhnicheskaya Informatsiya; Series II (6) 1970 : 14-21.

1788 Sommar, H. G. and Dennis, D. E.

A new method of weighted term searching with a highly structured thesaurus.

Proceedings of the 32nd *Annual Meeting of the American Society for Information Science, San Franciso, 1-4 October 1969.* Volume. 6. Westport, CT : Greenwood Publishing, 1969 : 193-198.

1789 Spang Hanssen, Henning.

Multilingual problems in scientific and technical information and documentation.

Tidskrift for Dokumentation 33 (2) 1977 : 13-15.

Discusses the multilingual problems associated with abstracts in controlled languages, and subject indicators-word-like indicators in thesauri.

1790 Spink, A.

Term relevance feedback and mediated database searching : implications for information retrieval practice and systems design.

Information Processing and Management 31 (2) March-April 1995 : 161-171.

Examines the effectiveness of search terms identified by users and intermediaries from retrieved items during term relevance feedback.

1791 Srinivasan, P.

Optimal document-indexing vocabulary for MEDLINE.

Information Processing and Management 32 (5) Sept. 1996 : 503-514.

Explains the use of MeSH in text retrieval.

1792 Srinivasan, P. et al.

Vocabulary mining for information retrieval : rough sets and fuzzy sets.

Information Processing and Management 37 (1) Jan. 2001 : 15-38.

Explains how rough sets and fuzzy sets help in vocabulary mining.

1793 Stalcup, William S. and Petrarca, Anthony E.

Automatic vocabulary control and its evaluation in computer-produced indexes.

Information revolution. Proceedings of the 38th ASIS Annual Meeting, Boston, Massachusetts, October 26-30. Volume 12. Ed. by Charles W. Husbands and Ruth L. Tighe. Washington, DC : American Society for Information Science, 1975 : 73-74.

Describes the use of machine-readable thesauri in automatic vocabulary control.

1794 Starr, J.

Content classification : leveraging new tools and librarians' expertise.

Searcher 7 (9) Oct. 1999 : 10-18.

Examines importance of automatic thesauri and other similar

tools such as taxonomy and classification in IR.

1795 Steiner, W. A.

Thesaurus problems : thesaurus problems as exemplified by the Index to Foreign Legal Periodicals.

International Journal of Law Libraries 2 (1) March 1974 : 5-13.

1796 Still, Julie.

A comparison of online search strategy formation as presented in British and American textbooks.

Microcomputers for Information Management 13 (3-4) 1996 : 301-310.

Discusses keyword and controlled vocabulary searching as presented in the UK and US textbooks.

1797 Still, Julie.

Cultural differences on online search strategy formation.

National Online Meeting 1991. Proceedings of the 12th National Online Meeting, New York, 7-9 May 1991. Ed. by Martha E. Wliams. Medford, New Jersey : Learned Information, Inc., 1991 : 385-389.

Reports a study conducted to investigate impact of cultural differences on using controlled or uncontrolled vocabularies.

1798 Still, Julie.

The anthropology of online search strategy formation : a study of four countries.

Online and CD-ROM Review 20 (2) April 1996 : 59-66.

Presents results of a survey conducted to know the influence of culture on user's IR skills, which indicated that users from different cultures have different tendency towards using controlled vocabulary.

1799 Studwell, W. E.

The three camps : the present and possible future status of subject access in online catalogues.

Behavioral and Social Sciences Librarian 14 (2) 1996 : 61-64.

Examines the future of LCSH in the context of subject access in online catalogues.

1800 [The] subject enhancement of OPAC records and the need for multilingual access.

Vine (90) March 1993 : 33-35.

Explains the potential of controlled vocabulary for multilingual access to OPACs.

1801 Sutton, E. and Foulke, L.

Coverage of anthropology by major electronic indexes : a comparison.

Reference Services Review 27 (2) 1999 : 134-157.

Compares eight databases covering anthropology considering various criteria including availability of controlled vocabulary.

1802 Tague, Jean M.

User-responsive subject control in bibliographic retrieval systems.

Information Processing and Management 17 (3) 1981 : 149-159.

Reports a study carried out to test the effectiveness of user vocabulary.

1803 Tarker, Barbara.

The SMOKING AND HEALTH Database.

Medical Reference Services Quarterly 6 (4) Winter 1987 : 53-63.

Reports the development of the Smoking and Health database and the use of controlled vocabulary.

1804 Tatalias, Jean.

Attitudes and expectations of potential end user online searchers.

National Online Meeting proceedings 1985: *New York, April*

30 - May 2, 1985. Compiled by Martha E. Wliams and Thomas H. Hogan. Medford, New Jersey : Learned Information Inc. 1985 : 457-462.

Presents results of survey, which indicates that users require thesaurus among other things for effective online search.

1805 Taylor, B. L.

Chenhall's Nomenclature, the Art and Architecture Thesaurus, and issues of access in America's artifact collections.

Art Documentation 15 (2) 1996 : 17-23.

Explains Chenhall's Nomenclature for Museum Cataloguing and ATT's role in enhancing access to America's artifact collections.

1806 Tedd, Lucy A.

Report on a visit to European computer-based information services.

Program 13 (2) April 1979 : 47-57.

Describes use of thesauri at European computer-based information services.

1807 Tenopir, Carol.

Full text database retrieval performance.

Online Review 9 (2) April 1985 : 149-164.

Examines the retrieval performance of full text databases and role of controlled vocabulary.

1808 Tenopir, Carol.

Human or automated, indexing is important.

Library Journal 124 (18) Nov. 1999 : 34 and 38.

Argues the importance of controlled vocabulary in automatic indexing.

1809 Terry, J. E.

Consistency between indexers using the Euratom Thesaurus.

Harwell : Atomic Energy Research Establishment, 1970. 7p.

1810 Thirion, B. and Darmoni, S. J.

Simplified access to MeSH tree structures on CISMeF.

Bulletin of the Medical Library Association 87 (4) Oct. 1999 : 480-481.

Describes use of MeSH in the development of online catalogue of health Internet resources for French speaking health and medical professionals.

1811 Thomas, Sarah E.

Use of the CAB thesaurus at the National Agricultural Library.

Quarterly Bulletin of the International Association of Agricultural Information Specialists 30 (3) 1985 : 61-65.

Explains the procedure adopted, difficulties faced and alternations made while using the CAB thesaurus at NAL.

1812 Tieman, R.

Boeing accelerates era of plane English.

Financial Times 28 July 1999 : 14.

Asserts the importance of controlled vocabulary for the communication of aircraft industry.

1813 Tillotson, J.

Is keyword searching the answer?

College and Research Libraries 56 (3) May 1995 : 199-206.

Discusses how keyword searching and controlled vocabulary searching are offered and explained in currently available OPACs.

1814 TINlib—two applications.

Vine (78) May 1990 : 4-9.

Reports experience of using thesaural control enabled library software called 'TINlib'

1815 Toth, I. A.

Coordinate indexing with descriptors for information retrieval on Uniterm and Peek-a-Boo cards in the technical library network of the meat industry.

Tudomanyos es Muszaki Tajekoztatas 15 (10) Oct. 1968 : 734-750.

1816 Toy-Smith, V.

Core records : is this the answer to cooperative cataloging?

Journal of Educational Media and Library Sciences 36 (2) Dec. 1998 : 143-161.

Discusses thesauri as one of the essential elements in the development of core records.

1817 Trautman, Rodes and Flittner, Sara vonx.

An expert system for microcomputers to aid selection of online databases.

Reference Librarian (23) 1989 : 207-238.

Describes the development of an open-ended classification system for online databases with nine attributes each one of which has a controlled vocabulary.

1818 Trubkin, Loene.

Auto-indexing of the 1971-77 ABI/INFORM database.

Database 2 (2) June 1979 : 56-61.

Described controlled vocabulary based auto-indexing.

1819 Turner, J. M.; Hudon, M. and Devin, Y.

Organising moving image collections for the digital era.

Information Outlook 6 (8) August 2002 : 14-18.

Various aspects of organization of moving image collection are discussed including terms found in related thesauri.

1820 Turner, N. B.

Baffled, befuddled or bemused : testing students' use of the online catalog.

College and Undergraduate Libraries 9 (1) 2002 : 71-79.

Explains that controlled vocabulary is one of confusing factor for the undergraduate users of OPAC.

1821 Turski, W. M.

A correspondence between thesaurus-based and multi-attribute retrieval systems.

Information Storage and Retrieval 8 (6) Dec. 1972 : 309-313.

1822 Turski, W. M.

On a model of information retrieval system based on thesaurus.

Information Storage and Retrieval 7 (2) August 1971 : 89-94.

1823 Tuttle, M. S. and Nelson, S. J.

A poor precedent.

Methods of Information in Medicine 35 (3) Sept. 1996 : 211-217.

Comments on J. J. Cimino's article entitled 'formal descriptions and adaptive mechanisms for changes in controlled medical vocabularies'.

1824 Ungurian, O.

The problem of the choice of a retrieval language for the Polish information system.

Aktualne Problemy Informacji Dokumentacji 19 (1) 1974 : 14-20.

1825 Ungvary, Rudolf.

Application of the thesaurus method to the communication of knowledge.

International Classification 10 (2) 1983 : 63-68.

Explains how thesaural displays are useful in teaching / communication.

1826 Van Camp, Ann J.

The MeSH vocabulary file and CHEMLINE : online sources of chemical nomenclature.

Medical Reference Services Quarterly 3 (1) Spring 1984 : 1-17.

Describes usefulness of MeSH and CHEMLINE (chemical terminology for free-text searching) for indexing and searching various databases.

1827 Van Hern, Linda J.

A hedge for searching nutrition and disease on MEDLINE.

Medical Reference Services Quarterly 3 (2) Summer 1984 : 31-42.

Describes use of a hedge i.e. list of terms used in searching nutritional aspects of disease on MEDLINE.

1828 Van Why, Carol B.

Machine assisted reference service : the MELSA experience.

Occasional Papers of the Minnesota Library Association (2) 1982 : 11-14.

Describes the Assisted Reference Service programme considering thesauri and other things.

1829 Vardy, D. A.; Gill, R. P. and Israeli, A.

Coding medical information : classification versus nomenclature and implications to the Israeli Medical System.

Journal of Medical Systems 22 (4) August 1998 : 203-210.

1830 Vasiljev, Anatol.

Enhancement of the subject access vocabulary in an online catalogue.

*Tools for knowledge organisation and the human interface. Proceedings of the 1st International ISKO Conference, Darmstadt, (*Germany) *14-17 August 1990. Advances in knowledge organization, no. 1/2.* Ed. by R. Fugmann. Part I. Frankfurt/Main : Indeks. 1990 : 163-170.

Explains role of thesauri in increasing effectiveness of OPAC.

1831 Vernimb, C.

A computerised information system faces its customers.

Euro Spectra 9 (1) March 1970 : 11-19.

Discusses usefulness of thesauri in managing computerized bibliographic information.

1832 Vernimb, C.

Indexing rules for the Euratom Nuclear Documentation System (ENDS).

Luxembourg : European Atomic Energy Commission, Euratom, 1969. 40p.

Gives rules for indexing with the use of thesauri.

1833 Vernimb, C.

Retrieval optimization by feedback.

Handling of nuclear information. Proceedings of the symposium organized by the International Atomic Energy Agency and held in Vienna. 16-20 February 1970. Vienna : IAEA, 1970 : 221-226.

Asserts the importance of thesauri in optimizing retrieval.

1834 Vernimb, C.

The importance of a thesaurus in retrieval.

Nachrichten fur Dokumentation 20 (3) June 1969 : 128-134.

1835 Vickery, Brian.

Classificatory principles in intelligent interfaces.

*Tools for knowledge organisation and the human interface. Proceedings of the 1st International ISKO Conference, Darmstadt, (*Germany) *14-17 August 1990. Advances in knowledge organization, no. 1/2.* Ed. by R. Fugmann. Part I. Frankfurt/Main : Indeks. 1990 : 14-20.

Explains how the structures of vocabulary control tools help to develop intelligent interfaces for online searching.

1836 Vizine-Goetz, D. and Mitchell, J. S.

Dewey 2000.

Journal of Library Administration 34 (1-2) 2001 : 103-109.

Discusses OCLC's research in various aspects of online DDC including linking DDC's terms with other thesauri.

1837 Vlasova, V. F.

Binominals in descriptor languages in document retrieval systems.

Nauchno- Tekhnicheskaya Informatsiya; Series II (8) 1972 : 20-23.

Discusses the concept of binominals in thesauri.

1838 VTLS to work with OCLC to extend WorldCat.

Advanced Technology Libraries 31 (4) April 2002 : 1.

Describes various types of helps including thesaural help provided by Virginia Technical Library System to the OCLC for developing the WorldCat.

1839 Waddington, Murray.

The AAT application protocol.

Art Documentation 8 (4) Winter 1989 : 178-180.

1840 Wagers, Robert.

Search Inform and Learn Inform-two new search aids from Data Courier : a review.

Database 5 (2) June 1982 : 51-53.

Describes Data Courier's Search Inform User Guide and Learn Inform Audio Training Kit, which used controlled vocabulary lists and other search techniques.

1841 Walker, Richard D.

Geo Archive Online.

Database 1 (2) Dec. 1978 : 35-45.

Explains the use of controlled vocabulary used for indexing and searching of information from GeoArchive online database.

1842 Wall, R. A.

Intelligent indexing and retrieval : a man-machine partnership.

Information Processing and Management 16 (2) 1980 : 73-90.

Suggests a method of distinguishing overlapping hierarchies in thesauri.

1843 Wan, T. L. et al.

Experiments with automatic indexing and a relational thesaurus in a Chinese information retrieval system.

Journal of the American Society for Information Science 48 (12) Dec. 1997 : 1086-1096.

1844 Wang, W. and Rada, R.

Experiences with semantic net-based hypermedia.

International Journal of Human-Computer Studies 43 (3) Sept. 1995 : 419-439.

Discusses thesauri and other link types useful for representing application domain concepts.

1845 Wanger, Judith.

Education and training for online systems.

Annual Review of Information Science and Technology. Volume 14. Ed. by Martha E. Wliams. New York : Knowledge Industry, 1979 : 219-245.

Traces the need for user training for using online systems and their thesauri.

1846 Weinberg, Bella Hass.

Indexes to the journals of the American Jewish Historical Society significance, coverage, and format.

Judaica Librarianship 10 (1-2) Spring 1999-Winter 2000 : 14-17.

Critically evaluates the indexes and the controlled vocabulary of the journals of the American Jewish Historical Society.

1847 Weinberg, Bella Hass.

Indexing after the millennium 5 - future conditional.

Indexer 21 (2) Oct. 1998 : 62-63.

Examines the future of indexing and suggests that the indexers must improve their skills in areas such as thesaurus creation for Internet searches.

1848 Weinberg, Bella Hass and Cunningham, Julie A.

The relationship between term specificity in MeSh and online postings in MEDLINE.

Bulletin of the Medical Library Association 73 (4) Oct. 1985 : 365-372.

Reports a study carried out to test the assumption of an inverse relationship between term specificity and the number of postings in on-line databases.

1849 Weintraub, I.

The terminology of alternative agricultural searching AGRICOLA, CAB and AGRIS.

Quarterly Bulletin of the International Association of Agricultural Information Specialists 37 (4) 1992 : 209-213.

Asserts need for controlled vocabulary for alternative agriculture.

1850 Weintraub, T. S.

The Dual-Thesaurus Catalog : MeSH and LCSH.

Technicalities 12 (12) Dec. 1992 : 10-12.

Describes feature of a catalogue maintained by using both MeSH and LCSH.

1851 Wellisch, H.

A flow chart for indexing with a thesaurus.

Journal of the American Society for Information Science 2 (3) May-June 1972 : 185-194.

1852 White, M.

Intranets aren't always the solution.

Digital Publishing Strategies 2 (3) Nov. 1997 : 6.

Suggests the development of integranets – the next generation of intranets as a solution to Intranets and discusses various essential elements of integranets including thesauri.

1853 Whitelock, P. J.

A descriptor bank of social science terms.

International Classification 9 (3) 1982 : 145-151.

Asserts the need for the creation of a descriptor bank of terms to be used in social science thesauri and explains uses of the resultant bank of terms.

1854 Wiggins, Richard.

Yesterday's headlines.

Library Journal; Net Connect Spring 2002 : 26-27.

Presents results of newspaper website's survey, which identified lack of thesaurus and other lacunae in newspaper's archival databases.

1855 Wildemuth, B. M. and Moore, M. E.

End-user search behaviors and their relationship to search effectiveness.

Bulletin of the Medical Library Association 83 (3) July 1995 : 294-304.

Reports a study aimed to know if there is any relationship between searchers behaviour and search effectiveness, which concludes that searchers underutilized the controlled vocabulary.

1856 Wilkes, A. and Nelson, A.

Subject searching in two online catalogues : authority control vs. non-authority control.

Cataloguing and Classification Quarterly 29(4) 1995 : 57-79.

1857 Willett, Peter.

Document retrieval experiments using indexing vocabularies of varying size. II. Hashing, truncation, digram and trigram encoding of index terms.

Journal of documentation 35 (4) 1979 : 296-305.

1858 Williamson, Nancy J.

An experiment in classification : based on William Goffman's 'indirect method' of information retrieval.

Cataloging and Classification Quarterly 1 (1) Fall 1980 : 3-21.

Narrates William Goffman's indirect method's advantages in planning search strategies in computerized ISRS based on controlled vocabulary.

1859 Wingert, F.

An indexing system for SNOMED.

Methods of Information in Medicine 25 (1) Jan. 1986 : 22-30.

Explains automated indexing based on the Systematized Nomenclature of Medicine (SNOMED).

1860 Wright, L. W. et al.

Hierarchical concept indexing of full-text documents in the Unified Medical Language System Information Sources Map.

Journal of the American Society for Information Science 50 (6) 1 May 1999 : 514-523.

1861 Xrefer launches xreferplus digital reference library.

Advanced Technology Libraries 31 (2) Feb. 2002 : 8-9.

Xreferplus is a digital reference library, which includes thesauri and other reference works.

1862 Yerkey, A. Neil.

A cluster analysis of retrieval patterns among bibliographic databases.

Journal of the American Society for Information Science 34 (5) Sept. 1983 : 350-355.

Presents results of cluster analysis carried out with the help of ERIC thesaurus.

1863 Ziegler, Herbert J.

Roche Integrated Reaction System (RIRS) : a new documentation system for organic reactions.

Journal of Chemical Information and Computer Sciences 19 (3) August 1979 : 141-149.

Describes a computer assisted reaction documentation system, which is based on a thesaurus of formulae with structural descriptors.

Section V

Literature on online thesaurus

Some thesauri are available online. This section lists literature about online thesaurus.

1864 Bates, Marcia J.

Design for a subject search interface and online thesaurus for a very large records management database.

ASIS'90. Information in the year 2000 : from research to applications. Proceedings of the 53rd Annual Meeting of the American Society for Information Science, Toronto, Canada, 4-8 November 1990. Volume 27. Ed. by Diane Henderson. Medford, New Jersey : Learned Information, Inc., 1990 : 20-28.

Describes steps in the designing of an online thesaurus for managing a very large database.

1865 Black, K.

Access personnel management on CD-ROM.

Managing Information 1 (6) June 1994 : 55-56.

Describes Institute of Personnel Management's CD-ROM database called 'Access Personnel Management' and its online thesaurus.

1866 Camp, A. J. V.

The MEDLINE integrated thesaurus on BRS.

Online 16 (6) Nov. 1992 : 99-102.

Describes the features of the MEDLINE Online Thesaurus as implemented on the BRS

1867 Huang, M. H.

Developing an ideal online thesaurus display format.

Bulletin of the Library Association of China (53) Dec. 1994 : 125-136.

Provides design of an ideal online subject and author thesaurus.

1868 Jachna, J. S.; Powsner, S. M. and Miller, P. L.

Augmenting GRATEFUL MED with the UMLS Metathesaurus : an initial evaluation.

Bulletin of the Medical Library Association 81 (1) Jan. 1993 : 20-28.

Presents results of a comparative study of experienced and novice users online bibliographical searches carried out with and without online thesaurus help.

1869 Lambert, N.

Plastic spaceships.

Searcher 2 (9) Nov.-Dec. 1994 : 43-49.

Describes online thesaurus and other features of Derwent's World Patents Index's Enhanced Polymer Indexing system.

1870 Morton, D.

Refresher course : expanding your outlook.

Online 18 (3) May 1994 : 77-79.

Describes how to use the EXPAND command of the online thesaurus.

1871 Platt, N.

Ethnic NewsWatch watches ethnic, minority, and native news.

Database 21 (1) Feb.-March 1998 : 29-31.

Describes Ethnic NewsWatch (a full text database of newspaper, magazine, and journal articles on the ethnic, minority and native press) and its online thesaurus.

Section W
Evaluation of thesauri

Number of thesauri have been constructed and used by different LIS professionals and institutions. Thesauri are produced as vocabulary control tools. This tool i.e. thesaurus is evaluated for assessing its strength and weaknesses. Certain criteria are applied for evaluating thesauri. The literature in this section deals with need for evaluation of thesaurus and criteria used for the evaluation of thesaurus.

1872 Cochrane, Pauline Atherton and Owens, Leslie Ann.

Thesaurus evaluation.

Cataloging and Classification Quarterly 37 (3-4) 2004 : 87-102.

Examines thesaurus assessment methods.

1873 Congreve, Juliet.

Subject access.

OPACs and the user. Proceedings of the 3rd Anglo-Nordic Seminar, April 1990. London : British Library, 1991 : 40-42.

Reports a Middlesex Polytechnic, research project, aimed to evaluate a front-end thesaurus to navigate users through subject searches in OPACs.

1874 Damerau, Fred J.

Evaluating computer-generated domain-oriented vocabularies.

Information Processing and Management 26 (6) 1990 : 791-801.

1875 Damerau, Fred J.

Generating and evaluating domain-oriented multi-words terms from texts.

Information Processing and Management 29 (4) July-August 1993 : 433-447.

1876 Elhanan, Gai. et al.

Auditing concept categorizations in the UMLS.

Artificial Intelligence in Medicine 31 (1) May 2004 : 29-44.

Presents an auditing technique to find errors and inconsistencies in the Unified Medical Language System.

1877 Hjerppe, Roland.

A framework for characterizing systems for knowledge organization : a first basis for comparisons and evaluations.

*Tools for knowledge organisation and the human interface. Proceedings of the 1st International ISKO Conference, Darmstadt, (*Germany) *14-17 August 1990. Advances in knowledge organization, no. 1/2.* Ed. by R. Fugmann. Part I. Frankfurt/Main : Indeks. 1990 : 21-34.

Presents a framework for characterizing and evaluating classification schemes and thesauri and compares some thesauri.

1878 Krautwurst, J.

Evaluation of a thesaurus by means of information-theoretical tools.

Nachrichten fur Dokumentation 20 (2) April 1969 : 68-72.

1879 McCulloch, Emma; Nicholson, Dennis and Shiri, Ali.

User evaluation of a pilot terminologies server for a distributed multi-scheme environment.

Online Information Review 28 (4) 2004 : 273-283.

Reports on a user-centered evaluation of a pilot terminology service developed as part of the High Level Thesaurus project at the Centre for Digital Library Research in the University of Strathclyde in Glasgow.

1880 Pokras, Yu L.

A method of measuring cohesion of descriptors in an information retrieval thesaurus.

Nauchno- Tekhnicheskaya Informatsiya; Series II (6) 1970 : 22-24.

1881 Reisner, P.

Evaluation of a 'growing' thesaurus.

New York : IBM Watson Research Center, 1966.

Section X

Thesaurus literature available on the web

Today a large amount of literature is available on the Internet websites. The following section lists articles, which are available on different websites. Entries in this section provide title of the article and its URL.

1882 ADL thesaurus protocol.

http://www.alexandria.ucsb.edu/thesaurus/protocol/

1883 American Society of Indexers.

Thesauri online. Prepared by Jassica L. Milstead.

http://www.asindexing.org/thesonet.shtml

1884 Aslib *thesauri collection.*

http://www.aslib.co.uk/osis/thesauri.html

Partial listing of print thesauri held in the Aslib library collection.

1885 Ballew, Randy.

Relational data structures for extensible thesauri [PowerPoint presentation].

http://www.calacademy.org/research/informatics/taf/proceedings/ballew/tsld001.htm

1886 BUBL Links/ 5:15. Catalogue of Internet resources : thesauri.

http://bubl.ac.uk/link/types/thesauri.htm

1887 Busch, Joseph A.

Thesauri for knowledge-based assistance in searching digital libraries [PowerPoint presentation].

http://alexandria.sdc.ucsb.edu/~lhill/busch/soergel/index.htm

1888 Chemical Abstracts general subject vocabulary helper.

http://www.cas.org/vocabulary/index.html

1889 Communication Canada.

Theaurus bibliography.

http://en.thesaurus.gc.ca/bib_e.html

Part of a group of pages on the Government of Canada core subject thesaurus which also includes the thesaurus itself and introductory material on thesaurus principles and use.

1890 Compiling a functional thesaurus to merge with Keyword AAA.

http://www.records.nsw.gov.au/publicsector/rk/rib/mergeaaa.htm

1891 Constructing and using thesauri & term lists.

http://www.slais.ubc.ca/resources/indexing/database1.htm

1892 Controlled subject vocabularies and thesauri.

http://sims.berkeley.edu/courses/is202/f97/Lecture11/index2.html

1893 Controlled vocabulary and the Internet.

Reoirt of the Subject Analysis and Retrieval Working Group Conference, 29th September 1999.

http://cendi.dtic.mil/pres_arc.html

1894 Craven, T. C.

Introductory tutorial on thesaurus construction.

http://instruct.uwo.ca/ca/gplis/677/thesaur/main00.htm

1895 Daniel, Ron Jr.

RDF and thesauri, [PowerPoint presentation].

http://nkos.slis.kent.edu/daniel_dl99abstract.htm

1896 Developing a functions thesaurus.

http://www.naa.gov.au/recordkeeping/control functions thesaur/contents.html

1897 Developing the next generation of standards for controlled vocabularies and thesauri : initiative commenced in 2003 to revise the current standard.

http://www.niso.org/committees/MT-info.html

1898 Getty vocabularies download center.

http://www.getty.edu/research/conducting_research/vocabularies/download.html

1899 Gold : a thesaurus browsing system.

http://www.csd.uch.gr/~chrysos/diploma/index.html

1900 Government of Canada core subject thesaurus – bibliography.

http://en.thesaurus.gc.ca/bib_e.html

1901 Green, R.

Relational thesaurus : modeling semantic relationships using frames.

http://www.oclc.org/oclc/research/publications/reviews96/green.htm

1902 Guidelines for constructing a museum object name thesaurus.

http://www.mda.org.uk/holm.htm

1903 Hagedorn, Kat.

Extracting value from automated classification tools : the role of manual involvement and controlled vocabularies.

http://argus-acia.com/white_papers/classification.pdf

1904 Harping, Patricia.

Documenting & access : indexing with the Getty vocabularies.

http://cendi.dtic.mil/presentations/harpring.PPT

1905 Hart, Quin J.

The CERES/NBII thesaurus partnership project.

http://ceres.ca.gov/thesaurus/

1906 Hodge, Hail.

Systems of knowledge organization for digital libraries : beyond traditional authority files.

http://www.clir.org/pubs/reports/pub91/pub91.pdf

1907 Hoy, Marian

Understanding official government terminology : natural language searching and government thesauri.

http://www.naa.gov.au/recordkeeping/gov_online/agift/gov_term/intro.html

1908 International Terminology Working Group, sponsored by The Getty Information Institute.

Guidelines for forming language equivalents : a model based on the art & architecture thesaurus.

http://www.chin.gc.ca/Resources/Publications/Guidelines/English/

1909 Introduction to vocabularies.

http://www.getty.edu/research/conducting_research/vocabularies/introvocabs/

1910 Jing, Yufeng and Croft, W. Bruce.

An association thesaurus for information retrieval.

http://www.cs.umass.edu/Dienst/UI/2.0/Describe/ncstrl.umassa_cs/UM-CS-1994-017?abstract=thesaur

1911 Johnson E. H. and Cochrane, P. A.

A hypertextual interface for a search's thesaurus.

http://www.cds.tamu.edu/DL95/papers/johncoch/johnncoch/html

1912 Kosovac, Branka.

Internet / intranet and thesauri.

http://irc.nrc-cnrc.gc.ca/thesaurus/roofing/report_b.html

Investigates the current use of thesauri for retrieval of networked information, more specifically, for indexing and searching Internet and intranet resources.

1913 Larson, Ray R.

Thesaurus design and development, [PowerPoint presentation].

http://www.sims.berkeley.edu/courses/is202/f98/Lecture10/index.htm

1914 Leighton, H. V. and Srivastava, J.

Precision among WWW search services (search engines) : AltaVista, Excite, Hotbot, Infoseek and Lycos.

http://www.vinona.msus.edu/library/webind2/wi2pt1.html

1915 Lopes, M. I.

Principles underlying subject heading languages : an international approach, 61st IFLA General Conference , 20-25 August 1995. Proceedings.

http://ifla.inist.fr/IV.ifla61-lopm.htm

1916 Matthews, B. M.; Miller, K. and Wilson, M.D.

A thesaurus interchange format in RDF.

http://www.limber.rl.ac.uk/External/SW_conf_thes_paper.htm

Proposes thesaurus interchange format in RDF to capture semantic relations.

1917 Metadata for the ADL Feature Type Thesaurus.

http://www.alexandria.ucsb.edu/gazetteer/FeatureTypes/FTT_metadata.htm

1918 Middleton, Michael.

Queensland University of Technology : controlled vocabulary guide.

http://www.fit.qut.edu.au.InfoSys/middle/cont_voc.html

1919 Milstead Jessica L.

Aubout thesauri.

http://www.bayside-indexing.com/Milstead/about.htm

Defines thesaurus, explains the need and process of thesaurus construction.

1920 Milstead, Jessica, L.

How do I build a thesaurus.

http://www.asindexing.org.thesauri.shtml

1921 Milstead, Jessica L.

NISO Z39.19 : Standard for structure and organization of information retrieval thesauri.

http://www.bayside-indexing.com/Milstead/z39.htm

Paper presented at the Taxonomic Authority Files Workshop, Washington, DC, June 23, 1998.

1922 Milstead Jessica L.

Use of thesauri in the full-text environment.

http://www.bayside-indexing.com/Milstead/useof.htm

1923 Milstead, Jassica L.

Workshop on electronic thesauri : planning for a standard : report workshop on November 4-5, 1999 in Washington, DC to investigate the desirability and feasibility of developing a standard for electronic thesauri.

http://www.niso.org/news/events_workshops/thes99rprt.html

1924 Morville, Peter.

How do you build a thesaurus?

http://www.ddj.com/documents/s=2879/nam1012433845/index.html

1925 National Library of Canada.

Thesauri and controlled vocabularies.

http://www.collectionscanada.ca/8/4/r4-280-e.html

Includes a section on terminology used in the federal government of Canada as well as links to thesauri, classification schemes, controlled vocabularies, geographic names, subject clusters and taxonomies.

1926 Networked Knowledge Organization Systems / Services (NKOS).

http://nkos.slis.kent.edu/

Discusses the data and functional model for enabling

Knowledge Organization Systems such as thesauri, classification systems, and gazetteers as distributed, interactive services on the Internet.

1927 Schatz, Bruce R. et al.

Interactive term suggestion for users of digital libraries :using subject thesauri and co-occurrence lists for information retrieval.

http://dli.grainger.uiuc.edu/papers/schatzDL96.htm

1928 School of Computing, University of Glamorgan.

FACET project : thesaurus based access to multimedia collections - faceted retrieval tools.

http://www.glam.ac.uk/soc/research/hypermedia/facet_proj/index.php

Investigates the ways in which access to a thesaurus can be used by searchers to formulate searches of an indexed collection, and ways in which search terms can be expanded automatically to include additional terms more or less closely linked to the initial term by relationships in the thesaurus structure.

1929 Soergel, Dagobert

Enriched thesauri as networked knowledge bases for people and machines.

http://www.dtic.mil/cendi/presentations/cendisoergel.pdf

1930 Soergel, Dagobert.

Functions of a thesaurus / classification / ontological knowledge base.

http://www.clis.umd.edu/faculty/soergel/soergelfctclass.pdf

1931 Taylor, Mike.

Zthes : a Z39.50 profile for thesaurus navigation.

http://www.loc.gov/z3950/agency/profiles/zthes-02.html

1932 Thesauri and taxonomies : an international conference and workshop.

http://www.multites.com/conference03.htm

A conference sponsored by multites as part of their 20th anniversary celebration in London in 2003.

1933 Tillett, B. B.

International shared resource records for controlled access, authority control in the 21st century : an invitational conference.

http://www.oclc.org/oclc/man/authconf/tillett.htm

1934 USGS gateway to the earth : controlled vocabulary project.

http://alexandria.sdc.ucsb.edu/~lhill/usgs_terms/usgs/USGSMainPg-retired.htm

1935 Weinberg, Bella Hass.

Thesaurus design for information systems - seminar report.

http://www.allegrotechindexing.com/article02.htm

1936 Will, Leonard.

Thesaurus principles and practice.

http://www.willpower.demon.co.uk/thesprin.htm

1937 Zeng, Marcia Lei and Chen Yu.

A multi-thesauri management system with web interface.

http://nkos.slis.kent.edu/zeng_dl99abstract.htm

A PowerPoint presentation.

1938 Zlotchenko, David.

On-line searching aids : automatically growing thesaurus as a tool for discovering semantic preferences of intranet users,[online thesis].

http://www.oars.utk.edu/~zlotchen/thes/

Section Y

Websites providing access to actual online thesauri and websites providing information about actual thesauri

Some thesauri are available only in hardcopy format. However there are some thesauri which can be accessed on the Internet. This section provides name and URLs of thesauri available on the Internet.

1939 AGIFT *Australian Governments' Interactive Functions Thesaurus.*

http://www.naa.gov.au/recordkeeping/gov_online/agift/extract.html

It is a thesaurus supported by the National Archives of Australia to provide description of government information online.

1940 AGRI/AGRISANASTO [Thesaurus of the Agricultural Library at the University of Helsinki].

http://www-db.helsinki.fi/triphome/agri/agrisanasto/Welcomeng.html

1941 AGRICOLA Subject Category Code Scope Notes.

http://laurel.nal.usda.gov:8080/agnic/cc/

1942 Agrovoc.

http://www.fao.org/agrovoc/bar.htm

1943 AOHST : Australian Occupational Health and Safety Thesaurus.

http://www.nohsc.gov.au/ohsinformation/libraryservices/default.htm

1944 APAIS Thesaurus [Australian Public Affairs Information Service].

http://www.nla.gov.au/apais/thesaurus/index.html

1945 Aquatic Sciences and Fisheries Thesaurus.

http://www4.fao.org/asfa/asfa.htm

1946 Archaeological Objects Thesaurus.

http://www.open.gov.uk/mdocassn/archobj/archcon.htm

1947 Art and architecture thesaurus : browser.

http://www.shiva.pub.getty.edu/att_browser/

1948 Art & Architecture Thesaurus : user's guide to the AAT data releases.

http://www.getty.edu/research/tools/vocabulary/aat/guide/AAT-Users-Manual.html

PDF version at : http://www.getty.edu/research/tools/vocabulary/aat/AAT-Users-manual.pdf

1949 ASFA Thesaurus.

http://www.csa.com/htbin/ccfdisp.cgi?fn=/wais/data/thes/asfithes.ccf&sl=A&fmt=5&ldtag=TR

1950 Asia - Vegetable Thesaurus.

http://www.nre.vic.gov.au/trade/asiaveg/thes-00.htm

1951 Assessment of the AAA Keyword Thesaurus.

http://www.naa.gov.au/recordkeeping/control/KeyAAA/aaa/intro.htm

1952 Astronomy Thesaurus.

http://msowww.anu.edu.au/library/thesaurus/

Compiled by R. M. & R. R. Shobbrook, provides multilingual access : English, French, German, Italian, and Spanish.

1953 Australian Emergency Management Terms Thesaurus.

http://www.ema.gov.au/ema/rwpattach.nsf/viewasattachment Personal/07D1F0ED1B8663F4CA256C8A0008E41A/$file/AEM_TERMS_THESAURUS2.PDF

1954 Australian Pictorial Thesaurus (APT).

http://www.picturethesaurus.gov.au/

1955 Australian Thesaurus of Educational Descriptors.

http://www.acer.edu.au/library/catalogues/edthesaurus.html

1956 Australian Transport Index Thesaurus.

http://www.arrb.com.au/index.php?option =content &task= view&id=14&Itemid=35

1957 Australian Women's Weekly Subject Thesaurus.

http://wwwfp.cc.flinders.edu.au/WWIndex//thesaurus.html

1958 Biocomplexity thesaurus.

http://thesaurus.nbii.gov/

Developed through a partnership between the NBII (the U.S. National Biological Information Infrastructure) and CSA, as a merger of the CSA's *Aquatic Sciences and Fisheries Thesaurus*, *Life Sciences Thesaurus*, *Pollution Thesaurus*, and *Sociological Thesaurus*, with the *CERES/NBII Thesaurus*.

1959 Bioethics Thesaurus.

http://www.georgetown.edu/research/nrcbl/ir/appd.pdf

1960 BIOSIS controlled vocabulary : lists.

http://www.biosis.org/training_support/reference_shelf/list_toc.html

1961 The British Museum Materials Thesaurus.

http://www.mda.org.uk/bmmat/matintro.htm

1962 BZZURKK - The Thesaurus of Champions.

http://collection.nlc-bnc.ca/100/200/300/ktaylor/kaboom/bzzurkk.htm

1963 CAB Thesaurus.

http://194.203.77.66/

1964 CALL Dictionary and Thesaurus.

http://call.army.mil/call/thesaur/index.htm

The CALL (Center for Army Lessons Learned) thesaurus, maintained by the US Government, contains military terminology, codes, names, etc.

1965 Canadian Literary thesaurus.

http://thesaurusalpha.org/thesaurus/index.htm

1966 Canadian subject headings.

http://www.nlc-bnc.ca/6/23/

1967 Canadian Thesaurus of Construction Science and Technology.

http://www.nrc.ca/irc/thesaurus/welcome.html

TC/CS was prepared by the IF Research Group, University of Montreal for the Government of Canada, Department of Industry, Trade and Commerce (now called Industry Canada).

1968 CATIE Thesaurus [Thesaurus of Canadian 'Community AIDS Treatment Information Exchange'].

http://www.catie.ca/thesaurus.nsf/

1969 CERES thematic thesaurus

http://ceres.ca.gov/thesaurus/

The Californian Environmental Resources Evaluation System and National Biological Information Infrastructure (NBII) Biological Resources Division (BRD) are collaborating on the development of an Integrated Environmental Thesaurus and Thesaurus Networking Tool Set for metadata development and keyword searching to facilitate access to a variety of electronic data describing California's environments.

1970 CHID Alzheimer's Disease Thesaurus.

http://chid.nih.gov/

1971 The Cooks Thesaurus.

http://www.foodsubs.com/

1972 Curtin Keyword Thesaurus [derived from the Keyword AAA Thesaurus].

http://www.curtin.edu.au/curtin/dept/rao/records_management/keyword_thesaurus.htm

1973 DEH Thesaurus.

http://www.deh.gov.au/about/deh-thesaurus.html

It is produced by the Australian Department of Environment and Heritage.

1974 DTIC Thesaurus.

http://www.dtic.mil/stinet/str/indexthes.html

Created by Defense Technical Information Center.

1975 EET (European Education Thesaurus).

http://www.eurydice.org/TeeForm/frameset_en.HTM

Joint product of the European Commission and the Council of Europe.

1976 eHealth Thesaurus.

http://www.hc-sc.gc.ca/ohih-bsi/res/thesaurus/thesaurus_info_e.html

Maintained in Canada by the Office of Health and the Information Highway (OHIH) to index material on health care and health information, telecommunications technology, including health technologies, the Internet and computers, and branches of telehealth services.

1977 English Heritage and Adlib Information Systems Ltd.

HITITE : illustrated thesaurus.

http://hitite.adlibsoft.com/index.html

Provides a way of finding thesaurus terms for monuments by specifying a combination of characteristics. HITITE is an on-line thesaurus of monument terms illustrated with images from the National Monuments Record's archive, and augmented with additional indexed information.

1978 Envoc thesaurus.

http://p5uni.ii.pw.edu.pl/envoc/

The thesaurus for INFOTERRA databases. (INFOTERRA : formerly the International Referral System of the United Nations Environment Programme) is the Global Environmental Information Exchange Network, established in 1975 by UNEP to "facilitate the exchange of environmental information within and among nations".

1979 ERIC Thesaurus.

http://ericae.net/scripts/ewiz/amain2.asp

1980 Eurovoc.

http://europa.eu.int/celex/eurovoc/

A multilingual, polythematic thesaurus focusing on the laws and legislation of the European Union (EU). It may be used in the areas of law, legislation and politics. Eurovoc exists in 11 official EU languages (Danish, Dutch, English, Finnish, French, German, Greek, Italian, Portuguese, Spanish and Swedish).

1981 Family Thesaurus Online.

http://www.aifs.org.au/institute/info/html/index.htm

This thesaurus is produced by Australian Institute of Family Studies.

1982 Feature type thesaurus for Alexandria Digital Library.

http://www.alexandria.ucsb.edu/~lhill/FeatureTypes/

Terminology to categorize named locations.

1983 Florida Environments Online Thesaurus.

http://palmm.fcla.edu/lfnh/thesauri/feol2/index.htm

1984 Food Safety Thesaurus.

http://www.nal.usda.gov/fsrio/fsresearch.htm

1985 Gateway to the Earth Thesaurus.

http://geo-nsdi.er.usgs.gov/term

1986 GEM Controlled vocabularies.

http://www.geminfo.org/Workbench/Workbench_vocabularies.html

Supports description at Gateway to Educational Materials (GEM).

1987 General Multilingual Environmental Thesaurus, GEMET.

http://www.mu.niedersachsen.de/cds/etc-cds_neu/software.html

1988 Getty Thesaurus of Geographic Names.

http://www.getty.edu/research/tools/vocabulary/tgn/

1989 Getty Thesaurus of Geographic Names : User's Guide to the TGN Data Releases.

http://www.getty.edu/research/tools/vocabulary/tgn/guide/TGN-Users-Manual.html

PDF version at :

http://www.getty.edu/research/tools/vocabulary/tgn/TGN-Users-Manual.pdf

1990 Global Legal Information Network (GLIN) Thesaurus.

http://lcweb2.loc.gov/glin/indxhlp.html

1991 HASSET : Humanities and Social Science Electronic Thesaurus.

http://dasun1.essex.ac.uk/services/nhasset.html

1992 Health and Aged Care Thesaurus.

http://www.health.gov.au/thesaurus.htm

Developed by Australian Department of Health and Aged Care Library using MeSH.

1993 Health and Ageing Thesaurus.

http://www.health.gov.au/internet/wcms/Publishing.nsf/Content/health-thesaurus.htm

1994 Health Promotion Thesaurus.

http://www.nigz.nl/methp.html

It is a four language (English, French, German, Dutch), thesaurus maintained by The International Union for Health Promotion and Education.

1995 Health thesaurus.

http://www.healthinsite.gov.au/search/thesaurus_search_new.cfm?access=standard&visitorName=

1996 Historical Thesaurus of English.

http://www2.arts.gla.ac.uk/SESLL/EngLang/thesaur/homepage.htm

1997 Illinois Researcher Information Service (IRIS) Keyword Thesaurus.

http://carousel.lis.uiuc.edu/~iris/thesaurus.html

1998 The International Thesaurus of Refugee Terminology.

http://refugeethesaurus.org/hms/home.php?publiclogin=1

This thesaurus is in English, French and Spanish for refugee- and forced migration-related information terminology.

1999 ITS Thesaurus.

http://www.nas.edu/trb/about/itsthes.html

The ITS (Intelligent Transportation Systems) Thesaurus is based on the TRT (Transportation Research Thesaurus).

2000 Keyword AAA : Thesaurus of general terms.

http://www.records.nsw.gov.au/publicsector/rk/aaa/Keyword AAA.htm

2001 LACBD subject thesaurus.

http://www.usc.edu/isd/archives/arc/lacbd/subject/index.html

This thesaurus is used with the Los Angeles Comprehensive Bibliographic Database.

2002 Legislative Indexing Vocabulary (LIV).

http://www.loc.gov/lexico/servlet/lexico?usr=pub-35:0 &op =frames&db=LIV

2003 Materials Thesaurus.

http://www.mda.org.uk/bmmat/matintro.htm

2004 Medical Subject Headings (MeSH) Indexing Tips.

http://healthlinks.washington.edu/howto/medindexing.html

2005 MeSH : Medical Subject Headings maintained by the US National Library of Medicine.

http://www.nlm.nih.gov/mesh/meshhome.html

2006 Multilingual Egyptological Thesaurus.

http://www.ccer.ggl.ruu.nl/thes

2007 NAIC Thesaurus.

http://naic.acf.hhs.gov/database/thes.cfm

It is the U.S. Dept of Health & Human Services Thesaurus of child abuse, child welfare, and adoption terms for Clearinghouse Document records of the National Adoption Information Clearinghouse.

2008 NAL Agricultural Thesaurus.

http://agclass.nal.usda.gov/agt/search.htm

2009 NAL Animal Use Alternatives Thesaurus.

http://agclass.nal.usda.gov/altrntvs/index.htm

2010 NASA Thesaurus.

http://www.sti.nasa.gov/thesfrm1.htm

2011 Nelson, Stuart.

The role of the Unified Medical Language System (UMLS) in vocabulary control.

http://www.dtic.mil/cendi/presentations/nelson.ppt

A PowerPoint presentation.

2012 Nelson, Stuart.

The Unified Medical Language System. [PowerPoint presentation].

http://www.nlm.nih.gov/mesh/presentations/tafumls/index.htm

A PowerPoint presentation.

2013 NIAAA : Alcohol and other drugs thesaurus : a guide to concepts and terminology in substance abuse and addiction.

http://www.etoh.niaaa.nih.gov/AODVoll/Aodthome.htm

2014 Nikolai, Ralf.

GenThes : a general thesaurus browser for Web-based

catalogue systems : a step towards component based catalogue systems.

http://www.computer.org/proceedings/meta/1999/papers/49/rnikolai.html

2015 Object Names Thesaurus.

http://www.mda.org.uk/archobj/archcon.htm

Records object names in the British Museum, using standard thesaurus relationships, as well as explanatory notes; architecture based on ISO 2788.

2016 Occupations Thesaurus — Register of Australian Archives and Manuscripts (RAAM).

http://www.nla.gov.au/raam/occup.html

2017 OECD Macrothesaurus.

http://info.uibk.ac.at/info/oecd-macroth/

2018 The Plumb Design Visual Thesaurus.

http://www.plumbdesign.com/thesaurus/

2019 POPIN Population Multilingual Thesaurus.

http://www.cicred.ined.fr/thesaurus/thesaurus_a/

2020 ProQuest Controlled Vocabulary of Subject Terms.

http://www.umi.com/proquest/cv-controlled-vocabulary.shtml

2021 Public Health Thesaurus.

http://www.phthesaurus.org.uk/index.html

2022 ScOT.

http://scot.curriculum.edu.au/

Schools Online Thesaurus is a product of The Le@rning Federation project, an initiative of State and Federal governments of Australia and the New Zealand government to create online interactive curriculum content.

2023 Seattle City Clerk Thesaurus.

http://clerk.ci.seattle.wa.us/~public/newtoc.htm

2024 The Southwest Thesaurus.

http://www.swt.arizona.edu/

2025 SPIN Thesaurus [Sponsored Programs Information Network].

http://www.fas.lsu.edu/osp/spin/mythez.html

2026 Spindrift Music Thesaurus.

http://www.spindrift.com/Thesaurus/index.html?page=/Thesaurus/ThesIntro.html&mainFrame

2027 Statistics Canada Thesaurus.

http://www4.statcan.ca/english/thesaurus/index.htm

2028 Thesaurus of Ethics in the Life Sciences.

http://www.drze.de/BELIT/thesaurus/index_html?la=en

2029 Thesaurus for the Australian Transport Index.

http://www.arrb.com.au/index.php?option=content&task=view&id=14&Itemid=35

Devised by the staff of the M G Lay Library at ARRB Transport Research and available as pdf file.

2030 Thesaurus for the herb.

http://www.uky.edu/~lhjeng00/herbweb/

2031 Thesaurus for Graphic Materials II (Genre and Physical Characteristic Terms).

http://lcweb.loc.gov/rr/print/tgm2/

2032 Thesaurus for Graphic Materials I (Subject Terms)

http://lcweb.loc.gov/rr/print/tgm1/

2033 Thesaurus of Economic, Social and Cultural Rights.

http://shr.aaas.org/thesaurus/?OpenFrameSet

Online version of the Thesaurus created by S. A. Hansen for the Science and Human Rights Program of the American Association for the Advancement of Science, and Human Rights Information and Documentation Systems, International (HURIDOCS).

2034 Thesaurus of Geographic Names.

http://shiva.pub.getty.edu/tgn_browser/

2035 Thesaurus of Occupational Therapy Subject Headings.

http://otbibsys.aota.org/pdf/thesaurus.pdf

2036 Thesaurus of Sociological Indexing Terms.

http://www.csa.com/edit/sociothes.html

2037 UK Archival Thesaurus (UKAT).

http://www.ukat.org.uk/

2038 UNBIS Thesaurus [United Nations Bibliographic Information System].

http://lib-thesaurus.un.org/LIB/DHLUNBISThesaurus.nsf

2039 UNESCO Thesaurus.

http://www.ulcc.ac.uk/unesco/index.htm

2040 Unified Medical Language System (UMLS).

http://www.nlm.nih.gov/pubs/cbm/umlscbm.html

2041 The Union List of Artist Names Browser.

http://www.getty.edu/research/tools/vocabulary/ulan/

2042 Union List of Artist Names : User's Guide to the ULAN Data Releases.

http://www.getty.edu/research/tools/vocabulary/ulan/guide/ULAN-Users-Manual.html

PDF version at :

http://www.getty.edu/research/tools/vocabulary/ulan/ULAN-Users-Manual.pdf

2043 Victorian local history thesaurus.

http://210.15.209.254/thesaurus/index.htm

Lists subject terms used in Royal Historical Society of Victoria cataloguing projects.

2044 Vocabulary of Basic Terms for Cataloguing Costume.

http://www.mda.org.uk/costume/vbt00e.htm

This thesaurus is in English, German and French and it is developed by ICOM: International Committee for the Museums and Collections of Costume; it includes garments and accessories, and terms are accompanied by pictorial representations

2045 VOCED.

http://www.voced.edu.au/thes.htm

This is a thesaurus of terms used in the field of vocational education and training research and policy.

2046 WorldBank Thesaurus.

http://www.multites.com/wb/

2047 Zoological Record Subject Thesaurus.

http://www.biosis.org/zrdocs/zr_thes/subjthes/index.html

2048 Zoological Record Systematic Thesaurus.

http://www.biosis.org/zrdocs/zr_thes/systthes/index.htm

Section Z

Websites listing thesauri

Like most other subjects there exist various websites that list thesauri. This section provides names and URLs of thesaurus listing websites.

2049 Betz, Anne.

Classification schemes and thesauri on-line.

http://www.fbi.fh-koeln.de/institut/labor/Bir/thesauri_new/indexen.htm

Provides an annotated lists of thesauri (by subject and language)., classification schemes and thesaurus management software.

2050 Koch, Traugott.

Controlled vocabularies, thesauri and classification systems available in the WWW.

http://www.lub.lu.se/metadata/subject-help.html

A list of sources of terms for expressing the subjects of documents, compiled for use in the subject fields of Dublin Core metadata.

2051 Links to online thesauri, term lists & classification schemes.

http://www.slais.ubc.ca/resources/indexing/database1.htm

2052 Middleton, Michael.

Controlled vocabularies.

http://sky.fit.qut.edu.au/~middletm/cont_voc.html

Provides a list including bibliography, classification schemes, database of thesauri, thesaurus building & use, thesaurus sites and thesaurus software.

2053 Stephenson, Mary Sue.

Indexing resources on the WWW : database indexing, controlled vocabularies and thesauri.

http://www.slais.ubc.ca/resources/indexing/database1.htm

A bibliography of Web sources arranged under the following headings : constructing and using thesauri and term lists; links to online thesauri and other related websites.

2054 Technical Advisory Service for Images.

Controlling your language - links to metadata vocabularies.

http://www.tasi.ac.uk/resources/vocabs.html

Provides an sntroduction to the concepts of thesauri, subject headings, word lists, classifications and name authority lists, and links to more than 60 vocabulary sources.

2055 Thesaurus-related literature and resources.

http://www.darmstadt.gmd.de/~lutes/theslit.html

2056 Thesaurus-related research groups.

http://www.darmstadt.gmd.de/~lutes/thesgroups.html

2057 University of Strathclyde, Glasgow HILT project.

A-Z of thesauri.

http://hilt.cdlr.strath.ac.uk/hilt2web/Sources/thesauri.html

2058 University of Toronto Library.

Subject Analysis Systems (SAS) Collection.

A North American Clearinghouse for classification schemes, subject heading lists, and thesauri, and the major world collection in the English language, including multilingual thesauri containing English language sections.

Overview of SAS : http://www.fis.utoronto.ca/resources/inforum/sas.htm

Catalogue access via : UTCAT. http://www.library.utoronto.ca/resources/utcat.html

2059 Web thesaurus compendium. prepared by Barbara Lutes, Darmastadt University of Technology.

http://www.ipsi.fraunhofer.de/~lutes/thesoecd.html

Lists thesauri and classification schemes and has some other references to thesaurus-related literature.

2060 Willpower Information : Information Management Consultants Publications on thesaurus construction and use including some references to facet analysis, taxonomies, ontologies, topic maps and related issues.

http://www.willpowerinfo.co.uk/

2061 wordHOARD.

http://www.mda.org.uk/wrdhrd1.htm

Is a series of WWW pages prepared by the Museum Documentation giving information about thesauri and controlled vocabularies, including bibliographies and lists of sources.

Index

Note: 1. The index contains entry word followed by entry number.

2. Index entry is made under the first author's name only, when there are more than one authors.

3. Index entry is made under the name of the institution, in case of corporate author

4. For an anonymous document the index entry is made under its title.